FIRE IN HIS HEART
by
Harry R. Hall

PUBLISHED BY FREE ENTERPRISE SERVICES, INC.
SARASOTA, FLORIDA,

Library of Congress Catalog Card Number 80-70388

ISBN 0-943636-00-0

"Find me good men who understand what it
is to love God and love his children.
Find me men with fire in their hearts
and wings on their feet."

From *The Shoes of the Fisher-man* by Morris West (permission of William Morrow and Co., Inc., Publishers)

CONTENTS

INTRODUCTION

In 1959, at the age of 35, he was in his ninth year of employment at a major university. His salary was $6200 a year. At that point of his career he decided to go into business. With borrowed money, he built a small FM radio station at a time when FM radio sets in use accounted for only eight percent of total receivers. For the first year, the gross revenues were $12,000.

By 1978, he had finessed that operation into a public corporation owning and publishing six daily and sixty-one weekly newspapers in seven states, plus printing and typesetting plants in three states and one foreign country. Gross revenues approached $40 million.

In 1974, he established a separate, wholly owned private corporation and purchased one metropolitan daily newspaper, fifteen suburban non-daily papers, and 50 percent ownership in a worldwide news gathering organization serving numerous networks and two hundred TV stations, in seventy countries. The corporation was involved further in non-media investments. His personal financial status had changed from a subsistence level to eight figures.

This story of individual enterprise in action illustrates how the private enterprise system works for enterprising individuals who put it to work for them. It is an age old success story as new as tomorrow's latest venture into the business world by an ambitious individual who believes that dreams can become realities. This is not a How To book, limited to telling how to do one specific job in general terms. It is a living, breathing, pulsating case history of a skillful entrepreneur. It tells, in specific terms, what he achieved in moving from a meager beginning to a position of affluence and influence. It shows how he handled the many growth problems. It is a How It Was Done book. The interrelated actions and reactions can be valuable lessons to any entrepreneur who wants to benefit from the hard earned experience of someone else.

Deprecation of the free enterprise ideology, beginning in the 30's, fostered the concept that individualism in this mass society was outmoded; that opportunity for personal advancement was confined to the massive public and private bureaucracies; that entrepreneurs were a part of an American mythology, romanticized by distant time.

For almost half a century, official government policies were more punitive than inducible to independent self-lifting effort. Excessive regulatory restrictions, burdensome reporting procedures, strangling taxes, and governmental intrusion into the mechanics of the free market economy served to dampen the entrepreneurial ardor, to discourage risk taking, to belittle rugged individualism, and to undermine the public's confidence in private business motives.

Federal policy gave precedence to welfare economics over entrepreneurial self help. Dependency on government for security supplanted the protestant work ethic resulting in a diminished public awareness of the vital role of entrepreneurs in building the fabulous economic structure of the nation.

In spite of these formidable barriers, entrepreneurship is not dead, is not ailing, is not a relic of the irretrievable past. The spirit of the entrepreneur is too inextricably woven into the fabric of the American character to be disentangled, even by unsound government policies. Today it survives, prospers, flourishes, and is on the threshold of the brightest future in its incredible history.

Respected analysts predict that the entrepreneur will become the new American folk hero of the 80's. Welfarism has failed to maintain the dynamic economy created by the early day entrepreneurs. This realization has prompted a changed public perception of the role of small private enterprises in the creation of jobs and higher standards of living.

Out of the more than eleven million business firms in the nation, excluding farms, 10.8 million are classified as small business, measured by the Small Business Administration size standards. Small enterprises account for 48 percent of the private production of goods and services in this country. Small entrepreneurial operations have been responsible for more than half of the new product and service innovations developed since World

War II. Authenticated studies show that small business enterprises bring their innovations to the marketplace faster than the large multi-plant corporations. A study by the National Science Foundation reveals that small companies produce 24 times more innovations per research dollar than the large firms.

Most of the energy-related innovations of the twentieth century have been introduced by small enterprises. Many of the small companies became big business as a result of these developments. Examples: air conditioning, the gasoline engine, the electric light.

Small business accounts for 60 percent of the nation's total employment. Business firms with 100 employees or less account for 80 percent of new job opportunities. Businesses with 50 employees or less generated 56 percent of all jobs in the United States from 1969 to 1976. These small companies are expected to create new jobs for an even greater proportion of job holders during the rest of this century. Small business operations provide a livelihood, directly or indirectly, for more than 100 million Americans even though 98 percent of the nation's business firms, excluding farms, have sales of less than $1 million, 82 percent have sales of less than $100,000 and 62 percent have sales of less than $25,000.

Entrepreneurship offers no guarantee of financial success. The only guarantee is the opportunity to try. More and more people are taking advantage of that opportunity. Increasing annually for the past two decades, the number of new incorporations each year has passed the half million mark. According to the record, about one third fail within the first year. Half of them fail within five years.

The change in the political climate in 1981 also changed official federal attitudes toward business. A new administration displayed confidence in the entrepreneurial approach; believed that a nation of entrepreneurs was willing, eager and ready to take risks to improve their own position and to strengthen the nation. These beliefs were bolstered by enactment of an extensive program of incentives designed to encourage entrepreneurs.

One of the problems during the past fifty years has been the growing problem of finding venture capital to finance new ideas, new processes, new products and new services developed by small entrepreneurs. One large step to relieve this barrier was taken in 1978 when Congress passed the Steiger Act lowering the individual capital gains rate from 49 percent to 28 percent. Total venture capital available for fledgling enterprisers during the three year period from 1978 to 1981 exceeded the total for the preceding decade. In 1981, a new economic package reduced the rate from 28 percent to 20 percent, a boost for the aspiring. entrepreneur as well as the small enterpriser eager to expand. Coupled with enactment of the Small Business Investment Act that eased restrictions on Venture Capital firms, wealthy investors, pension funds, universities and corporations were provided with new incentives to enter the risk capital field. Foreign investors had additional reasons to seek investment opportunities in increasing numbers. It is a fitting compliment to the free enterprise system that these foreign investors view America as an oasis of economic stability in a world desert of instability.

This new flood of risk money focuses on smaller enterprises with good growth potential. The record shows chance of greater return ranging from 25 to 30 percent where investors provide seed money in such enterprises in exchange for shares of stock. The new exotic fields of genetic engineering, the high technology developments, computers, electronics, and the many new communications devices in television have attracted particular consideration. Interest is not limited to these areas of endeavor. It depends on the individual and the particular proposal more than the product or service.

Additional incentives for entrepreneurs in business or planning to go into business are:

—A 25 percent tax cut for individuals over a three year period and reductions in the corporate rate over a two year period.
—Lower capitalization for starting new enterprises.
—Regulatory relief reducing the time consuming, costly paper work for useless reporting to a swarm of federal agncies.
—Revision of estate tax laws to ease the tax burdens on family-owned businesses. This encourages continuity of family ownership.
—Simplified rules for writing off certain business assets, including real estate, buildings, equipment and light vehicles.

The reversal of public policy to encourage the private business system reflects a new public attitude favorable to entrepreneurship. Nothing demonstrates this change more than the interest of college students. Back in the 60's and early 70's many students went through the idealistic phase. Business was number one on the hate list. Altruistic and egalitarian values dominated their thoughts and actions. Now, surveys reveal a sharp reversal. More and more young people are thinking about careers that offer opportunity for personal economic success.

The number of colleges and graduate schools offering courses in how to start and conduct a business has jumped from fewer than ten in 1967 to more than 150 in 1980. These courses veer abruptly from the traditional Business Administration curricula. Practical, project-oriented, these working sessions are designed to provide the budding or the practicing entrepreneur with everyday How To do the job information. Some of the schools are equipped to provide seed money to students with carefully developed plans to start a business.

One of the outstanding programs is sponsored by the Center For Entrepreneurial Development at Carnegie-Mellon University in Pittsburgh. Originally funded by corporate and public contributions, it is now supported substantially by contributions of its graduates who get seed money to start a business. One of the participants founded Compuguard, a computer-based energy management company. In a relatively short time, he paid back the $40,000 seed money and contributed $90,000 to the revolving fund. Later he sold the business for $6 million. This is just one of the numerous successful ventures of the participants in this fifteen week course, organized by Professor Dwight Bauman in 1971 because he was concerned that the engineering and business schools were not developing entrepreneurs.

The early day entrepreneurs had no such training schools. They succeeded or failed by trial and error taught in the university of hard knocks. Today, the sources for guidance and assistance to the entrepreneur are manifold. The Entrepreneurship Institute with headquarters at Worthington, Ohio was established for the purpose of assisting and encouraging entrepreneurship and new enterprise development. It is an independent, international, non-profit organization. Under the leadership of William McCrea, Chairman of the Board, the Institute conducts practical seminars around the nation on how to create and manage a new growth company. All aspects of business management are covered. Resource leaders for these programs are drawn from the ranks of successful entrepreneurs, senior corporate executives, private investors, venture capitalists, lawyers, accountants and other well-qualified specialists engaged in new enterprise operations at the day to day working level. The Institute publishes a newsletter keeping members up to date on developments and providing contacts in the entrepreneurial community.

Numerous non-profit membership organizations provide a wide variety of services to aid business firms at any stage of development and with any type of operating problem. The Chamber of Commerce of the United States and many State and Local Chambers sponsor conferences, seminars, clinics, and offer specialized staff assistance. Meetings on special problems permit members to share experiences as well as to take advantage of the most skilled professional counsel.

Special purpose trade associations at the local, state and national level proffer assistance in Know How peculiar to the particular industry or business of their particular area of interest.

The U. S. Small Business Administration publishes many documents on all phases of operations for small business and sponsors dozens of meetings in all parts of the nation to promote small business in development and to aid in operational problems.

Showing entrepreneurs how to be successful has become a thriving enterprise in its own right. A large number of entrepreneurs have pursued successful careers in spotting trends, searching out new business opportunities, reporting success stories and publishing How To information.

Enterprise Publishing, Inc. of Wilmington, Delaware, specializes in publication of legal self-help and business How To books. The company was organized by Ted Nicholas when conventional publishers rejected his first book entitled *How To Form Your Own Corporation Without a Lawyer for Under $50.00*. Publishing it himself, establishing his own advertising agency and doing his own promotion and distribution, he sold over 300,000 copies. It is still selling. Enterprise Publishing has sold more than 500,000 copies of seven How To books authored by Ted Nicholas as well as thousands of copies of other noted authors, writing on different aspects of business operations. *The Ted Nicholas President's Letter* is published twice monthly for subscribers. It provides business and personal planning ideas for the corporation President. *How To Succeed in Your Own Business* is a taped seminar of 78 minutes length, recorded live at the State University of New York at Albany.

Ted Nicholas is another entrepreneur who has made several fortunes in his own business operations. He has refined these techniques into a practical system and developed a home study course called *Opportunity Unlimited*. This course has helped thousands of people to profit from the lessons learned by Ted Nicholas in his experience.

Bookstores offer a multiplicity of publications aimed at the entrepreneur. Numerous magazines feature regularly the case histories of individuals with ideas that they put to work, accumulating their own wealth in the process.

All entrepreneurs do not strike it rich overnight. Some do not make it at all. Others fail and keep trying until they do make it. Some fall by the wayside early in the operational stage of the new born business. Some remain small by the nature of the business. Some prefer to remain small. Some have a tough struggle to survive year after year. None of them would give up the independence, the privilege of making their own decisions, setting their own work pace, maintaining their own lifestyle. Pride of ownership and freedom of self determination are rewards in themselves. Many entrepreneurs enjoy high incomes and acquire all the accouterments that mark success in the modern society. Thousands of others join the million dollar income class, some in a relatively short time.

Max Fisher of Detroit did just that. His father was a poverty-stricken immigrant peddlar when he first came to this country. By the time Max had finished school in 1930, his father had acquired a small reclamation plant, cleaning the crud out of used crankcase oil collected at gasoline service stations. Max went to work as a $35 a week salesman. In 1938, he acquired a fourth partnership in a refining company. Developing a new process for producing premium gas out of cheaper crude oil, he built one of the largest independent gas station chains in the Midwest. The Ohio Oil Company, now known as Marathon, paid $37 million for the chain.

From there, Max Fisher continued his successful business career in real estate, office buildings and apartment houses and various other investments. His net worth has been estimated at $100 million and still counting. For years he has been advisor and confidant to big business executives, powerful national political leaders, international figures as well as recognized internationally as a generous contributor to worthy causes, an unsurpassed fund raiser, a civic leader and one of the wealthiest men in the nation.

Anthony Rossi, an Italian immigrant, worked as a fruit picker, a farmer and operated a small restaurant before he organized a small fruit processing plant in Bradenton, Florida in 1946. Starting with fifty employees, the company grew to become the state's sixth largest manufacturing employer with 3800 employees at the peak season. By that time, Tropicana had become the world's largest producer of 100 percent chilled orange juice claiming a major share of the $2 billion citrus market in the United States. In 1978, Beatrice Foods, the world's largest food company, acquired Tropicana for a half billion dollars.

Jay Van Andel and Richard DeVos were founders of the Amway Corporation in late 1959, operating out of the basements of their homes for the first year. Then they converted a small gas station in Ada, Michigan into a combination office and print shop. At the beginning they sold a few household products directly to the consumer. In 1980, Amway is the world's second largest direct sales industry, an international business operating in thirteen nations with sales in excess of $1 billion. With headquarters in Ada, Michigan covering a 300 acre site, the company requires six million square feet for manufacuturing plants, laboratories, offices, warehouses and other services. As one of the top privately owned enterprises in the world, Amway owns, in addition to the direct sales business, the Mutual Broadcasting System, the largest radio network anywhere, with 950 affiliate stations, a fifty thousand watt radio station in both New York City and Chicago, Nutrilite Products, Inc., a seven hundred room hotel, plus three office buildings in downtown Grand Rapids, Michigan, and the Peter Island resort in the British Virgin Islands.

Amway has 6000 employees and 750,000 distributorships worldwide. Amway distributors operate their own businesses, selling directly to retail customers and assisting other interested people in becoming distributors. Amway products are available only through Amway distributors. Amway products form six separate groups: Home Care, Personal Care, Nutritional, Housewares, Personal Shoppers Catalog and Commercial. As independent operators, Amway distributors can market any or all of the products. Products are sold and delivered to homes or places of business.

Under this system, each distributor is an entrepreneur. Each is free to establish goals for size and income based on each individual's effort and ability. Amway is one of the world's largest producers of entrepreneurs.

According to the Statistics of Income released by the Internal Revenue Service, the number of people reporting personal adjusted gross income of $1 million or more increased from 903 in 1973 out of 80 million returns to 2041 in 1978 out of 90 million returns.

It is estimated that 600,000 Americans had a net income of $1 million or more in 1980. The number is increasing at a 10% rate annually. Studies of these records reveal that most of the new millionaires are self made. They gained the affluent status by their efforts rather than by inheritance. This is consistent with the history of entrepreneurship.

With so much attention focused on the gigantic corporations, transnational conglomerates and multi-billion dollar mergers between the mega-organizations, there is an inclination to forget that these mammoth economic institutions were once small business firms, sired by entrepreneurs of paltry means. They did not start as we know them today. Over a period of time, they grew into the powerful industrial, commercial, and financial organizations that we take for granted. Their founders are remembered as millionaires, philanthropists, and in some cases, ruthless scoundrels with lavish lifestyles.

The tradition of poor boy makes good was initiated by these rugged individuals. Today, John D. Rockefeller is remembered as the world's richest man of his day. Few recall that he was the son of a penniless peddler. At age sixteen, he started his climb to fame and fortune as a clerk in a small produce company. Ambitious, a planner, an organizer, he formed a partnership in a grain commission house. At age twenty-three, he used his profits to enter the oil business, buying and selling kerosene from the coal mines in Pennsylvania.

Fifteen years later, he controlled oil refining, distribution and transportation in the United States and much of the world's oil trade.

Andrew Carnegie is remembered as the world's second richest man and for his generous gifts to educational and cultural interests. A member of an impoverished immigrant family from Scotland, he started to work at age thirteen as a bobbing boy in a cotton mill for $1.20 a week. He went to work for the Pennsylvania Railroad for

$35 a month. On the advice of some of his supervisors, he borrowed money to buy shares in the Woodruff Sleeping Car Company. From there he became the steel magnate credited with developing the steel business in the United States. He sold his Carnegie Steel holdings to a group headed by J. P. Morgan. It became U. S. Steel Corporation.

In the early 19th century, a raucous sixteen year old entrepreneur named Cornelius Vanderbilt operated a rickety ferry between Manhattan and Staten Island. He ferried farm produce and passengers. He went on to become the railroad tycoon, Commodore Cornelius Vanderbilt, the first of the Vanderbilt dynasty.

Dozens of others began under similar humble circumstances—entrepreneurs starting with little more than an idea, an abundance of energy, an unshakable self confidence and a hard-nosed sense of practicability that spurred them to learn the tricks of their chosen trades better than anyone else at the time. They laid the foundation for the prodigious growth of these enormous business establishments that are household words, now, throughout the civilized world.

Under dissimilar conditions, laws and practices, the tradition continues, multiplied by the hundreds of thousands of individual enterprises running the gamut of products and services demanded by an insatiable public. Remove the contributions of these entrepreneurs from the world economy and the productive machinery would come to a job-crunching halt.

Today, an infinite number of entrepreneurs could be selected as models of business achievement, civic responsibility, public service and personal rectitude. Their names would emblazon a vast hall of success as beacons of inspiration for all future generations. I have selected just one of these present day entrepreneurs for this story. His name is John McGoff. Similar to his counterparts in countless communities throughout the land, he has become a successful business leader and an influential citizen in relative anonymity except in his own area of operations where he has been subject to more publicity about some of his activities than he sought or deserved.

In addition to being a good example of modern entrepreneurship, he is a non-conformist, an iconoclast, a civic leader, a patron of the arts, a patriot, an ordinary American citizen with an extraordinary record that is shared here. He has been called America's most controversial publisher by some of his critics; a publisher who has made unique contributions to the advancement of journalism by some of his supporters. His enemies swear at him. His friends swear by him. When annoyed, he swears at anything around at the time.

His ascendency to a position of affluence and influence through his own efforts is emblematic of the thousands of ambitious, self-motivated, independent men and women in this nation who make the American dream come true, day after day, year after year.

John McGoff's career makes a fascinating story, in its own right. For the purpose of illustrating his particular way of putting the free enterprise system to work for him, I have selected incidents, events and developments that have influenced most directly the direction and ultimate course of his career: his successes, his failures, his strengths, his weaknesses, his ideals, his ideas, his personal qualities, his character traits, his relationships with his associates, his actions under stress, his private family life, his public business behavior.

As this story unfolds, it serves as a symbol of the legions who conceive opportunities that abound around them and react in their own particular way.

John McGoff was selected for this story, primarily, because he reflects the spirit of entrepreneurship with a high degree of fidelity. One of the better definitions of entrepreneur states, "One who undertakes to start a business or enterprise, usually taking full control and risk." Even that splendid description fails to reflect the spirit that we have learned to associate with the name— a spirit signifying boldness, daring, venturesomeness, initiative, courage, energy, drive, independence, desire to achieve, growth, success in the traditional American way. The spirit of the entrepreneur transcends quantitative measurement. It is intangible. It cannot be counted but it accounts for everything else that counts in success or failure.

As Rome erected physical barriers to repulse the invading hordes, Cicero went around admonishing his fellow Romans, "Look not to the walls of Rome, but look to the spirit of men." So it is with this story of John McGoff, the entrepreneur. Look to the spirit of this man. Look to that indomitable, fervent spirit that drives him to seek new walls to climb for his own gain and for the highest good of his nation. Look to the fire in this man's heart and kindle one for yourself.

Harry R. Hall

Acknowledgments

During the course of writing this book, I talked and corresponded with numerous individuals familiar with the subjects covered in the text. I express gratitude to all who contributed to the information bank.

I acknowledge, with special appreciation, the cooperation of others who rendered specific services on numerous occasions:

* John McGoff's associates, employees, friends and family members who gave written and oral information with permission for direct quotation. Since they are identified in the text, names are not listed here.
* Michelle Lower and Sharon Mitchell of the Panax corporate staff for search and reproduction of various records and reports needed from time to time.
* James Barrett, Martin Rauscher, George Graff and Sally Dorer of the Michigan State Chamber of Commerce staff for their promptitude in responding to special requests.
* Lynne Peck Rutan, The American Society of Travel Agents, New York, for literature on the International Travel Business.
* James A. Bunce, the Travel Bureau, Department of Commerce, State of Michigan, for facts and figures on Michigan's tourist industry.
* United Steel Workers of America, Pittsburgh, Pennsylvania, for publications relating to union history.
* A. M. Griffin, General Manager—Personnel, J. and L. Steel Company, Pittsburgh, Pennsylvania, for Peter McGoff's employment record.
* William J. McCrea, Chairman, The Entrepreneurship Institute, Worthington, Ohio, for copies of the Entrepreneur and other publications of the Institute.

* Dee Kinzel for reading the original manuscript and making constructive comments for improvement.
* If I have missed anyone deserving special mention it is inadvertent. Facts, figures, dates, conditions prevailing at given times and places were gleaned from a variety of sources, such as:
* Encyclopedia Britannica III.
* Michigan, a History of the Wolverine State by Willis F. Dunbar, published by William B. Eerdmans Publishing Company.
* History of the Third Infantry Division in World War II, edited by Donald G. Taggart.
* Road to Rome, a Fifth Army booklet describing action from arrival in Italy until entering Rome.
* Anzio Beachhead, American Forces in Action Series, Department of Army, Washington D.C.
* Anzio by Wnyford Vaughan-Thomas, published by Longman's London.
* Command Mission by Lt. General Lucien Truscott, published by Dutton.
* Calculated Risk by General Mark Clark, published by Harper.
* 50 Great Pioneers of America Industry, a News Front Year Periodical, published by C.S. Hammond.
* The Age of The Moguls by Stewart Holbrook, published by Doubleday.
* The Enterprising Americans by John Chamberlain, published by Harper and Row.
* The Entrepreneurs by Robert L. Shook, published by Harper and Row.
* The Enterprising Man, prepared by Michigan State University for U. S. Small Business Administration, Washington, D.C. Authors: Orvis F. Collins, Associate Professor, Graduate School of Business Administration, Michigan State University; David G. Moore, Dean, New State School of Industrial and Labor Relations, Cornell University; with Darib Unwalla, Assistant Professor of Management, College of Business, Michigan State University. Published by Michigan State University.
* The Organization Makers: A Behavioral Study of Indepen-

dent Entrepreneurs, by Orvis, F. Collins, New York State College at Buffalo; David G. Moore, New York State School of Industrial and Labor Relations, Cornell University. Published by Appleton-Century-Crofts, Meredith Corporation, New York, N.Y.
* The Power of the Corporate Mind, Abraham Zaleznik, Professor of Psychology, Harvard University; Manfred F.R. Kets de Vries, Associate Professor of Management Policy and Behavioral Science, McGill University. Published by Houghton Mifflin Co., Boston, Mass.
* Small Business Publications, U.S. Small Business Administration, Washington, D.C.

No direct quotes were made from these books, but they proved invaluable in providing proper background material and perspective on the subject of entrepreneurship. Other pertinent information was gathered from various newspaper articles over a period of years and from such magazines as Money, Forbes, Saturday Review, Newsweek, Fortune and similar publications that I read regularly. Much of the understanding of the subject is the result of personal observation through more than thirty-five years of association with entrepreneurs as an organization executive.

Grateful appreciation is made to the following for permission to quote from their publications:
* Reader's Digest for permission to use quote by Dorothy Wenzel from May, 1979 issue of Reader's Digest.
* Harcourt Brace Jovanovich, Inc. for quote by Dorothy Canfield Fisher from Her Son's Wife.
* Harper and Row Publishers, Inc. for quote by Channing Pollack from Guide Posts in Chaos.
* J.C. Ferguson Publishing Company for quote by Bruce Barton from the International Encyclopedia of Quotations.
* Antheneum Publishers for Quote from John Fitzgerald Kennedy from the book John Fitzgerald Kennedy by Hugh Sidey.
* Dodd Mead and Company for quote by Robert Service from The Law of the Yukon in The Collected Poems of Robert Service.
* A.M. Kelly, Publishers for quote by Louis Dembitz Brandeis from the book, Business: A Profession reprinted by A.M. Kelly, 1971.

Chapter 1

Forming the Mold

"One father is worth more than a hundred schoolmasters."

. . George Herbert

Cruising northward on the pellucid waters of Canada's Georgian Bay, the Global Star logged nine knots bucking a cool twenty-five mile wind. John McGoff and his guest, lolling on the sundeck of the luxury ship were lulled into a semi-hypnotic state by the throbbing cadence of the powerful B. W. Alpha diesel, the soporific rays of a blazing sun out of a cloudless sky and the rhythmic roll of the ship gracefully cutting through the undulations of an aroused bay.

"Adversity, suffering, deprivation, poverty, can all be great character builders if they are accepted in the right way," murmured McGoff. "Being poor is the most powerful incentive anybody should need to get as far away from it as possible."

Startled out of his somnolence as though a bucket of ice water had been dashed on his relaxed body, the guest bolted upright in his deck chair. Was McGoff talking in his sleep? No, he was awake, serious and apparently trying to make a point. Obviously, he was in a reflective mood. This talk of being poor sounded oddly incongrous in surroundings glistening with affluence.

Apparently, an incident a few hours earlier induced this train of thought. The Global Star had docked at Tobermory for some supplies— Canadian whiskey, steaks for a cookout that evening and a few other miscellaneous food items. A hundred cars were

1

waiting in line to board a ferry boat that would take them to a province attractions park on an island about an hour out in the bay. McGoff had walked over to a public building to call his office. A man standing in line to use the same pay station phone was admiring the Global Star.

"What a beautiful ship," he said as he turned to McGoff. "It's got a foreign flag. Must be one of them Arabs. They seem to have all the money these days. I wonder who owns it. You know?"

"Well, I know the cook," McGoff answered. He did not lie. He did know the cook. Also, he owned the ship. He did not mention that, unwilling to embarrass the man. At that moment he looked more like a friend of the cook than a luxury vessel owner. He might have been accepted as a deck hand. Owner? Never.

A walking cast encased one leg, broken in an accident a few weeks before when he jumped from the ship into a small tender. Dressed in worn rumpled slacks, a wrinkled shirt and a weather-beaten baseball cap, his stinging vermilion face revealed over-exposure of a sunsensitive skin.

The Global Star, sitting gracefully on the glimmering bay cushion was silhouetted against the verdantly forested mountains in the background. Posed like a model for a painting by noted marine artist James Cleary, the resplendent vessel seemed to flirt with the Canadian day vacationists attracted by her beauty and symmetry.

The Global Star, registered in the Cayman Islands, measures one hundred fifteen feet in length, has four decks, provides space to sleep thirty people, including eight crew members, weighs three hundred and twenty tons. The former Danish hospital vessel had been converted into a private luxury ship at a cost of one and one-half million dollars and still counting with each revolution of the mighty engine.

Light years separated McGoff's affluent life style and a poor family past. Recrudescence of early life memories, undimmed by time, kept him grateful for the distance between the two levels of living.

When John McGoff was a student at Michigan State University, one of his part time jobs was at WKAR radio station, owned and operated by the University. As a script writer, he earned sixty cents an hour for a maximum of twenty hours a week, or twelve dollars.

Robert J. Coleman, now retired, was the station's manager. He projected a severe demeanor but the gruff drill sergeant facade covered a subtle humor and a character as gentle as a whisper on a soft summer night. These qualities may not have been required as a condition of employment, but they were indispensible to his own emotional stability as he tried to present a high quality program to an intellectually oriented community using constantly changing part time student employees of dissimilar disciplines, diverse credentials and differing motivations.

Some of these student employees claimed that Bob Coleman was gifted with some kind of built-in receiving set that automatically cut him into any program at any time a script writer or announcer made a mistake. To them, it was uncanny, if not eerie, that he could identify a boner on the air with such accuracy and immediacy.

Most of them did not know that Bob's wife, now deceased, was the receiver. She listened to the station most of her waking hours. Discriminating in her listening tastes, a perfectionist in her expectancies, proud of her husband's position, she called Bob when she heard an error. He, in turn, confronted the offender, delivered a few thundering imprecations and forgot the entire incident. So, would the student, but neither ever revealed that fact to the other.

Clarence E. "Dusty" Rhodes worked with John at WKAR. In addition to his work at the station, Dusty was the golden voice on the public address system for Michigan State University home football games, a cherished duty he performed until 1975, a quarter of a century after his graduation. Dusty and John became close friends. Both of them developed an enduring friendship with Bob Coleman. This relationship was to have a decisive impact on McGoff's career, and consequently, on Dusty's career, although it was not apparent to any of them for another decade.

McGoff's middle name is Peter. His fellow workers at the station jokingly called him J.P., after J.P. Morgan. He acquired this friendly nickname because of his frugality and undisguised distatse for wasting anything—money, time, effort, talent or words. He was serious about his studies, but far from stuffy or boorish. Bouncy, cheerful, inclined to play practical jokes, he displayed a keen sense of humor, was well liked, performed his assignments efficiently. At that time, he did not drink, smoke or chase around as many of his classmates did in the freewheeling forties following World War II. He saved his money and hoarded his time for essentials.

Dusty Rhodes says, "Like many of us, John was dependent on the G.I. Bill and part time jobs because he was paying all his own expenses. With his several part time jobs during the school year and full time jobs during the summer, he was putting some money in the savings bank and making a few smart investments. Even in his student days he had a nose for money."

This was not the first time that McGoff had been chided for his thriftiness, nor was it the first time he had shown a bent for business. At eleven years of age, he acquired a paper route, saved his earnings until he had enough to buy a fully equipped Silver King bicycle, enabling him to enlarge his route, increase his profits and put more in his savings account.

An early radio buff, Pittsburgh's pioneer radio station KDKA had no more attentive listener than young John McGoff, riveted in front of the late twenties model Atwater Kent at any spare moment, enchanted by his favorite programs—Garry Moore of the N.B.C. Blue Network— Don McNeil's Breakfast Club—Club Matinee— all broadcasting live out of Chicago.

When he was thirteen, he withdrew some of his newsboy savings to pay his twelve hour long milk train fare to Chicago, staying at the YMCA a full week, sitting in the audience several hours at each of these shows each day.

Going on the trip alone with his own money lofted his confidence, bestirred a sense of self-reliance, whetted his secret longing for travel and new experiences. Purchase of the bicycle had excited a pride of ownership.

Reminiscing over forty years later, McGoff observes, "I suppose the thrill of buying that bicycle has never been surpassed. That first Chicago trip alone divulged a parental trust that inspired me to do nothing to betray that trust." He did not know what was happening at the time, but these experiences were building character.

Young John's money management traits surfaced again during his four years in the Army, all but a few months of that time in combat zones of the European Theatre of Operation. Most of his pay was allotted to his mother, who deposited all of it in the bank for him. A non-smoker, he stored cartons of cigarettes in barracks

4

bags when they were issued to combat troops, later selling them at premium prices and transmitting that money home for additional savings.

At the end of his freshman year at M.S.U. he worked sixteen hours a day, every otherday, as a fireman on the Bessemer and Lake Erie Railroad, hauling coal to the Upper Great Lakes and fetching back iron ore to the Pittsburgh steel mills. Earnings ranged from fifteen hundred dollars to eighteen hundred dollars a month during his university summer break.

On two other summer vacation periods, he worked as a house painter. During the school year, ten hours a week in the university paint shop earned extra dollars for savings, stocks or bonds.

Dave Merrell was John's roommate the first few years at M.S.U. Looking back, Dave recognizes many incidents that marked the emergence of John's entrepreneurial inclinations while he served as a student leader of the University Glee Club. Both Dave and John joined the Glee Club as freshmen. The Director of the Club welcomed John's rich baritone voice and "fine musical ear." His imitation of Bing Crosby would have amazed Bing, and probably made Bing's lawyer suspicious.

Dave Merrell says, "John's leadership qualities began to blossom through those years. His natural sense of humor and his growing outgoingness made him a lot of friends. Elected the student Business Manager, and eventually President of the Glee Club, he organized a spring concert tour, put the show on the road with numerous trips in Michigan and Illinois. These tours made enough money to buy new costumes, new music, and put the group on a paying basis for the first time."

John was elected Chairman of his Dormitory Committee for the University Spring Festival, an annual activity for dormitories, fraternities and sororities to compete for prizes as student-built floats drifted down the Red Cedar River corkscrewing through the boundless M.S.U. campus.

Dave Merrell recalls, with both admiration and amusement, "For two years, John organized this activity for Old Wells Hall. We won awards both years. He was innovative. The floats had humorous themes. John supplied the ideas. I was on the committee to implement them. To illustrate, one year the theme of the float parade was 'Popular Songs.' We selected the homeliest student we could find. What nature had started, we completed with makeup.

5

Dressed as a girl, this grotesque figure stood in front of a mirror while John, at the bandstand, sang 'The Way You Look Tonight', to some silly irrelevant lyrics which I composed."

By this time, good-natured needling by his college friends about this sparingness, (some called it parsimony) his entrepreneurship, his independence of thought were accepted in the same exuberant spirit that propelled his drive for achievement. After all, it was his life, his money earned by sacrifice of pleasures and extra-curricular trivialities. He was free to spend his time and money on his own priorities. The hell with what anybody else thought. At this young stage of his life he was inner-buttressed against the peer peonage that diverted so many others from more purposeful goals.

These individualistic inclinations went back farther than his university, or for that matter, his paper route days when members of his own family chided him for being too tightfisted with his few dollars. He was born to a tradition of hard work, strict· moral conduct, thrift, discipline and freedom to pursue life in his own way.

Life had never been easy for Peter McGoff, his father. It had been a harsh struggle from the beginning. Born in Johnstown, Pennsylvania in 1884 of a working class Catholic family, he left school after the seventh grade and went to work. That was not unusual at the turn of the century. A strong boy in good health in the lower income family was expected to share in its upkeep. Schools concentrated on the basic subjects of reading, writing, arithmetic, spelling, history, geography and hickory stick discipline. Peter learned his lessons well. He was accustomed to an iron discipline at home.

When Peter was old enough, he left home to seek employment in the steel mills at Lorain, Ohio. Although still a boy chronologically, circumstances made him a man in a hurry. In Lorain he worked hard. In time, he met Sarah Thomasine Robinson from Patton, Pennsylvania. Sally Robinson was born in Kentucky. John's brother, Dan McGoff, claims family roots shooting off into distant kinship with William Clark, of Lewis-Clark Expedition fame, as well as Robert E. Lee and Daniel Boone.

Sally's father was a prosperous contractor for many years. When Sally was in her late teens, her father suffered severe financial losses. She was staying with her sister in Lorain when she met Peter.

This chance meeting evolved into friendship, courtship and inevitably, marriage. In Lorain the first four children were born. Edward, number one, died in his infancy. William was born in 1910. Ruth came along in 1914. Robert arrived eighteen months later.

Dan was the blessed event in 1918 in Pittsburgh. John joined the family in Pittsburgh on June 29, 1924. A few months later, John was protesting his discomfort with shrill cries, flailing arms and pistoning legs. Peter looked down on the crib and mused, "Look at that little tyke fight. He has more fire in his heart than a blast furnace. I hope it is never banked."

Peter McGoff moved his family to Pittsburgh in 1917 looking for a better job. That first rented house on Edmund Street was to be home for the next twenty years. Known as the Bloomfield section, the neighborhood was occupied by working class people of varied ethnicity—Irish, Italian, German. It was convenient to the Jones and Laughlin Steel Company where many of them worked, including Peter. He was drawing near his fortieth year. His work in Lorain had been steady, but pay was low. Pittsburgh seemed to offer more choice of jobs with the numerous burgeoning steel mills advertising for help.

He was employed as a craneman in the Electric Department at the J. & L. Pittsburgh works from June 2, 1917 until March, 1920. His weekly earnings were based on a wage of twenty-six cents an hour, an increase over his previous wages. The work was steady.

He was discharged for insubordination about June 1, 1920. None of the surviving members of the family recall what he did to keep them in food, clothing and shelter for the two year period between discharge and re-employment at J. & L. They survived somehow, through his efforts. No federal, state, or local relief agencies provided any aid. Proud, independent, self-reliant, he would not have accepted any kind of charity, public or private, even if it had been available or offered.

Peter was re-hired by J. & L. on March 14, 1922. He worked as a craneman throughout the Pittsburgh Works Electric Department and the J. & L. Pittsburgh Works Blooming Mill Department until he was retired with pension on October 26, 1948.

From 1922 through the mid-thirties, his weekly earnings were based on a wage of thirty-one cents an hour. From the middle to the late 1940's, his earnings as a craneman were at the rate of $1.25 an hour, the highest level of his work life. Today the same job would pay a minimum of $10 an hour with numerous fringe benefits almost equaling, if not surpassing, the wages.

Work in the steel mills was rugged in the first half of the century. Grit, grime, dirt, dust, physical hazards were part of the price of a regular paycheck. Pittsburgh was known as the Smokey City. No place in the city was more smutty than the steel plants, inspiring Carl Sandburg to write his famous "Smoke and Steel" poetry.

Universal ecological awareness was to await several generations before its time arrived. Environmentalists were mute. The public expressed little concern about air, water or urban pollution created by uncontrolled industrialization. Research was academic rather than applied. As for general public understanding, ecology could have been an occult science, like magic or necromancy. Modern ecology as an interdisciplinary science did not come of age until 1942. Early studies were limited to interaction of organisms in plant and animal communities. Man, the dominant organism on earth, was not considered as a part of the interaction of living organisms. When Thomas Malthus postulated the theory that population boomed more rapidly than the capability of the earth to supply food, ecologists studied animal population dynamics and territoriality of nesting birds to test the theory.

In the steel plants safety rules were lax. Accident rates were high. Workmen's compensation awards were low. The Gompers craft union concept prevailed. Industry-wide bargaining did not start until the advent of the United Steel Workers of America, recognized by U.S. Steel in 1937 as the bargaining agent. Other steel companies held out until 1941.

Seniority, paid holidays, paid vacations, company-paid hospitalization, life insurance and other benefits were non-existent. Employees worked at the whims of the foreman. He was king.

Pay rates were higher than most other factory jobs. Work was steady, under normal conditions. Above the noise, workers could be heard singing:

"Go to steel mill

8

if wanta work
pays good money,
Gotta work
where jobs are."

Except for the interim between 1920 and 1922, Peter McGoff worked regularly, with considerable overtime, until the depression. These depression years from 1929 to 1935 hit the McGoff family hard. This was the most difficult time in Peter's career. Work was uncertain from day to day. Workers would line up for each shift. The foreman would call names of anyone needed for that day. If a worker's name was not called, there was nothing to do but go home and hope for the next day. Any worker getting two days a week was considered lucky, or suspected of being a favorite of the foreman. Peter McGoff worked only one or two days a week during the depression.

The McGoff family managed. Some neighbors were less fortunate. They did not work at all for long periods. Of the four surviving members of the family, older brother Robert McGoff has the most vivid recollection of the depression from the time it started with the stock market crash in 1929 until various New Deal economic pump primings and preparation for World War II triggered a resurgence in the economy.

Born in 1916, Bob spent his teen years in the depression. Now retired at age sixty-five and living on a farm at Murryville, Pennsylvania, he recalls the period with a mixture of solemnity and lighthearted pleasure.

"These were bad years," he declares. "We were poor—very poor— but we had a spirit that even bad times couldn't faze. We wore patched up clothes to school, church or anywhere we went. There was no choice. We couldn't afford anything else. We were in a depression, but our family wasn't depressed. Most of our friends and neighbors were going through the same experience. We didn't waste any time brooding about it. We took it in stride and went right on living the best we could. My father had great faith. He took the attitude that we had been able to get by up to that point and we would continue to make it some way. It had no effect on our close family relations."

"Sure, times were hard," Bob recounts, "but we had barrels of fun, too. Our parents were not the kind to let setbacks interfere

9

with out homelife. Times had always been tough. The depression just made it tougher. If anything, we became closer. My father and mother believed in living a happy life. If they were worried about anything, they never let us know about it."

With nostalgic enjoyment in his voice, Bob conveys some of the simple activities that helped give happiness to everybody at the time.

"We used to have 'depression parties'. Neighbors would gather in our home for the evening. They brought their own food and pillows. We sat around the living room on the pillows. My mother played the piano. We had a singing family. All of us had good natural voices, although we never made anything out of it commercially. But we did enjoy singing, so on these depression parties we spent the evening singing everything from the old hymns to the popular hits of the day. Sometimes we played games. They might seem corny to the present generation, but they gave us a lot of entertainment and enjoyment and we never tired of the same things happening at the next party."

Bob remembers that one of the favorite stunts pulled frequently was to have someone sneak up back of you and place hands over the eyes until you guessed the name of the person. The part that got the biggest laugh was when the hands had been soaked in extremely hot water or when they had been held outside until they were freezing cold. The shocked reaction never failed to draw maximum applause. And it never grew old.

Bob chuckles as he relates another fond memory to illustrate one way they beat the hot, sticky, muggy summer days in Pittsburgh. "Since everybody had more time on their hands than anything else during the depression, a group of the neighbors would pack picnic baskets in the summer and chip in to get a truck to ride out in the country along the Ohio River. One of the favorite spots was on a shady bank overlooking the river. Somebody had smoothed out a dirt slide from the top of the hill to the river. After watering it down, the men and kids who could swim would use it as a mud slide. My father was a good swimmer. I can see him now as he'd take a long run, belly flop on that mud slide and shoot out in the Ohio River time and time again. Times were tough, but we enjoyed life and took care of ourselves."

Although Bob McGoff would not want to return to the conditions of that depression, he does wonder what has happened to the spirit that sustained them. He now reminisces, "We pulled through without being a burden on society. We had no unemployment insurance, no generous welfare programs, no food stamps, no medicaid or medicare or any of the many tax-supported things that people today consider rights, not just privileges. I wonder what happened to that spirit and pride that kept us going?"

Sally performed miracles with the meager funds, shopping astutely, preparing tasty dishes with what was available. It was necessary to skimp on the essentials and eliminate any semblance of luxuries. Everybody else in the neighborhood was doing the same. So nobody developed self-pity, least of all the McGoff family.

Peter McGoff's parents had been Republican. Sally's family believed in God, Country and Republicans. Peter shifted to the Democrats. He was convinced the Republicans had muffed it. In his mind, the complacent Republicans were responsible for the depression. Calvin Coolidge had said, "The business of America is business." A man of strong convictions, Peter had no reluctance in speaking his mind to anybody who would listen. Articulate, though not polished, there was never any doubt about where he stood on an issue. He admired Franklin D. Roosevelt, supported him in elections, defended him vehemently against critics. As far as he was concerned, Roosevelt was a divine deliverer of the working man in a floundering economy.

John recalls the heated discussions at the dinner table about the relative merits of Roosevelt's policies. John's sister and brothers were partisan to their mother's opposite point of view. Gentle, mildmannered, even-tempered, she never raised her voice. When Peter reached a point of uncontrollable explosiveness in his advocacy of the infallible Roosevelt, she would say, "Now come on, Peter," and leave the table. That was a signal to clear the table as well as the air.

John was too young to participate in the heated discussions. They left an indelible impression. He thought the tone was alarming.

A further illustration of Peter McGoff's independence pertained to his conversion from Catholicism to a church-going Methodist. Like many converts, his devotion, loyalty, and unwavering support of his adopted religion bordered on intolerance of any other faith.

Peter had been a hardworker all his work life. He had no choice because his jobs were hard, but he believed in giving a full day's work for a full day's pay. He shunned shortcuts. Elbert Hubbard's moralistic essay, *"Message to Garcia"*, mirrored his protestant ethic philosophy with a high degree of fidelity. At the same time, he believed the working man was the neglected element in the free enterprise system. He saw no conflict in loyalty to his employer and advocacy of a strong union, for, by, and of the employees themselves. In the early twenties a group of workers with the various mills in the Pittsburgh area did form what was called originally "The Independent Company Group". Company-dominated, weak in leadership, indoctrinated in the craft union concept, it disappointed the founders, frustrated the workers.

In 1936, John L. Lewis, aggressive President of the United Mine Workers, assigned Phillip Murray, one of his Vice Presidents, to organize an industry-wide steel workers union. Grafting the cells of the independent group as an embryo for a Steel Workers Organizing Committee, the effort culminated in the official chartering of the United Steel Workers of America. Phil Murray was elected its first President.

Concurrently, industrial unions were organized in the automobile, tire, rubber and electric products industries. In 1938, Lewis formed the Congress of Industrial Organizations, with these components as the charter base.

Energizing the new forces for election of public officials sympathetic to the unions, the C.I.O. revolutionized both national politics and the union movement. Bestowed with awesome political powers, John Lewis exploited his position to harvest a bountiful crop of demands from politicians and employers alike. A dominant figure of the Democratic Party, Lewis opposed Roosevelt's bid for a third term. Roosevelt's subsequent election was taken by Lewis as a personal repudiation. He resigned the C.I.O. presidency. Phil Murray succeeded him and served in that capacity until his death.

All of that is well-known history. Never appearing in the record is the role of anonymous volunteer organizers and supporters like Peter McGoff. Laboring tirelessly in the organizing campaign, supporting the leaders in battling lethargy and apathy of potential members, his voice carried weight with fellow workers. He held no paid or elective union office, but he remained loyal to the cause. His influence was substantial.

Peter McGoff was the dominant member of his family, but he was not domineering. Stern, decisive, opinionated, outspoken, he exuded affection for his wife and children. He nurtured a close-knit, compatible family. The family accepted his firm hand as a normal way of life. A bond of mutual confidence and trust prevailed. Tolerating no back talk from his offspring, he taught them to speak up about their convictions and views no matter how unpopular the opinion may be at any given time—and a view with Peter McGoff was a conviction.

He feigned no pretense of being a paragon of virtue, but he insisted on strict adherence to a code of virtuous conduct. Honesty, truthfulness, promptitude, obedience, integrity, trustworthiness, frugality! These were the eternal verities of his life—the ageless nineteenth century values—the immutable guidelines.

Today, John says his father's frequentative admonitions to be honest, to tell the truth, to fight for what you think is right and the hell with the consequences, became etched into his behavioral patterns at an early age.

Dan is a stickler for promptness for a sound reason. When he was in grade school, his teacher punished tardiness with equal time in the corner. One day, Dan lingered much too long after the bell rang. Detesting the punishment that he knew awaited him in the classroom, he went home, not realizing that his father was home too. Trying to sneak upstairs to his room, he stopped short when his father stormed in his stentorian voice, "Dan! What're you doing here?"

Hoping the truth would be rewarded with less painful punishment than a lie, Dan replied, "I'm not going to school today."

"Why?"

"I was late and don't want to stand in the corner."

In the late twenties, Dr. Spock's misguided theories on child psychology had not been inflicted on gullible parents. Peter McGoff held his own pre-Spock remedy for disciplinary problems—a remedy which produced more responsible adults than all the permissive miscreances that became the vogue a decade or two later. From his youth Peter learned from the receiving end the efficacy of a deftly applied razor strap.

Dan says, "He wielded that razor strap with such finesse that it would sting but not injure. A few strokes across the rear convinced me to return to school. He accompanied me. Each time I whim-

13

pered a protest, he administered another stinging reminder. By the time I got back, I was grateful to the teacher for letting me stand in the corner. My backside was burning too much to sit down then. I was never late again."

As a teenager, Ruth liked to dance, but a public dance hall was forbidden. To Peter McGoff, that was a place of wickedness to be avoided like the smallpox. Sitting on the front porch, she cried silently as other girls her own age passed on their way to the dance, dressed in knee-high skirts, rolled stockings and faddish painted butterflies on the bare knees.

"At those moments," Ruth relates, "I thought it was mean, but I could not muster up any lasting resentment. I loved my father dearly. I soon recovered from my temporary disappointment. There were many other redeeming pleasures in our home."

At age twenty-two Ruth was married. No alcoholic beverages were served at the reception. In his younger days Peter would imbibe at intervals although he was never habituated to drink. On one particular night, he overestimated his capacity. When he opened the front door at home, the floor seemed to undulate like Lake Erie in stormy weather. His young son laughed at Peter's comic attempts to navigate across the room to flop into his favorite chair.

The next morning his son went through the same antics with great glee. As Peter watched through bloodshot eyes, he said to his wife, "I don't want my son to think there is anything funny about me getting drunk. He won't see me out of control again. I want him to look up to me, not make fun of me. I'll never touch another drop. That's a promise."

That was it. Decisive, determined, stubborn, once he reached a decision, it was as irreversible as yesterday.

He had a will of steel.

His hobby was carpentry. Over a period of years, the basement workshop acquired a few power tools. On one occasion he cut off a finger. Wrapping it in a towel to keep the blood from spurting on his clothes, he walked to the hospital, refused anesthesia while the doctor performed surgery. He walked back home.

Later in life, he fell down the basement steps, breaking an arm in the process. Refusing Sally's pleas to go to a hospital, he filled a bucket with sand, selected a few pieces of wood for splints and insisted that Sally bandage it while he held the bucket of sand with the broken arm. It healed perfectly.

In the present age of laxity, life with such a strongwilled, unbending disciplinarian may sound draconian. Not so, say the surviving members of that household. Each of the four vow in almost identical words, "I have nothing but happy memories of my family life at home." Although living on a low income, nobody ever talked or thought much about it. Most of the neighborhood families were in the same income class. Laughter, song, joy, conviviality prevailed. Along the way Peter learned some magic tricks. He enjoyed nothing better than entertaining Dan's gang with his magic or leading them in songfests. He had a natural, melodious voice. Everybody in the family enjoyed singing.

A disciplined home. Yes! But a happy family. The kids developed normally—no hangups—no adolescent maladaptions—no antisocial behavioral problems—no immature ego-centered rebellion.

Sally, was known to everybody in the neighborhood as Mom, children and adults alike. Her home was an informal gathering place for the kids. Gentle, tolerant, kind, patient and understanding, Mom McGoff was a sharp contrast to Peter. Seldom raising her voice above its soft conversational level, she could project her displeasure by a slight, almost imperceptible change in expression or by a subtle comment.

Occasionally, Dan would become over-enthusiastic, or resistant to the order of the moment. At such times she was wont to remark, "Dan, sometimes I think they switched babies on me back in the hospital. You are so different from the rest of us." That was enough. Dan got the point.

That was Mom McGoff—sympathetic to Peter's principles, supportive of his methods but independent and self-assured in her own approaches to the same aims. She too had a strong will—a mind of her own. She accepted hardship, misfortune and physical pain with a stoicism that Peter could not surpass.

Helping her with the housecleaning one day, a neighbor handed her a loaded gun from a closet shelf. It went off as it was transferred from the lady to Sally. Noting that she was gravely injured, Peter took her in his arms and ran to the hospital. A petite female surgeon with peerless skills performed the life-saving surgery,

15

although the eye was lost and eventually replaced with a glass eye. Sally did not lose consciousness during the whole ordeal. She did not complain, harbored no bitterness. During her hospitalization and convalescence, neighbors prepared meals, cleaned the house and maintained normality in the McGoff's home life.

Radiating happiness, cheer and optimism to all around her, Sally was close to her children, particularly to Bill, the oldest, and John, the youngest. Bill was stricken with encephalitis lethargica, commonly known as sleeping sickness, in his middle teens. Although he recovered sufficiently for limited non-combat duty, progressive muscular weakness, lethargy and other deteriorating characteristics of the disease affected his physical capacity to function. Confined to institutional care, he remained mentally alert until his death. A voracious reader, he spent weekends at home discussing a wide variety of topics with the family members and friends.

John, the youngest, was the family favorite, but remained unspoiled. Being six years younger than the next to youngest sibling, he was relegated to a fringe observer, rather than an active participant in the group activities of his sister and brothers. Too young to take part, but too old to stash away in the corner, he developed his own interests. He learned to entertain himself, becoming a loner, but by no means an introvert. He enjoyed other people's company, but was not dependent on them to keep occupied or happy.

Sally, recognizing that the other kids did not want the little brother tagging along with them, spent most of each Sunday, after church, with John. In those days, the streetcar company sold an all-day pass for twenty-five cents, allowing unlimited travel to any place on the line.

John looked forward to these trips. He and his mother would go to the end of the line and explore the communities around Pittsburgh or visit different parts of the city, including all the tourist attractions. Possessing an intellectually inquiring mind, he was fascinated by the sights and the people. He could ask a thousand and one questions. The discussions with his mother, and other members of the family when he returned home, were enlightening, but more important, a whole new world opened its borders to his dreams with each new trip, each new discovery, each new morsel of knowledge. His mother's original idea was to keep him occupied.

She continued the Sunday streetcar outings because his enthusiasm was so contagious, his enjoyment so unrestrained. For John, these childhood experiences inspired a burning desire to travel to strange, faraway places—a yearning that has abided throughout his adulthood.

This was just one of the many simple, but deeply significant happenings that magnetized a close relationship of mother and son. As Walter Savage Lander wrote,

> "Children are what the mothers are,
> No father's fondest care
> Can fashion so the infant heart."

Today, Ruth Bliss Makon, John's older sister says, "John gets his gentleness, kindness, compassion, generosity and consideration for others from his mother. He acquired his drive, independence, stubborness and willingness to speak up on controversial issues from his father. There is a lot of both of them in him. They stand out in bold relief more distinctly as he gets older."

And so the mold was prepared, tracing all the delicate lines and patterns from the diverse personalities of a father and mother, joined in everlasting love and dedicated to the common cause of wholesome family rectitude. They provided the harmonic tonality and balance that shaped John McGoff's traits, qualities and character, preparing him to seek his rightful place in a cataclysmically changing world.

John McGoff was born and reared in a home, poor in material resources but rich in love and parental guidance. His moral moorings were secure. The harmonious family relations would be a model for his future family life. The memory of the poverty of his youth would be the motivating force in the development of his career.

Chapter 2

Forces Shaping the Future

*"There's a Divinity that shapes our ends, Rough-
hew them how we will."*
. . Hamlet—William Shakespeare

Behavioral scientists identify the home as the vital force in shaping character. A psychologically sound atmosphere in the home is conducive to psychological maturity as a child passes through the various cycles to adulthood.

In the early stages of life the child is dependent on the adult members of the family to establish behavioral patterns that determine future responses to institutional customs and demands. Ingrained in the character structure, these patterns direct whether a child develops confidence or diffidence, inner security or insecurity, a sense of responsibility or irresponsibility, affection or undemonstrativeness, eagerness or indifference, compassion or insensitiveness, and other basic linkages to life. These character traits occur initially, where learning from example is a natural process. Dolores Wengel has said, "Good character, like good soup, is made at home."

In Act II of "Ghosts", Henry Ibsen says, "It is not only what we have inherited from our fathers that exists in us, but all sorts of dead beliefs and things of that kind. They are not actually alive in us; but they are dormant all the same and we can never be rid of them. When I pick up a newspaper and read it, I fancy I see ghosts creeping between the lines. There must be ghosts all over the world."

18

Other forces unavoidedly assume equiponderance at certain stages of development: the school, the church, the community environment, the state of the economy, wars, peers, organized character building interest groups.

New forces outside the family were interjected into the shaping of John McGoff's future when he entered high school in 1935. The primary force was triggered by the family move to Edgewood, a Pittsburgh suburb. High school inflamed new interests, new outlooks, new ambitions, new hopes. The Glee Club uncapped an unusually gifted singing voice and a latent facility for showmanship that inspired the Glee Club to sparkling performances. His music teacher recognized a natural talent that needed encouragement. His infectious enthusiasm animated the entire chorus. Although he was shy and self-conscious at the beginning, he seemed to have a marvelous capacity to excel when the group was performing.

The Sea Scouts aroused a passion for the sea, boats, ships, and all their counterparts; a passion that has never been cooled. The Sea Scouts, at that time a part of the Boy Scouts of America, fostered good citizenship, physical fitness and character building through activities in sailing, general seamanship, power boat operations and water safety.

In 1939 young McGoff's consuming passion for ships was aroused further by a summer job on the schooner, Ida Mae, sailing out of Cambridge, Maryland, loaded with produce and canned goods destined for the West Indies and returning with bananas. The first job away from home tallied noticeable physical and mental growth. His father observed, "John is older than his years."

The new neighborhood sparked new confidence, overriding some of the self-consciousness about the family economic status; a sensitivity that had grown as he grew old enough to understand social status, and disturbed because he was excluded.

Recognition of his abilities gave self-assurance of his worthiness to compete successfully with students from more prosperous families. Self-reliant, inner motivated, emotionally stable, he was somewhat of a loner in high school, devising his own diversions as he had learned to do at home. Weekends found him rowing or sailing on the Allegheny, Monongahela or Ohio Rivers, weather permitting. The earlier streetcar rides were replaced with bike rides outside Pittsburgh, sometimes as far as one hundred miles away. Visiting smaller communities, he observed how others lived, worked and played, expanding his knowledge of people and things, satisfying to some degree, that restlessness for new experiences in strange places. On occasions a train trip with the family to Cleveland or Detroit or a side-wheeler steamboat trip to Buffalo added zest to life.

Today, McGoff extolls his father, his mother and the Sea Scouts as the most powerful forces in shaping his character, and his approaches to the hard realities of living and making a living.

Preferring history to all other subjects in high school, he devoured historical works with the avidity of a Renaissance scholar. Adept in spelling, he won several contests in school. When he entered high school, he gave no thought to college. It seemed out of his parents' means, and he had no particular ambitions for it. Before he reached his senior year, he had a craving for higher learning, realizing that any career appealing to him would require more than a high school diploma. This ambition and his election as President of his class incited an application to Penn State for admission. Approved a few weeks before his graduation in 1942, living history intervened to preclude entry to Penn State then or any later date.

Centuries before, Cicero said, "Thus in the beginning the world was so made that certain signs come before certain events."

For a decade, signs of coming events had been flashing luridly like neon lights, as Hitler screeched hatred for the Jews and all forms of democratic government in his bestial ascent to satanic power.

While McGoff was savoring the enjoyment of his high school days, the Nazi juggernaut demolished Poland, invaded Denmark and Norway, smashed Belgium, Holland and France, and trapped British Expeditionary Forces at Dunkirk.

With customary bombastic malevolence, fascist Benito Mussolini leaped on the seemingly unobstructable Nazi bandwagon, hoping to avenge past humiliations and latch on to a winner's share of the loot.

On December 7, 1941, the Japanese bombed Pearl Harbor. The United States promptly declared war on Japan, Germany and Italy.

So, inexorable forces unleashed by Hitler, Mussolini and the Japanese warlords heedlessly hurled John McGoff's future irretrievably away from Penn State.

A few weeks after his graduation, he was inducted into the Army at Fort Meade, Maryland, shipped to Camp Grant, Illinois for basic training and dispatched to Billings General Hospital at Indianapolis for special training as a medical technician. Dave Merrell had been through the same series of fast moving transfers, but did not know John during the three months basic training. Dave and John both volunteered for the special training. Dave was inducted at the end of his first year course as a pre-med student at Michigan State University. After arrival at Billings General, a practical joke incident blossomed into a lasting friendship. Dave recalls the beginning of a relationship that was to have an influence on their respective futures.

"John's irrepressible sense of humor which he has never lost, provides me with my clearest memory of that first impression. One night while we were both on duty as aid men in the wards, I received a call from a Colonel. I had never heard his name, but a buck private fresh from basic training does not ask any Colonel for an I.D. card.

"This Colonel ordered me to count the ward patients. One was reported missing, or so he informed me, in clipped military fashion. I grabbed my flashlight, made a hurried count and reported back by telephone as instructed. Abruptly, he told me to check again. Irately, he started to demand a third count when he burst into uncontrollable laughter. Only then did I recognize John McGoff as the phony Colonel."

This practical joke kindled a steadfast friendship that has endured the test of close and sustained association. At Camp Patrick Henry, the overseas staging area, Dave observed another unsuspected McGoff trait. After all these years, Dave expresses awe as he tells the story:

"We were standing around in the big room, waiting as Army units seemed to do most of the time. This burly, loud-mouthed, mean-looking G.I. swaggered in, spit on the floor and launched into a profane monologue about his prowess as a fighter. To believe him was to believe that the heavyweight champion cowered at the mention of his name.

"During my few months' acquaintance with John, I had been impressed with his verve, his sense of humor and his mild manner, but I was not prepared for the temper that exploded like gunpowder.

21

After the tirade had gone unchallenged for a while, John blasted suddenly and with vehemence, 'Shut your Goddam big mouth before I puke.' That was just for openers. This was followed with a string of profanities that left the braggart with mouth open and nothing coming out.

"A corporal lackey with him tried to interrupt, but John let him have it with the same fury. Everybody in the room was as amazed as I was. Here was this skinny, fuzzy-faced, high school kid ready to take on a bully, with no holds barred. We expected to see my new friend become a casualty before we left port. But, finally, everybody applauded. The intensity and conviction of John's verbal assault was enough. The troublemaker slinked out without another word."

Dave Merrell has seen that notorious McGoff temper flare on numerous occasions in these later years, but never with such surprising results.

At the staging area Merrell and McGoff were assigned to the Third Medical Battalion of the Third Infantry Division. They served together as litter bearers for the duration of the war.

The Third Infantry Division entered World War II with a tradition of gallantry established by victorious combat in World War I. Between wars the division performed wherever and whenever needed, divided between duty in trouble spots and routine post duty. Numerous military leaders who rose to high rank served with the Third Division at periods, including Generals Marshall and Eisenhower. Honor-laden since World War I, the division gained new luster in World War II for its role in some of the bloodier, most strategically decisive battles in the European Theatre of Operations.

Fewer than five months after John McGoff basked in the euphoria of grasping a diploma on the stage at Edgewood High School auditorium, he was a litter bearer crawling on the bloodstained beaches at Fedala, French Morocco and scrambling in the desert under deadly fire to deliver mutilated bodies to hospital clearing stations. Unexpected heavy casualties, shortage of equipment, transportation breakdowns hampered the rescue work when four transports were sunk in the landing off Fedala. This rude baptism of fire was the beginning of forty months of combat duty in some of the historically significant battles in modern warfare— Tunisia, Sicily, Palermo, Salerno, Cascino, Anzio, Cisterno,

Southern France, the Vosges, The Colmar Pocket, Nurenburg, Munich, Salzburg, Berchtesgaden.

Enshrined indelibly in the annals of military combat, these struggles stand boldly emblazoned in the history of man as classic examples of the capacity of the human spirit and body to adapt to barbarously inhuman conditions. No combatant group was subjected to a more severe test of human endurance than the litter bearers. Summarizing the exploits of the Fifth Army, Commander Mark Clark in "Road to Rome" states, "The litter bearers should be enrolled as the unsung heroes of the war." Paying tribute to all who served in the Third Division, General Lucien Truscott, Jr., said, "No condition of war has been unknown to you—barren beaches, desert sands, rugged mountains, vine-clad slopes, dense forests, marshy plains, torrid heat, torrential rains, winter snows, mud, ice—you know them all."

McGoff knew them all, remembers them all, survived them all. Anzio stands out most vividly. Anzio! A few square miles of beach and sand, thirty miles from Rome, at the foot of towering, graceful, treacherous, Colli-Laziali Mountains, controlling passage to Route Six and strategic highways of Southern Italy leading into Rome.

Anzio was the birthplace of Nero and Calugula. Augustus, the first Roman Emperor, was proclaimed "Father" of the Roman Nation at Anzio. It was at Anzio that Nero fiddled while Rome burned. Before World War II, Anzio was the site of a seaside resort for affluent Romans and a harbor for luxury yachts and commercial fishing boats.

Already secure in local history, this exclusive, obscure, little-known hamlet on the Tyrrhenian Coast was destined to have its name written in world history as the unlikely site of a savage military struggle that turned the tide of a major war. Anzio beach-head, recorded as a monument to valor and gallantry of the Armed Forces who fought there, is an embodiment of the horrors of suffering and human sacrifices of men under unpredictable conditions—a textbook study of the imponderables that thwart brilliantly-conceived tactics.

Components comprising the Sixth Corps of the Fifth Division, landed on Anzio without opposition on January 22, 1944. Intended as a diversionary surprise to wipe out hastily the scattered units of German General Kesselring's forces in the area, the maneuver was planned to gain control of Routes Six and Seven leading into Rome. Actually, the Anzio operation stretched out until April 27, 1944. Every known impediment and many unknown, occurred. Peaceful prewar Anzio turned into a pitiless deathway that made the reputed terrors of hell seem like a paradisical retreat by comparison.

At times, the weather turned savage. Freezing winds, accompanied by drenching, bone-chilling rains, held sway with relentless persistence. Continuous bombardment sometimes hit field hospitals, killing many of the wounded as they lay in the mud-sunken wards. Litter bearers poured the wounded into the clearing stations far in excess of capacity. Medical personnel never performed more nobly or humanely as they carried on to the brink of exhaustion, ignoring filthy clothes, blood-caked bandages, cold tasteless rations, sleepless nights and the ever-present stench of death.

In the "House of the Dead", Dostoyevsky wrote, "Man is a pliable animal, a being who gets accustomed to anything." McGoff and the thousands of men at Anzio did get accustomed to the execrable battlefield circumstances and the imminent danger of instant annihilation. He, like the others, went about his duties routinely, albeit fatalistically, stoically, unaffrightedly. He did not like it, but did not quail in the presence of suffering and death. He would never fear hell again. He saw it for four months at Anzio, in living color.

Citing a few incidents from memory dimmed by time, he recalls two of his closest calls. With some of his comrades in arms, he was walking down a road when an enemy plane streaked suddenly over the mountains, strafing the road. He dived into a ditch. All the others were killed. He emerged unharmed.

On another occasion, he dropped by a thickly weeded roadside from sheer weariness. His helmet fell on a slight ridge a foot away. Chunks of shrapnel shredded the helmet. He was untouched.

Dave Merrell laughs about another incident that illustrates adaptability of individuals under perpetual danger, but further shows McGoff's "tremendous sense of duty and commitment to any job he undertakes."

While off duty during a rare lull in hostilities, Dave, John and Herb Larkin, who worked together as litter bearers, sneaked down to the beach. On returning, their Master Sergeant was waiting for them.

"The old sarge was regular army, " says Dave, "and he was seldom seen without a medicinal cup of pure ethyl alcohol in his hand. Weaving on unsteady feet, he burped an AWOL charge against us. The next day was K.P. duty.

"After a few hours of scrubbing grease-laden field stoves, Herb and I took a rest and started to repeat a few old jokes to relieve the monotony. Without warning, John's nitro-glycerin temper went off. Castigating us more abusively than the Sarge himself, John continued to work until he had those beat-up old stoves glittering like polished diamonds. That is his way. When he tackles any job, big or little, he does it with an intensity that won't let him stop until it is done."

When a breakthrough at Anzio was still dubious, General Mark Clark visited the Third Division. McGoff was standing near the halftrack as Clark spoke. He recollects the General's closing admonition:

"We are fighting for our lives. Up ahead thirteen enemy divisions are throwing everything they have at you to break through our lines. Behind us is the sea. The ships that brought you here cannot return. We break through the enemy lines or we drown in the sea. There is no other alternative. There is no retreat."

Soon after General Clark's visit the allied forces did break through. General Clark rode in the lead jeep into Rome, and the Third Division was one of the first units to enter Rome in that historic triumphant parade.

Years later McGoff was in the audience at a Rotary Club meeting in Traverse City, Michigan, when Retired General Clark spoke. In a conversation with McGoff, the General said, "I recall well the visit to the Third Division at Anzio. We were in a desperate position. That breakthrough was a milestone in my life."

Rome had fallen. The Italian Campaign was history. But the war still raged. The Third Division moved on to spearhead the landing in Southern France, marching north and up the Rhone Valley, through the forests of the impassible Vosges Mountains culminating with the vicious fighting at The Colmar Pocket. Smashing the Siegfried Line, the Third Division was a key in the forces that bridged the Rhine, stormed Nurenburg, captured

Munich and Salzburg and finally knocked off Berchtesgaden as the war ended.

McGoff was with the Army of Occupation for another eight months. During the occupation duty, he organized leave trips to England, Scotland, Paris and Berlin, scrounging plane rides and accommodations to keep expenses at a minimum.

While in combat duty in Austria, troops were issued a carton of cigarettes daily. A non-smoker, McGoff hoarded his allocation. After the armistice, these cigarettes proved more precious than gold, at times selling for as much as two hundred dollars a pack. His savings account back home increased to more than ten thousand dollars as a result of these sales.

He was mustered out at Camp Kilmer, New Jersey in late January, 1946. His first act as a civilian was to buy his parents a home with $4500 of his savings. This was the first and only home they ever owned and they enjoyed it for the rest of their lives.

John embarked on his military service as a baby-faced, neoterical high school graduate. Fiercely patriotic, he burned with fervor for his country, believing passionately in the righteousness of the fight against the evil forces aligned against us. Thoroughly indoctrinated in the new deal philosophy as a result of his father's strong convictions, he admired Roosevelt, although he exhibited little interest in politics at the time.

Returning almost four years later, he had no reason to change these views. Proud to have served his country and proud of his nation, he had served faithfully, never shirking duty or complaining about assignments. As Plutarch said about Alcibiades, he could adapt himself to his company whether with good men or bad.

He came back unscathed, unsullied, unhonored. Except for the row of campaign ribbons, no special medals or citations for unusual acts adorned his chest. After all that service, he was a PFC until discharged, when he received his Corporal's stripes.

This was the result of a Presidential order to promote men with lengthy service one rank at discharge. The regimentation of military life did not unleash his leadership potential or latent capacity as a high achiever.

He came back as a man. Many of his basic qualities had emerged—adaptability, endurance, loyalty, emotional stability, courage, sobriety, independence, candor. Self-assessed as a loner,

26

he counted Dave Merrell as his one close friend from the long Army service. Close ties had been systematically avoided to obviate the pangs of loss due to death, disfigurement, mutilation and mental crack-up that he observed daily. He preferred no emotional involvement.

Now that his military days were a thing of the past, he turned his attention once again to higher education.

The G.I. Bill gave more flexibility in his choice and assurance of financing.

During their protracted conversations overseas, Dave Merrell had acclaimed the virtues of Michigan State. Dave re-entered Michigan State for the spring term of 1946; changing from pre-med to psychology. Torn between his original choice of Penn State and rejoining his best friend, John applied for admission to Michigan State. He had tasted just enough of world travel to sharpen his appetite for more. He had decided to prepare for a career in the foreign service of the State Department.

Immediately after the war all universities were inundated with applications from G.I.s whose education had been interrupted and from thousands of others who could now afford to go because of the G.I. Bill. Accommodations were inadequate to meet the demand. Only a limited number of out-of-state students could be accepted at State Universities. In due course, John's request was rejected.

Meaning to express nothing more than disappointment, he wrote to Dave Merrell. At this point, serendipity entered his life, the first of a succession of serendipitous episodes that would steer him to opportunities for advancement.

It happened that a close friend of Dave's family was an influential member of the Michigan State University Board of Trustees.

Dave avers, "This set up a situation for the one and only time where I had contacts that could be useful to both of us. Our family friend, Mr. Armstrong, was touched with my plea for my wartime buddy." John was admitted.

John McGoff's enrollment for the fall term in 1946 set in motion multifarious consequences of the utmost import on all aspects of his life; a culmination of his aspirations up to that time; a precursor of everything that would happen in the future.

It all started when two young G.I.s in training as army medical aids welded a bond of mutual respect and amity that was forged under the deadly fire of the battlefield and reinforced by close

27

association and common interests. It all started with an innocent practical joke.

Call it chance, luck, accident, fate, providence or destiny. Call it serendipity. Call it what you will. It does not matter. Being in the right place at the right time happens to everybody. Expecting one result and getting something better without explanation occurs in life. The wisdom, the judgment, the initiative, the common sense to take advantage of these fortuitous circumstances makes the difference in success or failure. As Sir Walter Scott wrote in "The Fortunes of Nigel",

> "Chance will not do the work,
> Chance sends the breeze;
> But if the pilot slumber at the helm
> The very winds that waft us towards the fort,
> May dash us on the shelves."

Chapter 3

The Pursuit of Opportunity

*"None of us knows what is ahead. The important
thing is to use today wisely and face tomorrow
eagerly and with the certainty that we shall be
equal to what it brings."*

. . Channing Pollack

John McGoff received his B.A. Degree in History and Foreign
Languages in 1950, the first college graduate in the McGoff family
tree. While he pondered the merits of a master's degree to enhance
his prospects for a State Department appointment, he was offered a
job at the university.

His extraordinary achievements as Student Business Manager
and President of the Glee Club had impressed Dr. John Hannah,
President of M.S.U. Hannah suggested him for Assistant Director
of Alumni Relations. Starr Keesler, Director, made the offer.
McGoff accepted. The salary was not staggering—$3500 a year.
Puny even by the pint-sized standards for non-faculty staff. Mate-
rially lower than McGoff had earned for three months work on
several summer vacations. That was not important at the time.
McGoff saw opportunity. He could pursue studies for his master's
degree. He could gain new experience, meet influential alumni,
travel. For the first time in his young life, he had many friends. He
enjoyed the associations at the university. He had nothing to lose,
and everything to gain, he reasoned.

One of the first members of the Alumni Association to give him
a boost was Dr. Jimmy Hays, M.S.U. faculty member and popular

29

with the Alumni Clubs around the state. McGoff mentioned to Dr. Hays that he was in the process of tapping his savings to buy a car, since his new job entailed visiting the clubs. Dr. Hayes advised, "Why do that? See my son. He is loan officer at the American Bank and Trust here in Lansing. Tell him I sent you. I will give you a good reference."

The five hundred dollar loan was used to purchase his first car—a two-door maroon Ford. Pride of ownership swelled again. In addition to travel in and out of the state, scheduled to permit graduate work, he was Assistant Editor of the Alumni magazine, conducted a weekly radio program, promoted out-of-state appearances for the Glee Club and solicited financial support for innumerable university interests.

Starr Keesler gave McGoff the highest job rating. Keesler, while working out of the University President's office on budget planning and control, recalled, "John McGoff was competent, hardworking, innovative, enthusiastic, eternally optimistic. He was a self-starter who worked on his own. He did not need prodding. To the contrary, it was necessary to hold him back, but he needed little supervision. Long hours, personal inconveniences and the rigors of heavy travel meant nothing to him."

On one occasion, Keesler recalls, McGoff aroused John Hannah's ire. Hannah had received reports that McGoff was collecting names for a petition opposing the adminsitration's plan to fire the Glee Club Director. Keesler was in a sensitive position when Hannah said, "Perhaps that young man has outlived his usefulness to us." When Hannah expressed an opinion, staff members listened. A strong administrator in the midst of building a great university, his suggestions were taken as commands most of the time. Keesler stalled for time. He did not interpret Hannah's suggestion as an ultimatum. He did talk to McGoff, who was not intimidated at all, insisted he was doing this as a graduate student on his own time and it had no relation to his job. He was not released. Keesler did not want to lose a productive assistant.

McGoff spent almost four years with the Alumni Association. High job ratings notwithstanding, the salary remained static. The Dean of Student activities held payroll authority over the Alumni Association. He refused salary increase requests for McGoff for personal reasons. He did not like McGoff. The job had no increment schedule. Neither Keesler nor McGoff was able to change the Dean's opposition.

Mired in this mucilaginous personnel imbroglio, he was rescued by Dr. Edgar Harden, Director of Continuing Education. Aggressive, ambitious, craftily astute in strategems of university politics, Dr. Harden appointed McGoff as an assistant with a salary increase to $4800 a year.

Kellogg Center is the headquarters for Continuing Education Programs. Built with a grant from the Kellogg Foundation, this center has full service facilities for conferences and meetings, including about two hundred hotel guest rooms. The Center sponsors seminars, conferences, conventions, and specializes in university made-to-order programs for associations, business, and professional groups, year round. It is a rare day, indeed, that Kellogg Center is not filled to capacity with some adult educational conference.

Dr. Harden later posted a distinguished record as President of Northern Michigan University and after retirement he was recalled to serve a two-year interim period as President of Michigan State University.

"When John was employed," says Harden, "we were experimenting with many new programs at Kellogg Center. John was the ideal selection for the job at that stage of development. He was eager to try new programs that we had not even considered. Always looking ahead, undeterred by difficulties, unaffected by criticism and full of original ideas, he worked incessantly. I gave him a great deal of freedom."

The job was exciting to McGoff. He promoted a Cap and Gown series. This developed into a popular and profitable music and drama program, bringing in prominent outside artists. Open to the public, the series attracted strong community support. In cooperation with the U.S. State Department, the Glee Club traveled to Europe. He arranged appearances for the Glee Club on national network shows, such as the Ed Sullivan and Dinah Shore programs. He initiated cultural workshops on and off the campus and organized a Drama Department.

One of the most popular attractions that he booked during his entire sojourn at Kellogg Center was Fred Waring and His Pennsylvanians. Fascinated by the brilliance of his performance, he was even more enchanted by the organizational efficiency, the promotional creativeness, the harmonious relations of the group, visibly happy to be working together and getting so much pleasure from each performance. Recognizing an affinity of interests, Fred Waring offered him a job on his staff. McGoff took a leave of absence from the university and traveled with the group for several months, learning about the innovative devices and techniques that made the Waring group so successful. He applied his new knowledge to his job when he returned and has found it useful throughout his career. He has remained a staunch friend of Fred Waring. He considers the experience one of the most productive of that stage of his development.

As one of the original Land Grant colleges, the multitude of Michigan agricultural organizations focalized state conferences at Kellogg Center. Dr. D.B.Varner, M.S.U. Vice President, successor to Ed Harden as director of all continuing education activities, asked McGoff to organize a program for the annual meeting of a particularly prestigious, politically potent, farm group.

Aware of Varner's flair for showmanship, McGoff resolved to produce a show worthy of Broadway. Special kaleidoscopic lights were installed. An elevated revolving stage was constructed. The best talent on the campus featured a gifted young harpist, accompanied by a brass section.

Woody Varner later served as President of Oakland University in Rochester, Michigan and then Chancellor of the University of Nebraska. He can recall no incident in all his career to equal the unexpected entertainment of that night.

"One of the most interesting and amusing incidents, although at the time it was hardly laughable, in my experience with John McGoff," reminisces Varner, "had to do with the staging of young harpist Harvey Griffin, who was a student at the university at that time. Harvey was a talented young musician. John liked to schedule him on the program there at Kellogg at every opportunity. With his true spirit of innovation, John rigged up a 'theatre in the round' concept and put Harvey in the center of the ballroom for this big event. It was a packed house and there in the center stood Harvey and his harp, spotted with colored lights. John had motorized the stage so that it would turn ever so slowly.

"All went well with Harvey Griffin's performance, at least in the beginning. The lights were focused, the harp began to play and the stage began to rotate. Unfortunately, the moment of truth struck. Someone along the line had failed to account for the fact that the electrical plug was fixed in the ceiling and each time the stage went around, it dragged Harvey and his harp down. He was great at that instrument while he was upright, but then came the electric cord and Harvey and harp went down again.

"This spirit of chaos and pathos caught the spirit of the crowd. Soon they were applauding vigorously as Harvey danced his way through the electrical arrangement. Finally, McGoff was able to disconnect the cord and Harvey finished his performance on a stationary stage. It was a dark moment for John McGoff. He was terribly chagrined but he pulled it off with his usual aplomb."

Today, McGoff chortles at mention of the incident. He remembers at one point of the concert, the cable caught a trumpet and threw it directly at Dr. Varner, who was embarrassed and furious at the moment, but after the audience responded so animatedly, Woody laughed as gustily as anyone else.

In evaluating the meeting, the leaders admitted that the unscheduled act saved the evening. These farmers had been in meetings for several days. They were seat weary. The artistically classical program would have induced slumber for many in the audience without the comedic relief.

This program is still discussed by the old timers at each gathering a quarter of a century later.

Dr. Varner says of his association with McGoff, "He was my assistant for cultural affairs. He was creative, brighteyed and bushytailed. He had more ideas than we could finance, but he had a knack, even then, of making things happen—with or without a budget. I would be less than honest if I did not share with you some of my sense of surprise at his extraordinary financial achievements. Little did any of us realize then, nor would we have predicted, that he would emerge as a mogul in the world of finance. He was a hard driving, effervescent and enthusiastic worker, but I saw little evidence that he was going to be a financial wizard. As a matter of fact, one of our problems was to figure out how to keep his programs solvent."

Margaret Hermina Evert, attractive, popular, intelligent, outgoing Home Economics major worked in one of the student cafeterias during her freshman year; the same year John was a Senior.

One day she stopped in the hallway to chat with an acquaintance. He introduced her to John, a fellow member of the Glee Club. Some time later this friend asked her to double date with John. Her first thought, she recalls, was, "Why don't you speak for yourself, John?" but she agreed anyway.

There was no sign of love at first sight or love at all for several years. The relationship was pleasant, casual, compatible. Dates were intermittent, always enjoyable.

"I was an ordinary student who liked college social life," Marge says in her cheerful, relaxed manner. "I seldom missed any of the major social events. John was a serious student more interested in studies and work. His social activities were limited."

Marge's father earned his mechanical engineer's degree in his native Germany, settling in Indiana when he migrated to this country. He moved to the Detroit area soon after Marge's birth in 1932. When Marge was thirteen, her mother died. Her father remarried. Marge took a commercial course in high school, preparing for secretarial work in her father's office. Her stepmother convinced her of the advantages of a college education and new career goals. Marge's future was altered appreciably. Stable, emotionally balanced, practical, Marge enjoyed university life. She was serious about her studies but did not consider pursuit of high grades of sufficient importance to encumber extracurricular activities. An average grade was no reflection against her sincerity or learning ability. It was a matter of values and application. The social and cultural exposures were a part of the educational process. She matured gracefully, sensibly, harmoniously.

Upon graduation, she was appointed to the teaching staff of Lansing's West Junior High School. Her relationship with John McGoff had grown from casual to close, to steady dating, to love. In 1955, five years after the first date, they were married in the chapel at M.S.U.

Dave Merrell was selected as John's best man. Dave and John had traveled different career roads since under-graduate associations. Dave continued as a full time graduate student earning his doctorate in psychology. Working full time at the university, John sought his master's degree as a part time graduate student. Their personal contact was infrequent. Inviting Dave to be his best man at the wedding, they both were amazed by a strange coincidence.

Dave's wedding date had been set just two weeks later. Each stood up for the other.

Marge continued teaching until Susan was born in March, 1957. After an appropriate time she returned to her teaching job. The second child, Tom, was born in July, 1961. Henceforth she devoted her time, talents, and efforts to being a full time wife and mother, family stabilizer, counselor, and inspiration for John. She performed with excellence in all of the roles. Three more children came in due time, spaced to allow for growing up in a wholesome family atmosphere.

David was born in February, 1966; Steven in June, 1968; and Andrew in 1971. At the age of eight, pictures show Andy as the spitting image of John when he was the same age.

Marge assumed her part of the partnership with no reservations. Just as John assumed the role of breadwinner, she accepted responsibility of homemaker. When they were married, John traveled a great deal. That increased markedly over the years. Generally, each absence was of short duration, but frequent. This created no problems, did not prevent a warm, healthy, close-knit, love-blessed family life.

From the beginning, John did not bring his work problems home. He seemed to have the capacity to shuck troubles when he left the office. Donning a cloak of undivided attention in the mundane affairs of the day with each member of the family, he loved to relax in an informal home life.

Marge soon learned to sense when tensions were seething beneath the facade of a carefree outer presence. She tried to create a smooth anxiety-free home atmosphere to fit any conditions. Even tempered, tactful, articulate, open in her relations with everyone, she learned when to discuss family problems and when to be quiet, when to encourage John to talk, when to respect anger as a human emotion that needs expression before it explodes violently from being bottled up too long.

The same understanding and patience held sway in her role as a mother, recognizing that irritations need to be aired to be cleared, that discipline can be maintained without being oppressive, that freedom can exist without permissiveness.

From the birth of Susan through the growing stages of Andy, Marge has displayed the qualities that were mentioned by Dorothy

Canfield Fisher in "Her Son's Wife": "A mother is not a person to lean on but a person to make leaning unnecessary." The result is a devoted family—secure, understanding, full of mutual confidence, trust, with none of the superficial trappings that complicate so many family relations.

In 1956, McGoff received his master's degree in History and Political Science. Two years later he was still plodding along in charge of special affairs in Continuing Education. The salary had increased to $6200 a year. Prospects for more rapid advancement were less than promising. His burning desire for a State Department career, flaming brightly when he entered the university, had smoldered, flickered and fizzled out in the incentive-thin atmosphere of academia. After more than a decade as a subject of a state bureaucracy, he chafed at the restraints on merit advancement, the tinsel pay for platinum performance for non-faculty employees without a Ph.D.

The empire building of each department at the University, the internal bickering for funds, the back-biting for special professional privileges, the arrogance of tenure—all these and more had become antithetical to his inclinations, his ambition, his mode of operations.

The cooperative promotions initiated by McGoff with the State Department quelled the idealistic views of federal service held before this practical exposure to the fumbling, cumbersome incompetencies, fostered by politicians and perpetuated by bureaucrats. He envisioned no future in any bureaucratic structure. For his own career, he figured the best way up was out.

Other changes were just as noteworthy. His political philosophy altered profoundly as he matured. Once a new deal disciple, he switched his allegiance to the Republican Party. His disenchantment with the Democrats had its roots in a natural conservative nature: belief in the Protestant ethic, puritanical devotion to hard work, thrift, self-reliance, personal independence, resistance to waste, disgust for slothfulness, resentment of growing welfare statism. These precepts were imcompatible with two decades of what he thought was a creeping socialism fostered by the Democrats.

Election of his war hero, General Eisenhower, to the Presidency, fueled his interest in politics, igniting into activism a latent interest in his chosen party and bringing harsh words for the party of his father. Believing that governmental intervention in business was a repudiation of freedom, he had grown into an articulate apostle of free enterprise long before he entered the business world.

These philosophical transmutations were not spur of the moment decisions, instigated by whim or fad. They defied trends. They crystallized over a period of years when liberalism was in vogue, younger people were flocking to the Democrats like crows to a cornfield, entrepreneurs were derided as unsavory characters of a crumbling past, security through government dependency was preferred to opportunity and risk.

McGoff's shift to the right typified a willingness, if not proclivity, to swim against the tide. This non-conformist tendency would be exposed, repeatedly, as his career advanced.

So he decided to go into business. He wanted to be his own boss. He leaned to the communications business. Believing that his demonstrated ability to raise money for the university would enable him to raise money for his own business, he discussed his plans with Bob Coleman, his friend at Station WKAR. At that time, Coleman and his radio associates were bullish on F.M. radio, predicting it was ripe for commercial exploitation.

Frequency modulation was not a new technical development. Edwin H. Armstrong, an inventor and pioneer in numerous electronic communications systems, laid much of the foundation of modern radio and electronics circuitry. He filed for patents for FM in 1933. The development of frequency modulation made possible the first clear practical method of high fidelity broadcasting. It eventually became the required sound channel in T.V., a dominant medium in mobile radio, micro-wave relay and space-satellite communications.

Armstrong's invention was acclaimed by scientists and engineers for its technical advancement. It eliminated static by modulating the number of waves per second, but it required a basic change in transmitters and receivers. It was snubbed by the radio industry.

Acquiring wealth and fame from his numerous inventions, Armstrong built his own station in 1939 at a cost of $300,000 to prove feasibility of FM as a commercial endeavor. World War II suspended promotion. Governmental regulations stifled renewed post-war attempts to proceed.

Litigation over patents sired interminable delays. Frustrated, ill, financially ruined, Armstrong committed suicide in 1954.

Mid-Michigan had no exclusive FM station in 1958. Some AM stations were broadcasting the same programs on FM, often offering this extra service to advertisers without extra costs to gain a competitive advantage. It was not until 1968 that the Federal Communications Commission ordered jointly owned AM/FM stations to broadcast independent programs in competitive markets.

In 1958, as McGoff mulled over alternatives of new career opportunities, he had no formalized education in private business, no specialized technical knowledge of FM radio. His personal finances were limited to the small joint savings he and his wife had accumulated by shrewd investments and frugal living. He could muster some money from his university friends and potential partners. That was restricted.

Add to these liabilities a limited, unmeasured audience for FM radio. Of all the radio sets in use then, ninety-two percent were AM. At this embryonic stage the other eight percent was owned by an elite listenership devoted to symphonic and classical music. The commercial response to an FM station was as unpredictable as a tornado's path. Raising capital under these conditions posed a Sisyphean task.

He could count some strengths to counterbalance the shortcomings. He had a flair for leadership. That could not be taught in formal courses. It could not be learned from "How To" books. He possessed an entrepreneurial spirit, daring to venture into unknown areas of endeavor, unafraid to fail and confident of success. He demonstrated a capacity to motivate others on numerous occasions in his university promotions. His integrity was unquestioned, an essential character trait that would take precedence over brilliance or academic degrees when dealing with other business executives. His performance standards were high, his tolerance quotient for mediocrity was low for himself and others. His optimism was balanced with a sense of realism and a contagious enthusiasm. He believed in himself, believed in his proposed service, had confidence in his associates. Some of the legendary tycoons of American business had started with fewer advantages.

He examined the obstacles. He saw barriers with open eyes. But the eyes served merely as instruments of transmission of an image to the brain, just as the lens of a camera lets in light to the film. With his brain he perceived opportunity.

Reminiscent of one of Carlyle's observations, the blocks of granite which would have appeared as obstacles in the pathways of a weaker person loomed as stepping stones to the strong-minded McGoff. Freedom to try. Expectations of achievement. Hope for financial gain. Opportunity to make his own decisions. Chance to compete for success. These were the incentives, the same incentives that had goaded countless Americans to fame and fortune.

When John McGoff became dissatisfied with his status in life, he did not waste his talents, energies or time in angry dissent against the established order, as many of his peers of that era were doing. He wanted improvement. He made no demands for destruction of the competitive enterprise system that the founding fathers had created. He put the system to work for him.

Having decided that it was time to change employment, he had four options: (1) to remain a job holder with another employer, (2) to join the unemployed ranks, (3) to become self-employed, (4) to become a job maker. He exercised his options by choosing to be self-employed and job maker.

In October, 1958, convinced that FM's time had arrived, he filed an application with FCC for a permit to operate a 100,000 watt station in East Lansing, Michigan. It was to be named WSWM/FM, acronym for Wonderful Sound, Wonderful Music. He recognized the risks. He accepted the responsibility. He did not wait for opportunity. He looked for it. He thought he had found it. He seized it. He made his own opportunity. That has been called the American way. It is the entrepreneur's way.

Chapter 4

The Struggle to Survive

"This is the law of the Yukon,
That only the strong shall survive;
That surely the weak shall perish
And only the fit survive."

. . Robert Service

In January, 1959, the FCC approved the application to operate WSWM/FM. Months of preparatory activity ensued, kicked off by purchase of over seven acres of land in the village of Okemos on Highway Sixteen, six miles east of East Lansing. A decaying old farmhouse was included in the purchase price of $13,000.

Magnetizing a working coterie from associates in the venture, all from Michigan State, laborers' clothing replaced office dress on evenings and weekends to remodel the dilapidated building, which had been used by Alcoholics Anonymous for a drying out center. If empty whiskey bottles hidden in the walls had been redeemable, the mortgage could have been liquidated on the spot. Gutting the interior, constructing new walls, laying new floors, reshingling the roof, smearing paint inside and out, the part time do-it-yourselfers turned the weathered shack into a combination transmitting station and office. Specialists were engaged to install the equipment and tower. The roof did not leak unless it rained hard. One of the early Board meetings of the fledgling Mid-States Broadcasting Company was adjourned hurriedly because of rain. Local residents identified the building as The White House.

McGoff left Michigan State University in May, 1959. WSWM/

40

FM went on the air on July 16, 1959, the first FM station in Mid-Michigan operating with no AM affiliation. At that moment, the world was McGoff's oyster, brimming with precious pearls, or so the euphoria of the occasion led him to believe. After an acute attack of reality replaced the exultation, he found the oyster lined with paste, not mother of pearl. The world could wait. The local community must be conquered first. An inauspicious opening was just the beginning of a long struggle for survival.

McGoff carried the dual titles of General Manager and Commercial Manager. He functioned as salesman, announcer, record spinner, janitor, goodwill ambassador and anything else that needed to be done. Though the seven original employees had some semblance of job assignments, the organization period was more experimental than routine. Everybody shared in the exigencies of the day.

The station featured symphonic and concert music. Strictly classical. No swing. No blues—stomp tunes. No rock and roll. No modern jazz. No country. Classicists loved it. Advertisers ignored it. Creditors blanched. Marge's teaching salary kept food on the table.

The first year gross income added to a grand total of $12,579. Debts mounted frightfully. It took no managerial genius to amass a huge deficit. It did require a rare acumen to keep operating with such emaciated revenues.

Several businessmen kept McGoff going. He sold himself better than his product. They had confidence in him. He assured them of his own confidence in a profitable future for FM broadcasting. After a shakedown period he spent most of his time calling on businessmen, met during his alumni association employment, to get enough money from week to week to meet the payroll. He was drawing no salary but he had to pay the other few employees to hold them. The records show he never missed a payroll for any of them.

Jim Anderton was one of his supporters. Jim was a steel executive, banker, civic leader in Lansing. He bought stock to meet the payroll on numerous occasions.

Harold Good, General Motors executive, was another of the payroll angels. His original interest was aroused when McGoff spoke at the Okemos Rotary Club in 1959. He was impressed by McGoff's openness, sincerity and convincing belief in the future of

41

FM, accepting an invitation to visit the new White House on the Hill at the edge of town.

Harold Good, retired for the past decade, says, "This was the beginning of a twenty-year association and a warm friendship that has continued to grow with the years. I soon became a minor investor and director.

"The public was just beginning to listen to FM," Good continues, "and revenues were slow. During the early days of WSWM there were a number of times when John would come to me and say, 'Harold, I'm going to need some help with the payroll this week.'

"As I preferred stock to cash repayment, I acquired my early financial interest in the company in this manner."

These were palliatives to relieve the payroll pain, but no cure for the operating deficit. In spite of some prestigious sponsors for hour-long symphony programs, the revenues were limited. Charges for time were low. C. Jon Holmes was an early subscriber. He bought a one minute ad per week for seven dollars and fifty cents. He attributes his rise in the insurance business to these ads. He talked about the effectiveness of his spot announcements to others, increased his time to five minutes a week, and kept the same spot for twenty years.

When he initiated the ads, he used the name C. J. Holmes. At a cocktail party at Michigan State, one of McGoff's associates suggested that he use C. Jon Holmes for his signature. "It has more class," he said. He tried it. The response was amazing. "It seems," he recounts, "that high income listeners responded to the name more readily and that was the type of prospects I wanted." Holmes became one of the best known and highest producing insurance agents in Mid-Michigan, soon qualifying for the Million Dollar Club, never missing the annual designation since that date.

When McGoff worked for the Alumni Association, he met Ty Gillespie, Vice President and General Counsel at Dow Chemical Company. Political and civic affairs were under Gillespie's supervision in addition to his legal responsibilities. Through Gillespie, he met Alden Dow, son of the founder of Dow Chemical, and one of the large stockholders but not an executive in the company. He had chosen architecture for his career and had become a renowned architect, a patron of the arts, well respected for his philanthropic and civic interests. On a McGoff visit, while seeking funds for a

42

university project, Dow had advised McGoff, "Get out of education. You will never make any money there. A young man with your talent and drive should go into business. If you need any help, let me know."

In 1961, when financial pressures advanced to the critical stage, McGoff talked with Gillespie who, in turn talked with Dow. A conference was arranged. Dow had followed McGoff's career. Complimenting McGoff on his good taste in trying to provide the public with a superior musical program, he asked, "How much do you need?"

"A minimum of $200,000," McGoff answered with an outward calm that belied an inward quaking.

"That should be no problem," Dow said instantly as he picked up the telephone. In McGoff's presence, he talked to Andy Hays at the American Bank and Trust in Lansing. "Andy, I want you to make a personal loan of $200,000 to my friend, John McGoff. I will guarantee the loan. Send me whatever papers you require."

McGoff, a heavy foot driver under normal conditions, collects traffic tickets faster than his windshield collects bugs. He pressed that accelerator to the floor on that ninety mile trip back to Lansing, trying to get to the bank before anybody had a change of mind.

Andy Hays was apprehensive. "I am sure, John," he explained, "you know this is an unorthodox procedure. With Alden Dow as your co-signer, the bank cannot lose anything, so you will get the loan." Without putting it into words, Andy implied that the bank had security but Dow was taking one hell of a chance. Six months later McGoff had difficulty in meeting the rather stiff payment schedule set at the bank. Dow took over the loan, establishing a repayment schedule for McGoff of $7,000 a year at one and one-half percent interest.

In January, 1978, McGoff presented to his benefactor a $62,000 check as the final balance on the loan that saved his business career. Dow made the loan on faith in this young man, the only security he had at that time.

"Alden Dow gave me survival money but, more important, his expression of confidence implanted a personal incentive through all those years. It prodded me to live up to his expectations," says McGoff today. "He has been friend, a sage advisor, a staunch supporter. I cherish the personal interest he has demonstrated so many times. He has been an inspiration to me."

43

When Dusty Rhodes graduated from M.S.U. with John in 1950, he went into radio and TV, working in several Michigan stations in a variety of jobs: announcer, morning disc jockey, farm reporter, news reporter, sports announcer, program director, advertising salesman, sales manager. In April, 1959, he acquired part ownership of WAMM/AM in Flint. Phil Munson, another M.S.U. graduate, was the other principal owner. Both Dusty and Phil had served as President of the Genesee County chapter of the M.S.U. Alumni Association. In August, 1960, Dusty, Phil and John met for lunch at the Farm Restaurant in Flint. At this luncheon they decided to pool their joint resources to build a total communications corporation. One barrier loomed. They had no resources.

"Our circumstances were no different from thousands of similar young men, long on enthusiasm and short of money and experience," philosophizes Dusty twenty years later. "We got the experience long before we acquired any money, but I think to this day we have never lost the enthusiasm and imagination.

"Of course, we had no definite plans on how to put things together," continues Dusty. "We met frequently after that, usually in some cheap hash joint where the food tasted like grilled tennis shoes, but where the owner would trade us food and an occasional drink for radio advertising. We were totally broke and usually had to fumble even to pay our own checks."

The two stations were as dissimilar as a diva and a rock and roll groupie. WSWM/FM was utterly uptown highbrow. WAAM/AM was strictly downbeat rock and roll. In Flint, Dusty and Phil sponsored Friday night dances for young blacks at an old movie theatre.

"This is the only way I could be sure of having soup and beans for my four (later five) kids. We'd take in maybe two hundred dollars at the door, pay the D.J., the rent and the cops. Phil and I would split the rest, usually fifty to one hundred dollars, get home at two a.m. and thank God we had not been mugged by one of our dance clients. John was in the same financial position but his high class listeners would not pay a buck on Friday night to watch somebody spin records."

On December 18, 1961, it was agreed that Dusty would join John on a day to day arrangement. He was called Sales Manager. The title was a hollow handle to impress potential advertisers and to boost Dusty's ego during a period when the future was as uncertain as the squirt of grapefruit at the breakfast table. Recalling the experience, Dusty says, "Selling the higher level program for WSWM after trying to peddle the crap we had to play in Flint was like finding gold in the streets. People in the Lansing area were receptive to the idea of good music for a change. Sales climbed. Things improved as we initiated a more balanced program.

"John spent most of his time selling stock to his friends to meet the payroll. He always had a special knack for separating people from money and making them happy at the same time. I hasten to add that not one—repeat not one—stockholder from those desperate days ever complained or had reason to be unhappy. This was proven later when they had opportunity to get their money back but stuck with us one hundred percent."

In the meantime, several other significant developments boded a brighter outlook for the future. At the 1961 Michigan State Graduation services, Alden Dow's son, Mike received his Bachelor's Degree in Mechanical Engineering. All through Mike's early years, it had been assumed by family and friends that he would join the Dow Chemical Company. Mike had worked at Dow during high school summer vacations. While attending Williams College, boredom with the liberal arts routine induced him to volunter for the Army to get his two years military service behind him. After training at the Army Signal Corps School, he was assigned duty in Germany for one year, serving in radio communications. Upon discharge, he enrolled at Michigan State University. Married in December, 1960, he graduated at the end of spring term in 1961 with a degree in Mechanical Engineering.

Mike was certain of two things when he graduated. He did not want to practice engineering. He did not want to work at Dow Chemical Company. He wanted to do something on his own. He had enjoyed the radio duty in the Signal Corps, gaining considerable knowledge in the technical phases. His father had introduced him to John McGoff. He knew that Mid-State Broadcasting was fighting for existence. If he knew anything about his father's loan to John, he never mentioned it, nor did he seek his father's approval to approach John for a job.

Money presented no problem. He needed an opportunity to design his own career independent of his family connections. Citing his interest in radio, aroused by his Army experience, he offered his services to McGoff. Tenaciously independent himself,

45

McGoff was attracted to this quiet, unassuming, soft-spoken young man. Mike joined the staff of the financially fragile company. This proved to be a mutually propitious move, manifested by Mike's cardinal role in growth of the company over the next thirteen years.

At the beginning, Mike had no title, performing a medley of duties as aptitude, interest and company exigencies prescribed. He sold and installed background music to business firms. One of the advantages of FM radio was the availability of additional channels, called subchannels, permitting simulataneous use with no interference to the regular station transmissions. These sub-channels result from the wide band features of the FM signal and cannot be received by the home FM sets. Selling piped-in music to business firms provided an additional source of income for the station.

Also, Mike directed the taping of a one hour, thrice a week cultural program of music, poetry and arts appreciation discussions. Eventually, he became involved in finance and administration leading to acquisitions and disposition of properties. In 1963, he was elevated to the Board, named Treasurer and Vice President, accepting the duties of Executive Vice President in 1967 where he served until he resigned in 1974 to give full attention to business firms he had acquired. He remained on the Panax Board.

Several years later, John learned that Mike's parents experienced considerable concern when Mike went to work at Mid-State Broadcasting. They were puzzled over McGoff's motives. Did he employ Mike in gratitude for favors received? Was it a disguised ploy to assure more financial help? At the time, they kept quiet, revealing nothing to either Mike or John.

Finally, years later, Alden Dow expressed his gratitude to McGoff. It enabled Mike to establish his own identity in the business world and find his niche in life.

In practice, John McGoff, Dusty Rhodes and Mike Dow functioned as a loosely knit management team. It was not organized with clearly defined responsibilities and sharply drawn lines of authority as advocated by leading management consultants, but was an effective team. The variegated personalities blended into a natural, free wheeling relationship, allowing full utilization of the strengths of each. McGoff was in unquestioned command, but the informal give and take with his trusted associates created a spirit that motivated each to high levels of performance. This spirit permeated the entire staff. Everybody shared the various tasks as needs arose.

A constant in success of any business executive is the ability to select strong, able assistants. It is said that Andrew Carnegie's tombstone is inscribed with these words:

> "Here lies a man
> Who knew how to enlist in his service
> Better men than himself."

From the beginning, McGoff demonstrated an ability to select proficient, superior assistants, not necessarily experienced in a particular specialty, but with the intellectual capacity and drive for rapid growth.

Fran Martin was one such case. He agreed to go to work for McGoff on New Year's Day in 1962. Fran recalls, "I was District Manager for Olan Mills Studios, making $26,000 a year. A friend told me about this new radio station. He arranged a meeting with McGoff who came to my home on New Year's Day. We talked informally. He was a most persuasive man. After a visit to the station, I accepted a job as an advertising salesman for $150 a week, which gives you some idea of McGoff's sales ability. Six months later to the day I was raised to $200 a week."

Fran Martin pays tribute to McGoff for his actions in the early days of the struggle for survival. With deep personal feeling he states, "Nobody missed a payroll in the tough going except John himself. The employees came first, then and now. He has never changed his attitude in relationship to employees. He was the driving force when we were small and struggling. He is the same today."

Libby Martin says, "John was kind, considerate, and friendly from that first meeting on that New Year's Day. He showed an interest in our family. He was ready to help any time we needed it. He has been a source of strength to me. Success has never changed him in that respect."

Soon after going into business, McGoff envisaged an FM network. He pursued this idea as one solution to a more saleable product. Lack of financing precluded immediate purchase of additional stations. He conceived the idea of an informal working arrangement with several other stations; a sort of symbiotic relationship, where they would cooperate to sell a package deal to

47

advertisers. Eventual integration of the voluntary participants into one organic structure was deferred until the concept could be tested.

The beginning of the mini-network seemed timely when a second broadcast property, WQDC/FM, went on the air at Midland, Michigan on September 29, 1961.

Alden Dow had been fascinated with McGoff's efforts to present a quality program appealing to the more refined cultural tastes. WSWM had been granted its license for thirty thousand watts, limiting its range. It was increased to 116,000 watts in 1963, but that still would not reach Midland, about ninety miles distance from East Lansing.) Dow persuaded some of his friends to join him in financing construction of an FM station in Midland. McGoff was asked to supervise construction and operate the station. Thus a network was born. WQDC was merged with Mid-States for fifty thousand shares of Class A stock in 1963.

On June 15, 1962, the third FM station joined the network with the acquisition of WABX/FM in Detroit. Mike Dow bought this station with his own money, assuming the duties of President; McGoff was Vice President. Operations were directed from the Lansing office as a part of the informal network.

The fourth FM station went on the air on October 28, 1962, when WGMZ/FM in Flint joined the network.

Programs for these stations emanated from WSWM in Lansing. The cooperative arrangement built a wider awareness of FM quality beamed at an intellectual and financial segment of society that AM stations seemed to ignore while they capitalized on the rock and roll fad of the younger generation. However, most AM stations made money while FM was still struggling.

Revenues did increase but not in the amounts commensurate with costs that doubled. All these properties were losing money, but at least losses were decreasing.

In searching for loans to purchase FM stations McGoff was referred to a bank in Cleveland. "FM radio has no loan appeal. Get into the more glamorous TV business or newspapers if you want to do business with us," officials told him.

In 1962, McGoff talked to Lee Doan, President of Dow Chemical Company, hoping to persuade Dow to sponsor a cultural program for the four station network. Lee Doan said, "John, the Smith Barney Advertising Agency in New York places all of our ads. I make no promises but will refer this proposal to the Agency and ask them to consider it."

Smith Barney Agency gave Doan a detailed report discouraging any Dow ad budget for FM in Michigan.

Analysts agreed to meet with McGoff and his associates. Citing demographics, they advised in blunt language, "All your eggs are in one basket. FM radio, at best, is a long struggle to break even. Drop the FM properties or add AM or TV stations to subsidize them. Some time in the future FM may become self-sustaining and profitable. You may be floundering for some years before that time arrives. It is not a good advertising buy at present. We cannot recommend your proposal to Dow Chemical."

That assessment was made in 1962 when FM stations were being licensed rapidly. At the end of the year, eleven hundred stations were on the air. Most of them were operated by AM stations primarily as a bonus offer for regular AM programs.

In 1939 Edwin Armstrong built the first experimental station because he thought the FM era was just around the corner. In 1958 Bob Coleman advised McGoff to go into business because he thought commercial FM was ready to turn the corner. He backed his belief by joining McGoff in the undertaking. In 1978, finally, FM radio turned the corner. Though still running behind AM radio in total revenues, FM captured more listeners in 1978 than AM. The 3019 FM stations in the nation claimed fifty-one percent of all listeners compared to the forty-nine percent for the 4519 AM stations. Individually, some FM stations had been profitable before then, but the industry now recognized that FM had arrived and was ahead. The static-free stereo sound attracted more than $700 million in revenues and increased by twenty-five percent in 1979, compared to about $2 billion for AM stations. FM stations collectively earned a substantial profit for the first time in 1976. Station KMET/FM, Los Angeles, California, was rated the most profitable radio station in the nation with pre-tax annual net income of $6 million.

In some cities FM has a marked audience edge over AM. In Washington, FM draws sixty-seven percent of the listeners, fifty-six percent in Philadelphia, fifty-two percent in Detroit. In New York, WKTV/FM displaced WABC/AM for the largest audience in the nation. Nothing illustrates the switch more characteristically than the sale of San Francisco FM station K101 in early 1980 for $12 million. The companion AM station K1Q1 sold for only $3 million.

Foresight by the advertising agency in 1962 is supported by the hindsight in the form of the record. McGoff's decision to follow the advice was sound. He did not have sufficient capital to afford losses that could have continued for the next fifteen or more years. Hundreds of FM stations today are operating profitably with his format expressed by his call letters, Wonderful Sound, Wonderful Music.

Scanning a broadcasting yearbook soon after the agency advice, Dusty Rhodes picked a name at random. He knew none of the brokers listed. He called Richard Shaheen, a broker in Chicago, with the primary purpose of learning how much investment would be required for a TV station. The call could not have been more propitious! Shaheen had just listed a TV station and an AM radio station in St. Joseph, Missouri. It was owned by Bing Crosby Enterprises, was making a good profit, was available on reasonable terms. Another recent listing of a radio station in Jefferson City, Missouri, owned by a family foundation, was suggested for consideration.

In May, 1962, McGoff, Rhodes and Dow chartered a single engine plane from a Flint leasing agency for the Missouri inspection trip, trading advertising for the rental fee. Agreeing to purchase the properties for $1.7 million, the conversation back home centered on one critical question: "Where the hell do we get that kind of money?" This was a McGoff modus operandi. Make a tentative commitment and then figure out where to get the financing.

It took sixteen months to answer the question. The ultimate answer came from the Pullman Bank and Trust in Chicago. Stringent terms were imposed. A loan of $850,000 for a term of eight years and six and one-half percent interest was to be secured by assignment of all capital stock of the Mid-States Broadcasting Corporation. Officers and directors were to be personally liable, if during the term of the loan, the corporation, through action of the Federal Communications Commission, lost licenses for any of the facilities. A checking account was to be established. As additional security, Mike Dow pledged a block of Dow stock.

Final purchase of station KFEQ/TV and radio station KFEQ/AM was made on September 1, 1963. KLIK/AM in Jefferson City was acquired for $228,823 in stock. On the same date, WGMJ/

AM, Flint, Michigan, became property of Mid-States for 2387 shares of Class A stock.

Tom Matthews was appointed General Manager of the Missouri operations. A veteran of sixteen years in the broadcasting industry in both commercial radio and television, his experience included sports announcer, program director, operations director, national sales manager and manager of one of the top forty market TV stations. The Missouri operation was an instant success. At the time of purchase the stations were earning a net profit of about $250,000 a year. Within a short period, the profit rate was doubled. The first year tripled profits. Within two years, annual profits quadrupled. Dusty Rhodes mused, "These stations earned money faster than we could lose it with our idealistic FM networks."

Mid-States' consolidation of properties continued in 1963 by acquisition of WABX/AM in Detroit for 81,354 shares of Class A stock and WQDC/FM in Midland for 50,000 of Class A stock. WAMM/AM, the Munson-Rhodes station in Flint, merged with Mid-States on December 31, 1963, giving outright ownership of one television station, five FM and three AM radio stations. One additional station, WMAX/AM in Grand Rapids was secured on January 2, 1965, for $200,000 in cash and $37,500 in notes.

Purchase of the Missouri properties accented the turning point, but after tiptoeing through red ink for so many years, there was no relaxation of effort to effect more profitable operations for the other properties. They were still losing money. Purchase of black ink for the bookkeeper was unmitigated joy, but the flow of red ink for the corporate bottom line was a reality that could not be ignored. It was the shotgun that forced the marriage of idealism with practicality. As Rhodes states it, with full concurrence of McGoff and Dow, "We programmed too much classical music at the beginning. It satisfied our souls and esthetic being, but even idealists have to pay salaries and bills. We were giving people what we thought they ought to have rather than what they wanted. A mix in the program appealed to a broader segment of the listening audience. The jazzed up program jacked up revenues."

During the early times when McGoff was wrestling with the problems of survival, his management style could be called catch-as catch-can. He believed then, and still believes, that employer and employee should enjoy their work. Once employees know what is expected he believes they should have freedom of action to do it. His style was effective. Morale was buoyant. Everybody

51

worked hard and enjoyed it. An informal atmosphere, unfettered by procedures or office manuals, allowed utilization of individual skills when and where they could be productive.

Everybody called everybody else by first name. Mr., Mrs., Miss, Ms. were as out of place as the plumber in Eisenhower's millionaires cabinet. This practice has endured as the company grew. Contrary to Aesop's maxim, familiarity did not breed contempt; instead, it seemed to abet a sense of responsibility and initiative.

McGoff's sense of humor, his disdain for executive pomp, and emphasis on performance for results rather than conformance to patterns promoted good human relations. His fiery temper fostered an expectancy of the unexpected.

Stories abound about the temper flares—usually most of them harmless and humorous—some more serious—a few with dollars and cents impact.

In the bitter cold of winter in 1963 he attended a business luncheon at the Detroit Metro Airport, driving into Detroit after the lunch. At four-thirty in the afternoon of that day, a visibly angry man appeared at the office demanding audience with "a Mr. McGoff," spitting out the name through clenched teeth and unveiled impatience.

When McGoff left the restaurant, his own furlined raincoat was missing, or so he thought. He could not find it on the rack. He sequestered another identical coat, though a different size, thinking that someone had taken his coat by mistake. Assuming that the owner would discover the error and exchange could be made, he left his card with the cashier. Actually, as frequently occurs, his coat had been moved as the rack filled. In his eagerness to get to the next appointment, his own coat had been overlooked.

The owner of the coat now in McGoff's presence drove to East Lansing to make the exchange, arriving before McGoff returned. About thirty minutes later McGoff bounced into the office bright and cheerful as a spring robin. He laughed heartily as the stranger thrust McGoff's coat at him, practically ripping his coat from McGoff's shoulders, expressing some uncomplimentary opinions about McGoff's intentions.

A few sentences later, McGoff's voice echoed off the office walls with, "Just a goddam minute. Who the hell do you think you are?"

"Who am I? Who am I?" shouted the fuming visitor. "I have just driven ninety miles to track down a character who stole my coat, and now he insults me!"

"I did not steal your goddam coat, but since you are so upset about your stinking time and gas money, here's a check for your trouble which could have been avoided entirely if you had sense enough to make just one telephone call. If I had wanted to steal a wornout coat that does not fit me, do you think I would have left my card? I'm the one who is insulted!"

He handed the man a personal check for thirty-five dollars which was shredded faster than a Watergate memo and thrown at McGoff's feet, accompanied by a gush of invectives that would have made a Marine drill sergeant sound prissy.

A few minutes later, McGoff stomped out, slamming the door, screeching out the driveway with reckless abandon. Fifteen minutes later, laughing, relaxed, loose as a smock, he called Dusty Rhodes.

"You know why this s.o.b. was so upset? He came to my house and waited an hour for me. Marge tried to calm him down but he seethed more rabidly by the minute. Roaring out of the driveway too fast, he skidded off the road, got stuck in the snow and had to call a wrecker to pull him out."

After all this outburst, McGoff does not know the man's name to this day.

These unpredictable incidents provided a fringe benefit at Mid-States Broadcasting in its tempestuous incipiency. Dusting off the old cliche, Dusty Rhodes says, "We did not make much money but we had a hell of a lot of fun."

While having fun, they laid the foundation for a solid business. That free, unbridled, undaunted spirit galvanized staff, investors, advertisers, bankers. McGoff faced the rough times with audacity and unflagging confidence. Some observers may have been dubious. Not once did he think of failure. From one stumbling FM station, built personally from the first watt up, he now controlled one television station, five FM and four AM radio stations. With the exception of the Missouri properties, the others were not breaking even, but the deficits were decreasing and manageable. John McGoff, the entrepreneur, had passed the first test. He had survived. He had expanded. He had learned how to borrow money for the expansion. He was on his way.

Chapter 5

Changing Directions

"Tomorrow to fresh woods, and pastures new."
                                    . . John Milton

After five years Mid-States Broadcasting had survived and grown but had not prospered. Three properties were profitable. Seven operations were losing money. The corporate balance still was recorded in red ink. Mere survival was not an accepted performance for an indefinite period.

Once again serendipity intervened. At lunch one day, during a casual conversation, Richard Milliman said, "John, why not get into the newspaper business?" At the time, Milliman was serving as the Press Secretary for Governor George Romney. A career journalist, he had left the Lansing Journal to join Romney's staff. A rather stern, reticent type, Milliman's personality was not what you expected in a sensitive public office.

Several bankers had mentioned newspapers as an alternative to radio. McGoff and his associates had given no serious thought to the prospects. They had learned the radio business the hard way: trial and error. The success of the Missouri purchases encouraged them to find additional radio stations. They believed in the ultimate success of their holdings in electronic communications.

Dick Milliman made a specific proposal. He knew the Mt. Pleasant, Michigan paper was for sale. He offered to resign his state office and manage the paper for McGoff. He felt more comfortable in newspaper work, preferring straight news reporting to the periphrasis of political life. Although Governor George

Romney was more direct than most politicians, political strategy frequently required the type of double speak intended to conceal rather than reveal.

In October, 1964, several months after the conversation, Mid-States purchased the Mt. Pleasant Times News, a daily paper, with a paid circulation of 4900. Mt. Pleasant, the county seat of Isabella County, is located near the center of Michigan's Lower Peninsula, about midway between Lake Michigan and Lake Huron on Highway 27 leading to the beautiful wooded hills, inland lakes and forests of the North Country. Home of the Central Michigan University, the shopping center for a prosperous agricultural section amplified by the tourist business, the community enjoys a balanced economy. In 1964, the population was almost fifteen thousand in a county of thirty thousand, both doubled since that date.

Purchase price was $527,000, a figure that prompted other newspaper publishers to sneer, "The guy must be crazy to pay that price. He will go broke fast!" Mike Dow says the paper made money from day one. In the financial deal, Mid-States bought all assets, including a sizeable cash reserve and then used the cash reserve as the down payment. This had advantages for both seller and buyer. Internal reorganization, eventual change from letter press to offset, an aggressive circulation campaign, concentration on publishing a paper that appealed to the local public, increased circulation to 6900 by 1966. The paper proved a bargain.

McGoff bought the paper from a longtime local resident, an unabashed devotee of the Barleycorn way of life. On the morning of the official closing of the exchange, he arrived late, claiming he was under doctor's care for a cold and was heavily sedated, attested by slurred speech and a sour mash breath.

The signing ceremonies consumed no more than five minutes. McGoff and Rhodes were eager to take over operations. The deal had been consummated several months earlier than anticipated. Milliman's resignation had not been accepted by Governor Romney. Dusty Rhodes was to exercise control until Milliman had completed his duties for the Governor. As soon as the final papers had been signed, the previous owner suggested a drink—and then lunch—to celebrate at the Chieftain Hotel, the food and fun landmark of the community. It was eleven a.m., so Rhodes and McGoff nursed a couple of beers for an hour while their host had four fishbowl martinis. At noon Dusty said, "What do you say we order," meaning food.

"Good idea, Dusty. Good idea! Hey, waitress, bring us another round."

Lunch eventually consumed, McGoff and Rhodes ordered coffee and their host asked for another martini.

"Listen dear," interrupted his wife, "You're going to drive home— remember—so why don't you just have an Imperial and soda, like me?", implying that would neutralize all the gin. Apparently it did. Dusty said, "We drove behind him in case anything happened. He drove down the right side of the road as straight as a frozen clothesline." And with that little ceremony, McGoff was initiated into the newspaper business.

In June, 1965, the Alma Record-Leader and Record Printing Company were purchased for $208,000 with no down payment but agreement to pay $1000 a month at eight percent interest. This paper was a weekly with a circulation of 4500. This weekly was converted into a daily in 1968 when the nearby St. Louis weekly Leader-Press was acquired and combined with the Alma Daily. Alma is located twenty miles south of Mt. Pleasant in an oil producing area and is the home of Alma College, a respected private institution.

In 1965 it seemed appropriate to change the corporate name to reflect more accurately expansion into the newspaper business. The original corporation was formed under the name of Mid-State Broadcasting of East Lansing, Inc. This covered the single FM station WSWM. A series of separate corporations were formed in building the informal cooperative network—Mid-State Broadcasting of Midland, Inc., and Valley Broadcasting, Inc., both of Flint. When these companies were consolidated in 1963, Mid-States Broadcasting, Inc. was born.

Following acquisition of the Missouri stations and the Mt. Pleasant Daily Time-News in 1964, a name was sought that would exclude the words broadcasting, publishing, communications or media to allow for a broad-based expansion in any classification, not just media or communications. McGoff turned to the William John Upjohn and Associates Advertising Agency for guidance. William Upjohn, scion of the pharmaceutical Upjohn family, had pursued his career outside the family business by starting an advertising agency in his hometown, Kalamazoo. Pirating some of the best creative writers from several national agencies, he had built a successful, innovative agency. He suggested a short, distinctive name, easy to remember, attention-arousing and subject to novel graphic design. Further, X should be in the first or last letters, using Xerox and Exxon as notable examples. So the computer was programmed to print out the maximum combinations with consonant, vowel, consonant, vowel and X. The list was presented to Mid-States for final selection. The name PANAX jumped out at McGoff and his board members. PAN is the Greek work for all-encompassing. AX is Greek for action.

All-encompassing action seemed to describe what the officers and Board were doing within a plan for growth. The logotype was an orange bar on top of a brown bar, placed beneath the name. The name and logo were accepted spontaneously and unanimously in July, 1965.

Soon after, it was discovered that certain security laws had been violated inadvertently while selling stock. McGoff had sold stock to more than three thousand individuals to keep the business alive. Now it was necessary to notify the Securities and Exchange Commission and the Michigan Security Commission of the error. Letters of recision were mailed to all stockholders, explaining the unintentional error and advising each stockholder that full restitution would be made if requested. Tension of a high degree attended the waiting period for claims. What if a majority of the stockholders wanted the money back?

The deadline passed. Not one stockholder asked for reimbursement— not one. A complete vote of confidence. The letters of recision purged the company of any violation. All stock was legalized.

Harold Good evinced the stockholders' reaction. He said, "None of these people ever invested money in the company because they were told that they would make a bundle of money or a fast buck. They invested because they believed in John McGoff and his objectives and wanted a part in development of what they believed to be worthy projects."

McGoff had no intention of similar errors committed through ignorance of legal procedures. Miller, Canfield, Paddock and Stone of Detroit was engaged as Legal Counsel. It was one of the largest and most prestigious firms in the state. A partner, Richard A. Jones, assumed responsibility for the new client, becoming

57

Secretary of the Panax Corporation in 1969. Few, if any, actions have been initiated by McGoff without consultation with Dick Jones since the law firm was engaged.

Each expansion step from the first FM radio broadcast in 1959 proferred an ineffaceable challenge, studded with the uncertainties and hazards of a business dependent on the changing whims of an unappeasable public. When McGoff started negotiations for three daily newspapers in Michigan's Upper Peninsula, the solidity of his capacity to persevere was exposed to an exacting test. Negotiations stretched over an eighteen month period. Discussion ran the gamut from comedy to tragedy. A jumble of issues assailed and frequently diverted attention from the main objective of purchasing the papers. McGoff and his associates had stalled deliberately to find financing for the radio and TV stations in Missouri but money was not the problem here. Numerous factors beyond his control or anticipations delayed the final decision month after disconcerted month. These intangible factors were linked to the character and traditions of the Upper Peninsula as well as the character, personality and problems of the owner of the properties. To understand McGoff's problem, it is necessary to understand these factors.

As ancient Gaul was divided into three parts, Michigan has two distinct parts: the Upper Peninsula and the Lower Peninsula are split by the Straits of Mackinac, the body of water connecting Lake Michigan and Lake Huron. These peninsulas have been called the two Michigans. Geographically welded to Wisconsin, the Upper Peninsula was inaccessible to the Lower Peninsula except by ferry until one of the world's engineering marvels, the Mackinac Bridge, was opened in 1957.

The U.P., as Michiganians refer to it, was granted to Michigan by a special Act of Congress in 1835 as compensation for the Toledo Strip, awarded to Ohio to settle a dispute between the two territories. A mapping error extended Michigan's southern boundary eight miles into Ohio territory. Armed forces were mobilized by both territories to enforce their respective border claims. Fortunately, they did not fire a shot. However, Michigan statehood was delayed for almost three years after the dispute was settled. Michigan had formed a state government early in 1835 but President Jackson did not sign the bill approving Michigan as a member of the union until late 1837.

Many Michigan leaders were indignant when Congress substituted the U.P. for the Toledo Strip, even though the U.P. area appended to the state fourteen thousand square miles, equal in size to Delaware, Connecticut, Massachusetts, and Rhode Island combined. It was a sparsely settled, remote wilderness more distant from Detroit than Washington, D.C. or New York City.

Disappointment turned into jubilation in 1844. Discovery of rich lodes of copper spawned America's first major mining boom. U.P. led the nation in copper production until 1887 when Montana assumed supremacy. Michigan mines reached their peak during World War I, but geologists claimed that less than ten percent of pure copper had been mined. Although copper mining has not been a major economic activity for the U.P. for years, a potential bonanza awaits the time when demands for copper raise prices to exceed costs of extraction sufficiently to make mining profitable again.

Iron ore mining opened another era of prosperity for the U.P. The Jackson mines at Negaumee, the National mine at Ishpeming, the Republic mine, with eighty-eight percent pure iron oxide, produced from 1871 until 1927. The Champion mine operated from 1867 to 1910. Michigamma mine produced from 1872 to 1905.

The Marquette Range, the Menominee Range, the Geogebic Range, were heavy producers until 1955. Additional mines at Ironwood, Iron Mountain and Crystal Falls, helped make Michigan the leading state for iron ore production until surpassed by Minnesota in 1900 when the great Mesabi Range outweighed Michigan in tonnage passing through the Sault Ste. Marie Locks to the steel mills in the east.

Lying dormant since the mid-fifties, iron ore mining was revived in Marquette County. Cleveland Cliffs and Associates with headquarters in Cleveland, built a billion dollar processing plant in the mid-seventies where ore is separated magnetically and rolled into pellets. Revenues for 1978 were over $293 million, with a net revenue of $41 million. Between 1977 and 1979, CCI and Associates invested $920 million in Marquette County.

From 1860 to 1900, Michigan's economy was dominated by the timber industry. The Upper Peninsula boom in harvesting, sawing and marketing lumber started in 1880. Original forests in the U.P. covered ten million acres with hardwood covering about half of this vast area. Copper, iron ore and timber settled the U.P. and helped build America. Europeans flooded the U.P. to work the mines and forests.

Cornishmen arrived in 1884, bringing with them the traditions of English miners. Tough, hard workers, fun-loving, hardened outdoor sportsmen, they made solid citizens. After the Civil War, the Swedes moved in to man the iron ore mines. Norwegians came by droves. An influx of Finns occurred around 1870. Later, they acquired land and pioneered farming the hostile U.P. climate. Rich in soil but short in growing season, the rugged Finnish stock adapted their crops to conditions and helped balance the economy. Irish, German, Italian and French Canadian migrants came at various stages of development.

Early in the twentieth century, fifty percent of the residents of Houghton County, center of the copper country, were foreign born. Ethnic newspapers flourished. In 1910, the Copper Country alone had nine weekly, five daily, one tri-weekly, three monthly and two quarterly publications. As late as 1930, over twenty-five percent of the U.P. population was foreign born.

These heterogenous groups, veritably an ethnic boullabaise, came to stay, bringing the skills and cultures of the old country, learning the new language, qualifying for citizenship, building churches, homes, schools, communities, and growing into solid American citizens.

Proud, independent, self-supporting, religious, provincial, suspicious of the motives of state government in Lansing, and all the Lower Peninsula, these rugged individuals became Upper Peninsulans first, Michiganians by coincidence. Periodically, proposals have surfaced to secede from Michigan and to form a new state of Superior.

The U.P. was hit hard by the 1930's depression and even harder after the forties and fifties decline in mining and timber industries. It has remained thinly populated. In 1978 the total U.P. population approached 330,000 people, interspersed at random over the 14,000 square miles of one of the largest, unspoiled, spectacularly beautiful areas of the nation.

Succeeding generations in the U.P. have retained the mistrust of Lower Michigan. State Legislators representing the U.P. districts learned early that an attack by a Detroit newspaper or a slight by the Lower Peninsula majority in the legislature was the most effective campaign strategy for re-election.

When McGoff bid for acquisition of the three most prestigious newspapers in the U.P., he bore the stigma of a lower peninsula outsider. Moreover, he bucked publishing custom of local family owned newspapers, revered generation after generation from the beginning. As one U.P. newspaper veteran observed, "McGoff was going upstream against tradition when he entered the U.P. newspaper publishing field. The papers were aggressive and tuned to the needs of the Upper Peninsula. He was walking into an inbred situation like a Montana cowboy making himself at home in a Boston parlor."

All newspapers with the exception of the Menominee Herald Leader were family holdings going into the third generation. The Osborns and related Pratts in Sault Ste. Marie, the Noyes family in Ironwood and Marinette, the Rice father and son combination in Houghton, the three generations of Russells in Marquette and Iron Mountain, John Norton in Escanaba. Although the Russell family was as prominently identified with the Upper Peninsula as Lake Superior, some resistance was expressed to "absentee ownership" when the Escanaba Press was acquired by the Russells. Frank Sr. lived at Iron Mountain, just seventy-five miles away and Frank Jr. lived in Marquette, equidistant from Escanaba and Iron Mountain.

The paper was purchased for $440,000, considered an exorbitant price at that time. Russell bought the paper from the Escanaba School Board, which inherited the paper and a radio station under terms of John Norton's will.

The family publishers wielded power in Michigan's history. Governors confided in Frank Russell Sr. on most of the controversial issues of the day. U.S. Congressmen from the district seldom, if ever, acted on an issue without similar consultation.

Linwood Noyes attended more newspaper conventions than any publisher in Michigan, serving on the Associated Press Board, President of the Newspaper Enterprise Association, and an officer with the Inland Daily Press Association.

Frank Knox, Vice Presidential candidate on the Alf Landon ticket in 1936, Secretary of the Navy from 1940 until his death in 1944 and publisher of the Chicago Daily News, was publisher of the Sault Ste. Marie News from 1901 until 1912. Chase Osborn of the Sault Ste. Marie paper served as Michigan Governor for one term beginning in 1911.

Frank Russell Jr., last of the Russell family to inherit ownership, was a peninsula leader in his earlier reign. He lost most of his following as progressive pursuit of outside pleasures took precedence over business. Frank never won any awards from the Temperance League for abstinence or moderation. Many of his friends despaired over the creeping virulence of copious consumption of inebriant beverages, but Frank heeded no advice.

Some fine accomplishments are attributed to his leadership. He was first to organize regular meetings of advertising and editorial executives of all Upper Peninsula papers, resulting in formation of the Upper Peninsula Press Association. Sound, hard-hitting programs on mutual problems and agreements on editorial policies on Peninsula-wide issues were effected.

Then the spouses were invited. Social activities nudged aside business sessions, until the meetings gradually deteriorated into meaningless gatherings between social affairs. The Press Association drowned in the overflow of festivities.

In 1954, soon after purchase of the Escanaba Press, Russell lured Jean Worth from the Menominee Herald to become the highest paid editor in the Upper Peninsula.

Starting his newspaper career at Menominee in 1922, immediately after graduation from high school, Jean Worth was recognized as a professional of superior worth. His experience ran the gamut of newspaper publishing, from taking the conference telephone calls that constituted the wire service reports in the twenties, to rewriting, to editor. In looking back, Jean says, "The newspapers had a role in the community then which has been changed drastically by radio in the 1920's and television in the 1940's. Printed matter had a quality of gospel. There was a dependency upon journals for information because of the absence of electronic communications except for the telegraph and dot-dash wireless. This operated on the Ann Arbor Railroad Ferries plying between Menominee and Frankfort in lower Michigan all year, cutting through iceflows in the winter."

After Jean Worth assumed the editorship of the Escanaba paper he traveled to the State capitol frequently, serving on various boards and commissions, including the Conservation Department Study Commission which created an official Department of Natural Resources, the Community-School Service Program, financed by the Kellogg Foundation and in later years the State Human Resources Council and George Romney's Citizens for Michigan.

Since these appointments provided opportunities for inside information, he wrote many of the editorials for the three Russell owned papers. He was respected in Lansing as an articulate spokesman for the U.P. point of view and equally respected in the U.P. for his knowledge and analysis of state issues. Retired since 1969, he served as a consultant for Public and Governmental Affairs for the Mead Corporation, a consultant to Panax and a feature writer for the Upper Peninsula Sunday Times.

Analyzing the Russell operations, Worth says, "I think it would be fair to say that Frank Russell was feared as a somewhat impulsive boss but my work with Frank was pleasant. We had been friends for years. I respected him as a publisher. His personal habits dimmed his brilliance. I was never an intimate of Frank Russell. Our relationship was strictly business. I wanted it that way and assume he did too.

"Any objective reading must rate our journals at that time as quite provincial, reflecting the tastes of their readerships with their limited interest in the outside world. Frank did not exercise tight control of his papers editorially. He had enthusiasm, like getting General Eisenhower elected President, but there was no day-to-day surveillance, guidance, accounting or review. I thing the readers liked the Russell papers. They were moral, not sensational, not immensely opinionated, or overly political. They were devoted to their communities' interest. They were better than most of the papers in the top of the Lower Peninsula and all of the U.P.; less insular. I guess they were a little more serious in their pontifications in the past."

At the Mining Journal in Marquette, largest of the U.P. papers, Wilbert H. Treloar was the General Manager. Appointed to this position in 1958, he had served in various editorial and business management capacities since 1925. Born and bred in the U.P., a graduate of Northern Michigan University, he taught school for four years before joining the Russell papers. Witty, deeply devoted to the U.P., a popular Master of Ceremonies for any meeting of any importance, Wilbert Treloar kept the Russell papers viable as Frank Russell's extra-curricular activities diminished his taste for the concentrated effort required for successful publishing.

Treloar met John McGoff and Mike Dow originally when he was asked to bring together some of the leading U.P. business executives to consider sponsorship of a Mid-States radio program called "Milliman on Michigan", prepared and taped at Lansing's WSWM and sold to outside stations.

McGoff learned of the availability of the Russell papers through his friend, Dr. Edgar Harden, then President of Northern Michigan University. McGoff had been appointed to the University Board by Governor George Romney in 1964. Harden convinced McGoff to go after the papers. He introduced him to Don Pearce, local real estate and insurance businessman and close friend of Russell. Pearce arranged the first meeting. A series of meetings followed—dragging out to months of frustration, agreements in principle, reversals of position, theatricals without rehearsal. McGoff gives Treloar major credit for ultimate consummation of the sale, through his patience, counseling, guidance to both parties, and understanding of Frank Russell's agony over the sale. The drawn-out discussions were not concerned so much with major disagreements between the seller and buyer, but with Frank Russell's internal struggle and changing moods.

Treloar says, "Frank was torn between family sentiment, loyalty to the three communities and the necessity to sell to meet his financial obligations. He blew hot and cold, changing decisions practically every week."

There were compelling reasons to sell in the opinion of close observers and friends. He found himself in an economic condition that made the sale mandatory. He had no one in his family prepared, qualified or interested in carrying on the business. Treloar believes, "In the final analysis, the latter reason was the most pressing and decisive."

Attorneys were called into the discussion early. Wheaton Strom of Escanaba represented Russell. Richard Jones of the Miller, Canfield, Paddock and Stone firm of Detroit represented Panax. The attorneys haggled over legal technicalities but studiously avoided Russell's billingsgate. He meant nothing personal. It was just a linguistic flavor that spiced his conversations.

Strom was dubious of McGoff's capacity to finance a $4 million deal. At several points in the negotiations, he counseled against the transaction. This doubt was dispelled when Sam Cohodas arranged a $100,000 loan to Panax for earnest money. Aside from assurance of the requisite financial resources, association of the name *Sam Cohodas* enhanced McGoff's bargaining position far beyond money considerations. An endorsement by Cohodas carried respect. He had become a living legend in the U.P. Arriving in the U.P. at the age of seven when his family emigrated to the United States from Poland at the turn of the century, the family had started a produce business on nothing but an idea and willingness to work. It developed into one of the nation's largest produce distributors. Sam, the last surviving brother, had been recognized as the leader and spokesman for decades.

In his eighties, when most men of means enjoyed the leisure of retirement, he built a substantial banking empire. Known nationwide as an outstanding leader in business, finance and philanthropy, Cohodas joined the Panax board in 1966.

The agreement to purchase was signed six months before the closing. During the interim period, Russell, for some inexplicable reason, signed a three-year contract with United Press International for wire service, even though an Associated Press contract had not expired. These three small town community papers needed two wire services about as much as they needed a readers' boycott.

After learning about the dual service when Panax took over operations, Dusty Rhodes convinced the UPI to defer services during the course of the AP contract with the promise of an exclusive five year contract when service was resumed. Everybody was happy. Before UPI could remove the machines, John McGoff and Mims Thomason, President of UPI, got into an argument in an after-lunch telephone conversation. Following a harsh exchange, Dusty Rhodes heard McGoff yell, "Thomason, you can take your goddam machines and stick them." Before slamming the receiver, he specified an intimate part of the anatomy where Thomason could do the sticking.

UPI sued Panax for non-performance of contract. Panax sued UPI for violation of the Sherman Anti-Trust Act. After Panax won two lower court decisions, the case was settled out of court. Ironically, a decade later, McGoff would be a partner with UPI in a worldwide news gathering operation.

By the time of the Cohodas sponsored loan, Russell had committed himself to sell to somebody, though he continued to protest such intentions to a variety of audiences at different times. He stalled Panax by offering to sell on a piecemeal schedule: Iron Mountain News first, then the Escanaba Press and within a few years, his pride and joy, the Marquette Mining Journal.

McGoff was adamant. All or none. After eighteen months with

65

the agreed price of $4,100,000, Russell's final condition was to close the sale on April 14, 1966. This date was for obvious tax purposes. The first payment was to be $1 million, with the second payment one year later, for another $1 million. The Commonwealth Bank in Detroit had agreed to the loans. The rest of the payments were scheduled over a period of years to be paid out of earnings.

Several of the participants recall the closing ceremonies vividly. Treloar, McGoff and Dow joined Russell at his hide-away lodge on Strawberry Lake, ten miles from Marquette. At Frank's insistence, no attorneys were present. The elaborate buffet table spread had a wide choice of beverages. Mike Dow was impressed when he remarked, "It looks like Frank is acquiring properties instead of giving up his family empire." Luncheon amenities over, Frank asked to be excused from the final review of the papers. No one mentioned it at the time, but all present silently recognized that he was churning inside and had neither appetite nor stomach for further particulars. When he was called back to the meeting, he signed without hesitancy. All the parties present let out a long breath in relief and gratitude for the end of a long, suspenseful human drama.

The Panax Corporation now owned the three top papers in Michigan's Upper Peninsula, the vanguard of a cavalcade of events leading to a new publishing domain.

Chapter 6

Triumphs and Defeats

"Great results cannot be achieved at once, and we
must be satisfied to advance in life as we walk—
step by step."

. . Samuel Smiles

McGoff's first action as the new owner was a master stroke.
Wilbert Treloar was appointed Publisher and General Manager of
the three U.P. papers. Deeply involved in the purchase negotiations, he respected McGoff and Dow. A free, easy relationship
budded and flowered into friendship and mutual trust. Treloar was
steeped in the Russell traditions, knew the staff of all three papers,
was aware of the trepidations about new ownership, particularly the
prevailing skepticism about a downstater. He recognized the uncertainties created by this change. Would employees retain their jobs?
Would it be necessary to call East Lansing to get instructions about
procedures, policies, editorial positions? Would McGoff abandon
traditional Upper Peninsula postures? Would Lower Peninsula
attitudes be forced on them? Would outsiders be put in charge?
What kind of shakeup would follow?

Accumulative rumors, misconceptions, disappointments fa-
thered morale problems during the eighteen months of on-again,
off-again decisions. Treloar had counseled patience, tolerance,
acceptance of the inevitable. Now he was to serve as the ambas-
sadorial bridge between the old and the new. No one was better
qualified. Fortunately, his new title implied authority as well as
responsibility.

Most of the anticipatory fears were unfounded. Over a period of time, new accounting policies, better equipment, new processes, uniform personnel practices, new benefits, new pay schedules, retirement plans, were instituted. The only immediate change pertained to placing local news on the front page. It had been the practice to use page one for state, national and world news. "It had to be a nine-day conversation story for local news to hit the front page," Treloar recounts. "Local leads were headlining pages two and three."

Dick Milliman, then publisher of the Mt. Pleasant Times and a Panax Board member, suggested front page prominence for local news. At first it was resented by the U.P. editors. Readers appreciated the recognition. It became an accepted practice. Today the editors say, "We have always done that."

By one of those happenstantial twists of events, eleven years later two U.P. editors split with McGoff because they claimed too much corporate office pressure for national or international features slighted local news coverage.

During the transition period, Treloar rendered a service of momentous import, probably his most valuable contribution to Panax generally and McGoff particularly. Traveling continuously between the three communities, forgetting the working day clock, listening, talking, advising, urging a chance for the new ownership, the trauma was minimized. Staff retained positions, minor problems were weeded out.

Jean Worth, Editor of the Escanaba Daily Press, was a worthy working associate for Treloar. No two individuals equaled their encyclopedic knowledge of the Upper Peninsula and its people.

Wilbert Treloar retired in 1967 after forty-two years service with the papers. He remained active after retirement. He served as a special consultant for Panax and several other business firms. His duties as a Panax consultant consisted of advising McGoff on Upper Peninsula developments, including political, economic, and higher education areas of interest. He worked closely with McGoff on Operation Action—U.P., a voluntary bi-peninsular organization concerned primarily with economic affairs. Treloar did not become involved in Panax operations but was available to general managers and editors for discussion of general policies.

He wrote a fascinating book, *Cohodas, the Story of a Family,* published by the Northern University Press.

McGoff plunged into U.P. public life with the zeal of a reborn evangelical. Visiting the cities frequently, he attended public and private meetings of all types, joined the U.P. booster organizations, met the industrial, business, community and intellectual leaders. As a charter member of the Northern Michigan University Board, he gained credibility and visibility. Worth says, "McGoff comes on strong. He impresses his personality on his company. He is an activist. He reads the latest books, is well versed on causes, has no reluctance to espouse controversial issues. He expects support for his directives, is testy in exposure to timidity or indecision of others. He is an entrepreneur in the old dimensions of the term—bold and adventuresome, investing in many ventures and always looking for more—sending people forth to be Davids in Goliathland."

After McGoff and his associates had analogized the relative merits of radio, TV and newspapers, they concluded that Panax should concentrate on acquisitions of newspapers while disposing of the radio properties. Financing was easier. Radio experienced some problems in the early sixties. Profits in 1961 were the lowest since 1939. The trend reversed in 1965. TV profit soared to about a thirty percent pre-tax return. Profits for radio operations improved but financing for small independent radio stations was compounded by the impact of TV on revenues and uncertainty of more restrictive government controls. The proliferation of radio stations in the more profitable markets discouraged McGoff. The discussion at the Federal Communications Commission to disallow cross-membership of newspapers, radio and TV in the same market area weighed heavily in the decisions to change directions.

Also, Panax profits from radio operations failed to meet expectations, exclusive of the Missouri stations. Added to the nonprofitability factor, the long lead-time between agreement to purchase and approval by the FCC delayed operations for many months frequently extending to a year or more.

Finally, the barrage of regulations were costly, nettlesome and downright meddlesome. To an entrepreneur, the minute by minute record of all air time and a blizzard of other reports seemed as unnecessary as they were irksome. McGoff said, "We decided to divest ourselves of government regulations and get into an enterprise where an inadvertent error would not jeopardize the entire operation or threaten disapproval of license renewal at a later date."

Divestiture began in February, 1966. Three radio stations were sold at a profit. WGMZ/FM in Flint was purchased by Metrocom, Inc., headed by Phil Munson for $60,000 in notes. Munson had joined Panax when he sold his AM station to what was then Mid-States Broadcasting in 1963. WQDC/FM, Midland was sold for $55,000 in cash to Habco, Inc. Ned Arbury, a Panax board member served as President of Habco. A week later, Century Broadcasting Corporation acquired WABX/FM of Detroit for $30,000 in cash and $70,000 in notes. All the transactions included assets and receivables.

Additional sales of radio properties were delayed until 1968, when three profitable dispositions whittled down the radio holdings. In April, 1968, Neal Mason paid $25,000 in cash and $190,000 in notes for all assets, excluding receivables for WAMM/AM in Flint. A few days later, WMAX/AM, Grand Rapids, was sold for $203,000 in cash for all assets, excluding receivables.

A profit approaching $250,000 was realized by the sale of the Jefferson City, Missouri radio station to Floyd Linn for $130,000 in cash and $445,000 in notes. This station had been a profitable operation from the beginning, but the decision to get out of electronic communications at a sizeable profit prompted the action.

An offer for purchase of the other two profit making Missouri properties KFEQ/AM and FKEQ/TV was accepted soon after, but it was not approved by FCC until the middle of 1969. I.S.C. Industries, a diversified holding company, paid $565,000 in cash, assets excluding receivables, for the radio station and $3.1 million in cash for the TV station. Profit exceeded $2 million.

WSWM/FM, the original station, was held until 1970, partly for sentimental reasons and because it became marginally profitable. Robert Liggett of Media-Media, Inc. bought the station for $256,000 with $64,000 as a down payment and the balance over a twelve year period. The name was changed to WFMK, the program switched to hard rock. The money rolled into Bob Leggett's pockets.

Going out of the radio business proved good business for Panax. The balance sheet and cash flow were regenerated. Money was available to expand the newspaper chain and several sizeable printing plants.

In mid-year, 1968, Panax purchased the Ypsilanti Press from Booth Newspapers, Inc. owner of daily papers in Ann Arbor, Grand Rapids, Jackson, Kalamazoo, Bay City and Muskegon, all the more populous cities in Michigan outside Detroit. The paper was not profitable for Booth, running at a loss of $70,000 a year. The Justice Department was threatening Booth with an anti-trust suit because of ownership of the Ann Arbor and Ypsilanti papers in the same market area. The Ypsilanti Press was treated like a stepchild of the Ann Arbor Press. Within one year after Panax bought the paper, it showed a profit of $250,000. In July, 1968, Panax acquired Inco-Graphics, a printing plant and the Ingham County News, a weekly, both located in Mason, Michigan, Ingham County seat, within about twelve miles of Panax headquarters. The purchase included the Holt Community News, serving a small bedroom community adjacent to Lansing. Total purchase price was cash of $195,000 and notes for $730,000 and 75,000 shares of Class A Panax stock. The properties were sold by owners James and Richard Brown. Jim Brown was elected a Panax Vice President and board member. Dick Brown remained Editor of the weekly Ingham County News. Three years later he repurchased the weekly for $200,000.

As Vice President, Jim Brown served in various capacities. He was elected a State Representative for two terms but lost his bid for the U.S. Congress in the Republican primary.

Inco-Graphics specialized in printing newspapers. At one period forty weeklies and twenty monthly publications were under contract, none of them owned by Panax. In late 1968, acquisition of Associated Newspapers actuated a pattern of growth for Panax. This group of Detroit Suburban weeklies in the western part of Wayne County included the Wayne Eagle, the Westland Eagle, The Garden City Guardian-Review, the Inkster Ledger Star, the Belleville Enterprise, the Romulus Roman and Legal Times. A combined circulation of forty thousand in a market area of more than a quarter million people, in a rapid growing suburban area augured favorably for subsequent growth of the papers. Purchase price was $635,000.

Over a five year period, beginning with his first newspaper venture in Mt. Pleasant, McGoff made an intensive study of the

71

city suburban area papers. He concluded that weeklies beckoned for profitable development. His observations and inquiries disclosed an erosion of the metropolitan dailies in the booming fringe cities enveloping Detroit and smaller cities with a multiplicity of separate municipal governmental entities. The more prolific population growth was in suburbia. Business development followed the population's drift from the center city.

Central city papers gave little more than cursory coverage to the sub-publics and displayed little interest in the area except for crime or some sensational occurrence. Token suburban sections were published to help circulation but they were obscured by core city dominance of the news.

Residents of these areas beamed with local pride, yearned for community identity, resented the practice of being lumped with the central city, responded to recognition. In Michigan, the Detroit suburban districts carried more political clout than the central city. Incomes were higher, providing more affluent, better educated, more sophisticated readers. It was McGoff's firm conviction that properly run papers in these areas could compete successfully for advertising and exert an influence in forming public opinion on critical issues of the day.

Procurement of the Associated Papers was the genesis of a studied plan to encircle Detroit. The Associated Papers proved stubbornly resistant to profit, although reorganization, consolidation of several of the papers, blitz sales campaigns, circulation drives, new printing processes, surgical economies in operating costs finally placed this group at the break even point by 1975. It had been a difficult task. Still, they fell short of expectancy.

Serving as his own broker, McGoff began a search for implementation of an encirclement program. Board members, staff, friends, alerted him to potential purchases. He checked out leads with a thorough, though at the time, brief investigation. He talked about the four P's as the basis for his analysis when considering an acquisition:

1. People
2. Potential
3. Profit
4. Paper

During the early seventies, a shortage of newsprint made this last point serious. Some of his earlier associates thought he was impulsive and feared he would overlook some of the basic details in his eagerness to expand. To some extent they were correct. Basically, mental acuity, decisiveness and unbridled enthusiasm were mistaken for impetuosity. Generally, his experience in assessing properties was favorable and denied any absence of forethought. In each potential acquisition, he examined the existing and potential market, the condition of plant and equipment, the performance of management and key personnel, the quality of the publication, the visible or hidden cause of success or failure of the pre-purchase ownership. The final evaluation pertained to what would be required to revivify the operation no matter what its status may be at the time.

McGoff possessed an inspired confidence in his ability to select management and professional personnel best equipped for any given situation to get favorable results, an essential characteristic of any entrepreneur. His batting average was not perfect. Sometimes he struck out. More frequently he guessed right.

On the last day of 1968, the Kalamazoo Printing Machinery Company was purchased for $100,000 in cash, $200,000 in notes and 75,000 shares of stock, earning a Panax Board slot for the seller, Adrian Vanderlinde. The company sold offset presses, camera room platemaking and composing room equipment and other graphic arts supplies. The company held exclusive contracts to represent certain domestic and foreign printing equipment manufacturers. This had the appearance of a logical diversification move.

Annexation of the Mellus Newspapers in the downriver section of Detroit occurred in October, 1969, for more than $2,700,000, through a stock merger. With a combined circulation exceeding seventy-one thousand, these papers incorporated the Allen Parker, The Lincoln Parker, the Southgate Sentinel, the Riverview Sentinel, the Ecorse Enterprise, the Taylor Tribune. Included in the group was a television magazine distributed weekly with the respective papers. In actuality, the deal was financed through the Commonwealth Bank which sold Mellus debentures at ten percent interest identical to the purchase price of the papers.

In 1970, aiming for further diversification and consistent with McGoff's natural affinity to the Upper Peninsula, Panax purchased fifty-one percent of the voting stock of a real estate development company in White Pine, Michigan. White Pine Copper Company had moved its international headquarters from New York state to White Pine during a short term boom in the copper industry. Formerly in the center of the copper mining country but idled for years, the community was unprepared for the sudden requirement of several hundred experienced copper miners. Busloads were transported daily from Ironwood and other communities, some requiring as much as a two hundred mile round trip for the workers.

Building a new model community with a modern shopping center, recreational facilities, churches, blocks of homes, and persuading the School Board to erect a new school, White Pines had a private urban renewal project that seemed a foolproof investment. At the dedication services, high level state officials proclaimed enduring growth and prosperity even though most of the newly erected houses were vacant at the time. The planners overlooked the character of these commuting miners. Time-hardened workers, many of them older immigrants or their offspring, they had deep roots in their respective communities. There was no assurance of job security. There had been sudden splurges of activity of other companies before with just as sudden shutdowns. These rugged individualistic skeptics had no intentions of pulling up stakes for new uncertainties in a new location. Conditions may have been tough back home, jobs may have been scarce, but by God, they were among friends, not strangers.

Aside from that, the daily travel was no burden. It was a pleasure. Many of them traveled in small buses, vans, station wagons, covered pickup trucks. On the way home they played cards, drank beer, engaged in the rough banter of miners. A fraternal esprit de corps soothed tired muscles, relieved the monotony of the job, relaxed tensions. And they joked about the jerry-built houses. They did not appeal to the artisans among them—prefabricated—trucked in from the outside—hastily assembled—devoid of individual style—no appeal. The word spread. No sale.

The project that looked so profit-promising in 1970 turned into a dead end loser in late 1971. Panax sold its interest and wrote off the small but unrecoverable loss at the end of the year.

Three major advances in 1971, however, improved markedly the Panax position. Harte-Hanks Newspapers, Inc., a major publishing company out of Texas offered McGoff $3 million for the

Ypsilanti Press. This unexpected windfall was too attractive to reject. The sale was consummated in September. The Ypsilanti experience had proven financially rewarding during the three years of operation. Doubling the original value enhanced McGoff's reputation for resuscitating newspaper properties drowning in a pool of red ink. It provided money for the next major move.

In November, the News-Herald group, seven weekly papers owned by the Wyandotte News Company, was merged with Panax. William Kreger accepted a Board membership. With a combined circulation of forty thousand, these additional seven papers solidified the market in the downriver area of western Wayne County.

Simultaneously, Panax took possession of the Macomb Daily and the Macomb Legal News in exchange for 250,000 shares of stock and a twenty year lease on the building. Three members of the McKee family, all heading other prospering business firms, joined the Panax Board—Mark T. McKee, Lucille McKee and Robert McKee.

The Macomb Daily, with a circulation of fifty-four thousand at the time was the only suburban daily in the seven county Detroit metropolitan area. It continued as the largest single Panax newspaper property with a projection of seventy-five thousand circulation by the middle eighties. Located at Macomb County seat, Mt. Clemens, it raised an effective voice in the northeast suburban section, winning a variety of Michigan Press Association awards annually.

Goethe observed that nature recognizes no pause in progress and development. McGoff knew no pause in his ambitions to duplicate his successes around Detroit. He turned his attention to the Chicago suburbs for his next major expansion.

In exchange for a block of stock, a Panax Vice Presidency and a seat on the Board, James A. Linen IV, son of the former President and Publisher of Time, Inc., sold to Panax a group of Chicago properties. This group included one daily, the Chicago Daily Calumet; two weeklies, the Harvey Bee News and the Calumet Day; four semi-weeklies, the Munster Sun Journal, Highland Sun, Griffith Sun and Route Thirty Sun; two tri-weeklies, the Calumet City Sun Journal and the Lansing (Ill.) Sun Journal and the Advertiser Shopper.

Completing the new properties were a printing plant, a typesetting company, an advertising agency, Promotion Management

Associates, and Suburban Publishers Press. Linen was given a contract to continue management of the Chicago properties. The papers gave Panax another hundred thousand circulation. The printing and typesetting plants handled all the Illinois Panax publications as well as contracting for outside work. Later, in 1975, Panax acquired Rantoul Press and a printing plant at Rantoul extending operations into Central Illinois.

In the meantime, two printing plants were acquired in the Detroit area—Keystone Publishing Company, the largest independent offset operation in Metropolitan Detroit, and its subsidiary in Lincoln Park, Wayne Graphics. The big plant was rechristened American Press Company. Containing fifty thousand square feet of floor space, the Detroit facility could utilize twenty-one offset presses, sheetfed presses and binding equipment.

Two years later, the Graphic Arts International Union, Local 981, called a strike after demanding a fifty percent increase and other concessions that Panax considered economically unfeasible. The plant was closed in June, 1974. Equipment was moved to other locations. McGoff said, "We decided to terminate operations of this plant because the unions ignored the impossibility of making a profit, the only way the free enterprise system functions. If there is no profit there is no reason for people to work or risk reputations and moneys necessary to provide the jobs for the union member."

Panax took a corporate loss of $465,000 for 1974 as a result of failure of this new venture. Another new attempt at vertical expansion failed to float to the end of its first year. Forming Panax Shipping, Inc., a wholly owned subsidiary, the freighter John P. McGoff carried newsprint from paper mills on Lake Superior to lower Michigan for use by Panax publications. Again this was a natural expansion since transportation by water cut costs, even though the shipping season for the Great Lakes was limited to the non-freezing months.

In May, 1973, the ship sank in the Caribbean. All cargo was lost. All the crew survived. The company was liquidated. Most of the loss was covered by insurance.

Tightening the grip on the Detroit suburban market, ten additional weeklies were absorbed in 1973 in the east and northeast sections. Identified as the Dawn group, acronym for Detroit Area Weekly Newspapers, these weeklies hiked circulation another one hundred thousand. At the time of sale of this family owned group of papers, Ben Nathanson speaking for the family said, "This is a difficult decision, but one that we think is in the best interest of my ten newspaper associates, companies, employees, customers and readers. It was relevant to find a company whose resources are greater than Dawn's in terms of technology, manpower recruitment, training, training facilities, management knowhow and financial capability."

Continuing, Nathanson praised Panax by saying, "Panax newspapers consistently earn recognition and awards on a local, state and national basis for their editorial, technical and typographical excellence. I have seen convincing evidence that Panax constantly makes an effort to recruit, hire, train, recognize and promote the people who make the firm what it is and what it will be in the future."

The Dearborn Press put Panax into the prestigious Dearborn, Michigan section of Metropolitan Detroit. The Miami Beach Times opened south Florida for subsequent expansion.

So in this step by step process the company grew, year after year. Growth induced more growth. Success emboldened the compulsive pursuit of more success. Between 1973 and the end of 1978, Panax affixed a dozen more properties in the Detroit suburbs through buying the Advisor and Community papers and securing a stronghold in the Dearborn section with addition of the Dearborn Heights Leader.

The Miami Beach Times was closed in 1975 but six additional papers and a printing plant in the Miami/Fort Lauderdale corridor established a foothold in this ballooning center. In 1972 McGoff invaded the high income Washington, D.C. megalopolis with its three million white collar residents and the highest percentage of specialized college graduates of any U.S. standard metropolitan area. The Globe and Advertiser newspapers encompassed ten weeklies with a circulation approaching 175,000 covering the Maryland, Virginia suburbs where much of the wealth is concentrated. As a supplement to the Globe papers the Washington Weekly was issued, featuring comment and strong editorial opinion on national political issues. Climaxing the 1978 growth period, Panax procured fourteen weekly suburban papers in Houston, Texas, with aggregate circulation of 200,000.

Two developments to improve products and markets gave McGoff particular pride of achievement. In 1977, the Morning Sun

77

made its sunrise appearance in the Mt. Pleasant/Alma communities as the first mid-Michigan morning newspaper for several decades. The Detroit Free Press had been Michigan's only morning paper. Combining the separate daily afternoon editions of Mt. Pleasant and Alma into one regional publication improved the quality of the flagship paper of the Panax chain.

Then in the spring of 1978, the newborn Sunday Times started publication to serve the Upper Peninsula. The scattered populations of the vast U.P. had been dependent on Detroit or Milwaukee for its Sunday reading. Except for periodic features on some phase of U.P. life, little coverage of events appeared in these papers. The distance hoisted circulation costs inordinately and thwarted advertising potential.

Response to a pilot Sunday edition of the Marquette Mining Journal in 1977 encouraged creation of an entirely new Sunday paper published exclusively for the Upper Peninsula. Starting a new paper requires a large capital outlay. A new $500,000 offset printing plant constructed in Powers, Michigan in 1977 handled all the printing for the Escanaba Daily Press, the Iron Mountain News and the Sunday Times. Located midway between these two cities, it became the headquarters for the Sunday Times. The first edition was published in March, 1978, with a press run of fifty-one thousand, increased to sixty thousand within a month.

This Sunday edition of the three established dailies was devoted to the interests of readers living hundreds of miles apart but having a much-vaunted pride in their peninsula and a shared passion for recognition. Although the operation was intended to be profitable over a period of time, a substantial deficit was budgeted for the first three years. Profit was the motivating force in creation of this new publication. Other factors led to the decision: pride of innovation, satisfaction of beating the big city competition, genuine regard for the people of the area. This move seemed a prudent gamble for long range dividends as well as amplifying the prestige of Panax and exerting additional influence in shaping public opinion on major state and national issues.

In the meantime, expedience dictated some divestments. The Associated papers, purchased in 1968 to spearhead the Detroit grid, were sold with no substantial gain or loss. The Kalamazoo Printing Machinery Company was sold at a loss in 1977. In June, 1978, Jim Brown, Panax Vice President and Director for seven years reacquired Inco-Graphics for $1,125,000 in cash, a $1 million, ten-year note at nine percent interest, certain real estate and assumption of $250,000 of outstanding liabilities.

Commenting on the move at the time, Brown said, "When you work with John McGoff for a few years, some of his spirit rubs off on you."

At the end of 1978, Panax growth reached its apogee, publishing six dailies and sixty-one weekly papers with a combined circulation of 925,000 in selected areas of Michigan, Illinois, Indiana, Texas, Florida, Virginia and Maryland. Printing and commercial typesetting plants were operated in Michigan, Illinois, Florida and South Africa.

Plans were approved for a press production plant for the Macomb Daily and all other affiliated suburban Panax newspapers in the Detroit operations. Going into full operation in May, 1980 at a final cost of $6,600,000, the plant was located on a five-acre site a short distance from the Macomb Daily building in downtown Mt. Clemens. Beginning in 1981 the new facility planned to accept large scale commercial printing. In addition to housing a new eight unit multi-color offset press, capable of printing as many as fifty thousand newspapers per hour, the center included new mailroom distribution equipment.

All this growth up through 1978, however, could not be equated with increased profit. Although net earnings approached $600,000 on net revenues of $39 million for the year, the net profit was possible only because of the sale of Inco-Graphics printing plant. Actual operations experienced a loss roughly equivalent to the listed profit. Growth was a contributing factor to the operating deficits:

- Costs involved in starting the new Upper Peninsula Sunday Times and subsequent budgeted losses for the first three years.
- High interest costs for loans incurred for the numerous acquisitions raising the net long term debt to $14.5 million at increased prime interest rates.
- Heavier corporate expenses for legal services.
- Logistical costs for supervision of operations in seven scattered states.
- Failure of operations in Texas, Florida and metropolitan Washington to produce anticipated profits.

79

A few intermittent failures along the way served as grim reminders that risk is a built-in factor of private enterprise. Financial gains in one operation can be offset by losses in another in a company such as Panax that never stopped striving for growth, never ceased taking new risks to achieve that growth. At times, these failures were the result of poor judgment, changing conditions in society, timing. At other times, uncontrollable events intervened in spite of anything management could do. This happened to Panax in an attempt to diversify.

In 1978, the Board approved two McGoff proposals that would appear, at first glance, to be incongruous. The commercial printing plants were profitable, but required large capital investments to stay competitive. Rapidly changing processes in printing due to advanced technology demanded replacement of machinery at an accelerated rate at a time that cost of money was alarmingly high. It was decided to sell the commercial printing plants when it was advantageous. Panax would remain primarily media-oriented. Sales of printing plants would provide money for new newspapers when opportunities arose.

Simultaneously, the Board approved the proposal to create a wholly owned leisure-service subsidiary to tap a share of the $20 billion cruise business. The cruise trade had doubled within a decade. Industry officials predicted it would double again by 1985, provided enough ships could be found to meet the exponentially increasing demand for space. More than 1.25 million passengers sailed from American ports in 1978. Once the exclusive privilege of the affluent, cruising had been discovered by middle class, vacation-bent Americans.

Analysis showed a cruise to be a bargain. A prepaid package cruise covering everything except personal choice expenditures for such items as shore trips, drinks and souvenirs was less expensive than land based vacations in many instances. Also, it eliminated traffic choked highways, hotel check-ins and other wearisome trivia. Aside from costs, the lure of the sea has always been irresistible.

With 1.25 million people begging somebody to take their vacation money, McGoff had no intention of being caught with his hands in his pockets. With typical entrepreneurial flair for capitalizing on an unsatisfied public fancy, he envisioned this new undertaking as a natural complement to newspaper publishing.

Panax publications were read by several million people each week. Other papers controlled by McGoff in a privately held corporation reached an equal number. They sold all kinds of products and services for other companies through the advertising pages. Why not sell one of their own services? Advertise Panax-sponsored cruises in Panax papers. The advertising would escalate the newspaper revenues. The avalanche of reservations would fill the cruise ship. A financial bonanza all around. Sound premise. Logical assumption. How could it fail?

It seemed feasible to lease a ship for a flat fee for each trip. It was impractical for Panax to borrow millions to purchase a ship and make long term commitments for crew. That could come later when profits from the cruise business warranted such outlay.

Chartering the Italian Costa Line's M.S. World Renaissance, an eleven day Caribbean Cruise was scheduled to leave Miami on January 22, 1979. Shore excursions were slotted for Cap Haitien, Haiti; San Juan, Puerto Rico; St. Maarten of the Dutch Windward Islands; Guadeloupe of the French Leeward Islands; Antigua, West Indies; St. Thomas, Virgin Islands; Puerto Plata, Dominican Republic; Nassau, Bahamas and back to Miami on the morning of February 2, 1979.

TFC, a California based tour agency, contracted to handle reservations and all arrangements. A new Vice President was appointed to direct the new leisure division, named Sun Seas, Inc. His career-long specialty in the travel industry had little impact on the planning for this cruise. Commitments were made before he assumed his new duties.

The M.S. Renaissance, built in France in 1965, carried 520 passengers and 220 crew members, had Greek registry and operated out of Miami. The ship's master and his top crew were Greek or Italian. The cabin and room stewards, many speaking punctured English, were drawn from the Caribbean—Honduras, Columbia, Panama, Haiti, Dominican Republic, Puerto Rico and the Miami Cuban colony.

Sailing with less than a break-even load authored no discernible concern by Panax officials. The inaugural cruise was calculated to generate future business. Enticing back home word of mouth good will by enchanted customers would more than compensate for initial promotion outlays.

A four hour shore excursion was scheduled for Cap Haitien on the second morning out of Miami. A sense of excited expectancy permeated the entourage when the local Harbor Pilot took over command of the ship for docking, in accordance with maritime law and custom.

Usually cruise ships anchored in the bay off Cap Haitien and passengers were transported ashore by tender. For some unexplained reason, someone decided to tie up at the wharf dwarfed by the leviathan vessel—four hundred ninety-two feet long, sixtynine feet high, eight decks towering over the single landing dock that seemed better equipped to accommodate the native-manned rowboats cluttering the harbor waters.

A huge, uncushioned concrete piling protruded from the corner of the pier, standing rigidly at attention like a Praetorian guard. With outward calm but apparent inward confusion, this native Harbor Pilot managed to maneuver the ship into this piling, blasting a jagged fifteen by twenty foot hole near midships on the starboard side, thirty inches from the water line.

Forced to use local labor and facilities, an estimated twelve hour delay for repairs stretched to forty-eight hours. The ship arrived at San Juan early Saturday, two days behind schedule.

A quartet of Federal inspectors boarded the ship at San Juan. At 7:30 P.M. the Captain announced, without elaboration, that the ship would return to Miami, the nearest port with adequate facilities to make additional repairs. The ship sailed at 8:00 P.M.

All the passengers were disappointed that the cruise had to be aborted. Most of them accepted the decision philosophically. However, a coterie of dissidents had been sulking since the two-day layover in Cap Haitien. Admittedly, Cap Haitien was not considered one of the Caribbean's premier ports of call. There was little there to attract the interest of the cruise members for more than the scheduled four hours. As the old proverb says, "Idleness is the mother of mischief."

These trumpets of discontent directed their resentment against Panax, sponsor of the cruise. John McGoff, several of his top executives and two Board members were passengers. The untimely accident was beyond their control. That did not deter several of the more vocal complainants from going to the Detroit newspapers when they arrived back home. The Detroit Free Press covered the story under the heading, "Voyage of the Dumped". The Detroit News had two lengthy byline features. One headline read, "Caribbean Cruise Rams Dock—It's Passengers Who Mutiny." The other story was captioned, "No Love Boat: Vacation Cruise Hits Legal Waves."

In May, after months of negotiations, Costa agreed to refund through Panax, seventy-five percent of the cruise fare or, at the option of each passenger, one hundred percent credit on any future Costa Caribbean Cruise until May 15, 1981. Without exception, passengers chose one of the options.

The hole in the Renaissance was repaired. The consequences of the accident and its adverse publicity could not be repaired. The Sun Sea Properties of Panax was dissolved. Panax wrote off more than $150,000 as a loss. An inauspicious beginning for 1979, the first of several serious setbacks that would alter the course of the company.

In October, 1978, Panax had decided to reenter the television business. Panax Television, Inc. was created as a wholly owned subsidiary. Agreement was made to purchase two television stations in Northern Michigan, subject to approval of the Federal Communications Commission. Stations WGTU-TV in Traverse City and WGTQ-TV in Sault Ste. Marie served an area in Northern Michigan composed of all or parts of twenty-seven counties in Northern Michigan and the Upper Peninsula. Purchase price was in excess of $1 million.

On May 31, 1979, the staff of the FCC Broadcast Bureau approved the license for purchase and further approved the application for a satellite TV station. Both parties were notified. On receipt of the instrument of public notice, Panax completed the contract agreement by making the down payment of $325,000. Management staff was employed. Transfer of operations to the new owners proceeded routinely.

In July, 1979, the full Commission, meeting in closed session, SET ASIDE the staff decision. In effect, this meant the application was in a pending status—not approved or denied. The FCC ordered the parties involved, seller and buyer, "to take whatever steps are necessary to revert to their status prior to the grant of the applications."

This action was unprecedented. Never before had the commission reversed the decision of the FCC Broadcast Bureau. The reason given for this unusual action by the Commission stated that the Justice Department was investigating John McGoff for ties to

South Africa in a matter unrelated to the TV application. According to press reports, the Commission acted to reverse the approval after the Media Access Project, a public interest communications law firm, had protested the routine granting of the license while McGoff was under investigation.

McGoff had not been indicted or charged officially. Numerous press stories had speculated about alleged ties to South Africa involving a loan to purchase newspapers. These stories claimed that McGoff had not reported the loan as required by law. He had denied any illegal or improper action at any time.

Officials of both companies involved in the transfer of the TV stations were shocked, confused and unprepared. Panax was in the anomalous position of owning the stations by virtue of legal purchase and deed and not owning the stations by order of the FCC. Michigan Television Network had sold the stations, accepted the down payment and distributed it to the stockholders, legally and in good faith. Trying to revert to the status prior to the approval of the application was like trying to put a scrambled egg back to its original form.

Panax withdrew the request to purchase rather than undergo the expense of endless legal action. The down payment was returned in February, 1980, more than seven months after it was made. No interest was paid. Panax had borrowed the money at prime rate plus. Legal fees, staff commitments during the short period of operations, interest costs, and other unavoidable expenses mounted to another $200,000 loss. The besmirched image was unrecoverable at any price.

The year 1979 was not a very good year.

Exacerbating these two major disappointments, the second quarter report disclosed continued loss in several operations. It was necessary to make some hardnosed decisions. Get rid of the unprofitable properties.

First Panax disposed of a foreign investment, Craft Press (Pty) Limited, located in Bophuthatswana, a small nation granted independence by South Africa. Entering this business in 1974 during a sustained effort by South Africa to train blacks in skilled jobs in what they called "Homelands", Panax owned eighty percent of the company. The other twenty percent was owned by the development company established by the government. Over a period of time Panax investment had been reduced to forty-two percent. This business was marginally profitable but not a significant part of Panax operations. In 1977 the company operated at a loss; a small profit was realized in 1978. In 1979 all interest in the company was sold. Technically, the managers and employees assumed ownership.

A small news distribution service, Media Services, Inc., in Washington was sold at mid-year; Sun Sea Travel Systems, a travel agency in Miami, was sold to another company owned and controlled by McGoff. Then in October, Panax peddled off its wholly owned subsidiary, Panax of Virginia, consisting of a number of weekly publications in the Washington area. This sale was limited to subscription lists and trade names of the specific newspapers and did not include property and equipment. These dispensations resulted in a combined loss of more than $100,000.

Next came the sale of Panax of Florida, including all newspapers and commercial printing operations, followed a few months later by sale of Panax of Texas. These disposals resulted in a pre-tax gain to Panax of $1,350,000.

By the end of 1979 Panax operations had been reduced to six daily newspapers and twenty-nine non-daily publications concentrated in Michigan and Illinois with a small group in Maryland in communities bordering Washington. Total combined circulation, daily and non-daily, averaged about 631,000. These retained properties permitted consolidation of operations into a smaller base in markets with past profitability and continued growth potential.

In the Virginia market, analysis showed it was a matter of timing. Panax acquired its papers about the time growth in the area had peaked, patterns were set, competition was established. In Florida, some of the earlier acquisitions met expectations. They were paying off. Losses in new properties acquired later overbalanced the profitable operations. Opportunity to sell at a gain and get rid of a corporate loser was a logical move.

In Texas, the original plan was to eventually purchase eight additional weeklies to equal or exceed circulation of the two metropolitan dailies. Rupert Murdoch, Australian publisher of the New York Post and various other papers, purchased these papers by his wholly owned subsidiary, News American Publishing, Inc., at a price that Panax considered unfeasible. Rather than continue a competitive struggle resulting in mounting losses, Panax sold the fourteen papers to Murdoch at a substantial gain.

Frank Shepherd, Panax Executive Vice President, said, "With the sale of the Texas group, Panax is now in the strongest position in its history financially and from a management-logistics standpoint. We intend to devote our energies and resources to making our present group of papers the pride of their communities and the industry."

McGoff said at the end of 1979, "In all, despite the current economic uncertainty, the company stands on the threshold of the new decade in good financial condition, with confident management, and ready to take advantage of new opportunities for further growth and expansion."

Chapter 7

Quest for Excellence

*"Each honest calling, each walk of life has its own
elite, its own aristocracy based on excellence of
performance."*

. . James Bryant Conant

Retreat from excellence in all phases of American society
during the past few decades triggered one of the most devastating
developments in the nation's history. For years, pursuit of excellence as a standard for individual performance produced unprecedented economic heights of living. In recent times acceptance of
mediocrity as a criterion for personal endeavor has denigrated the
quality of life, the national prestige, economic productivity. Mired
in mediocrity, the loftiest instincts have been detoured as ethics
came to be irrelevant, incidental and situational. Mediocrity has
infected all established institutions with a systemic poison, re-
lentlessly ravaging ideals and ideas of achievement. No institution
has escaped—not business, not religion, not government, not
labor, not education, not the professions. Still, a hard core segment
in society cherishes excellence as a guideline for performance,
keeps it alive as an ideal. These select bodies of all economic and
social levels refuse to prostrate themselves before the iniquitous
gods of complacency.

Characteristic of the entrepreneur, John McGoff strived for
excellence from the time he delivered the Pittsburgh Herald as a
preteen newsboy. He tottered on the brink of bankruptcy during his
first two years in radio broadcasting because he insisted on the

87

highest quality music program. His commitment came naturally. His father, Peter McGoff, never ascended the economic ladder past the first rung, but he had a fierce pride of workmanship. He considered himself as the "best damn craneman" in the steel industry.

So John's primacy of concern for excellence was rooted in his character. His application of excellence in his business was hinged on passionate convictions and anchored by constancy of purpose.

Harold Good, a retired General Motors executive, Panax stockholder and Board member, confirms McGoff's commitment to standards of excellence: "Panax is a reflection of John McGoff, his assignment of values, his original ideas, his willingness to take a calculated risk, his understanding that people are the most important asset in any business enterprise and his immutable belief in the free enterprise system."

Speaking of reasons for Panax growth, Good continues, "There is one major factor. John's prime objective in any venture has always been to supply a community need and to do it better than anyone else has ever done it before."

Jean Worth, retired editor of the Escanaba Press, a Panax consultant after retirement and frequent contributing writer for the Upper Peninsula Sunday Times commended McGoff for his aggressive efforts to improve print journalism. "Over a period of time as Panax expanded," asserted Worth, "he changed the appearance and character of the papers that he acquired. McGoff brought mechanical excellence to Panax papers. They were the best printed in the Upper Peninsula using offset presses with their great fidelity, laser transmission of photos, wire services, telex communications, route car delivery, optical character recognition (OCR) typesetting and centralized printing plants.

"However, the greatest change was in the staffing and in training staff," Worth elaborates. "McGoff was the most progressive element in the history of the U.P. journalism. He structured Panax so that it had officers assigned to its major divisions that included print, editorial, marketing, and other specialties.

"Editors were called to Lansing frequently to learn about state government where laws are legislated and administered. Trips to Washington familiarized the staff with the federal establishment. Of course," concluded Worth, "editors groused about being away too often, but I never heard anyone say the sessions were not helpful to performance. Everybody acknowledged that learning the intricacies of government enabled them to interpret developments more intelligently."

Worth specified Upper Peninsula papers to illustrate his points because he spent his entire career in the area, but he granted that indivertible attention to improvement applied to all Panax papers.

In encapsulated form, McGoff's personal philosophy on the subject is revealed in his own words:

"I learned a long time ago the value of a good sense of humor. Regardless of how right we might think we are, most of us find ourselves caught in some pretty stupid positions. That is the time to laugh, not cry. Always I have believed that business has to be fun. I look forward to every day. Two-thirds of my life is devoted to work; therefore, it has to be enjoyable. Failures in life result from people working in jobs that they do not like or feel they are not capable of handling.

"A job and a business should be challenging, pushing each individual to reach for new areas to conquer. It should be creative in the sense that each person has created something that no one else can emulate.

"I have heard many times that a newspaper is great because it has a beautiful plant or fine presses and computers. The most important ingredient in our company is people. They are not machines. With superior people, one can build an effective team to provide a better product. It is important—in fact it is necessary—for the boss to encourage his fellow workers to develop and grow. In our company, at least, we have ongoing training programs for people to develop, grow and advance.

"These training programs add to the cost of doing business. Some could say they cut into profits. I believe there would be no profits without qualified, well-trained, motivated, relatively happy personnel, and a program to give them opportunity to improve and experience the satisfaction of doing a good job."

This has been McGoff's guiding philosophy throughout his business career. Techniques were refined by experience. Goals were defined more precisely by time. Programs became structured, formalized and conducted by polished professional leadership. Basic concepts remained constant.

When the FM radio station was struggling for survival with a modicum of employees, he displayed a repugnance for the drift to mediocrity: "People make the difference. A quality product is dependent on qualified people. I need to select and hold the best people I can find if this business is to succeed."

He repeated that message time after time to business acquaintances as he beseeched them to buy stock or advertising to meet the weekly payroll. He was talking to profit-hardened business leaders, not academic idealogues. General Motors executive, Harold Good; steel executive, Jim Anderton; insurance excutive, Ned Arbury; architect, Alden Dow; dozens of executives of similar stature, including bankers and financiers.

These men responded with money, not because their clinically cold analyses promised any guaranteed returns. Indeed, there was reason to doubt the wisdom of the decisions by normal investment criteria, but here was a unique appeal. This man was committed to a quality product and high standards of performance. His belief in the profit motive was unshakable. He did not subordinate the economics of business but neither did he mention dividends or advertising values. He talked about people, services, business image, appeal to the noble interests of the public.

They did not turn him down. In turn, he never let them down nor did he wander from the basic principle that the right people in the right place at the right time makes the difference between success and failure in business.

This was not mere rhetoric. His words reflected his actions. Integrity, character, initiative, potential, compatibility were prerequisites for employment. As the company expanded, he inserted management development as an integral function of business, not an extra-managerial fringe activity to be initiated when budget permitted. Few publishers, large or small, allocated a higher percentage of total revenues to human resources planning and development. Securing, developing and utilizing the proven abilities of people was a touchstone of McGoff's management career.

Focusing on performance rather than pre-Panax experience, he encouraged self-development and rewarded demonstrated results.

Tom Madding endorsed the efficiency of the practice. As the executive in charge of the Florida operation at the time, he lauded the policy.

"Panax inherited me with the purchase of the Ypsilanti Press from Booth newspapers. At Booth, chief emphasis was on educational background and degrees earned in course. Promotions to the executive staff came from professionals, trained journalists or specialists in finance. With my experience limited to the printing field, I had no chance to move up to the executive office.

"At Panax, my advancement was determined by performance. This provided an incentive for top performance every day. I did not lose my identity. I was allowed to use my skills and abilities in my own way to accomplish certain goals established for my area of responsibility. I participated in setting realistic goals in our 'management by objective' program. Specialized help was available to me if I needed or requested it. I was not pestered or harassed. If I reached the goals, I was recognized and received a bonus. If objectives were not attained, experts from the corporate office helped me analyze the reason and I accepted responsibitlty for trying harder or accepted the consequences. The self-improvement programs and promotions from within the company gave additional incentives to do better. The strength of Panax was the emphasis given to the strengths of its people."

This program did not occur by instinct or accident. When the size of the company justified it, or even before if measured by traditional standards, McGoff turned to his World War II friend and erstwhile university roommate for professional guidance. After Dave Merrell received his doctorate in psychology, he gained valuable experience in working with business firms before joining Rohrer, Hibler and Replogle, Inc., highly regarded business consultants and specialists in planning and development of human resources. Dr. Merrell became R.H.R. Consultant for Panax. He designed pre-employment tests and an employee evaluation program.

In 1969, Joe Gross was employed as the Personnel Director. He met McGoff when they were serving on the Board of Control of Northern Michigan University. Tall, broad-shouldered, commanding in presence, Joe impressed McGoff with his intellectual honesty, his keen sense of analysis, his systematic approach to solution of university problems. Joe was invited to speak at McGoff's church. He was asked to take the battery of tests designed by Dr. Merrell for executive staff. He was labeled for an appropriate opening on the Panax corporate staff. A native Iowan, product of Lincoln University in Jefferson City, Missouri, graduate of the National Training School for Scout executives, Joe pursued a career with the Boy Scouts of America, serving four years as Scout

Executive at Dallas, Texas and completing his twenty-fifth year at Detroit when McGoff invited him to join Panax.

Appointment of Joe Gross posited on the record one more frame of reference to McGoff's uncanny ability to intuit executive potential in individuals unallied with the publishing business. Joe was a natural for Personnel Director. The job and Joe fit like the precision parts of a high powered motor calibrated to the thousandth of an inch tolerance.

A stickler for detail, disciplined to exactitude, a master organizer, he shared McGoff's ardor for excellence. He believed in the value of continuous on-the-job education as a means of self-improvement. He advocated positive non-material incentives to supplement pay and fringe benefits as primary motivating forces for high performance. From his Boy Scout experience, he knew that public recognition for personal achievement gave distinction, prestige and self-esteem beyond anything money could buy.

Through arrangements by Board members Harold Good, who had served as Personnel Director at Oldsmobile Division of General Motors, and Ed George, President of Detroit Edison, Gross spent considerable time at these two companies. He studied their policies, practices and procedures in recruiting, testing, interviewing, record keeping, training, promoting, increment schedules, fringe benefits, service recognition, performance evaluations and all other activities related to maximum development of human resources. Dr. Dave Merrell and his associates at R.H. & R. worked with him

A balanced, coordinated program evolved; extensive in scope; intensive in purpose; comprehensive in content; profound in depth; meticulous in execution. Goals were pinpointed. Ways of reaching the goals were drafted. Means of financing the programs were budgeted, methods of evaluating both the goals and ways and means were diagrammed.

A complete Human Resource program did not mature overnight. First things came first. It grew systematically, logically, improving with experience, expanding as the company expanded, responding to expressed needs and responses of staff. Recognizing that effective human relations should be personalized, the processes of interviewing, investigating references, testing and hiring procedures were standardized but administered informally. This avoided cold, impersonal bureaucratization.

An inclusive personnel records system permitted quick review of an employee's history from acceptance to termination of employment through color-coded ratings. Periodic evaluations measured development and indicated promotability potential.

A series of specialized skills conferences were held for each of the operating properties. Basic management seminars trained potential supervisors. Basic and advanced management conferences covered the gamut of responsibilities faced by managers. Production workers had their own problem-solving sessions.

Employees at all levels were recognized in appropriate public ceremonies for length of service and special accomplishments. An inhouse publication, "The Communicator", was devoted exclusively to company developments with written and pictorial recognition of employees and their local activities. When special honors were awarded, the newspapers where these honorees worked gave full coverage of the event. The program reached its pinnacle in 1977-78.

In 1978, a Washington Editorial Seminar on National Defense was instigated by McGoff's determination to devote more attention to national and international issues. He had encountered some resistance from editors already pressed to find adequate space for local/state news and syndicated features in their community-oriented papers.

In his introduction to the conference, he said:

"This conference symbolizes what makes Panax a very special newspaper organization. We care about the communities we serve. We care about the financial and moral health of the newspapers we publish. We care about issues larger than the ones usually relegated to community newspapers. We are not content to remain on history's sidelines, wringing our hands in anguish and frustration while the so-called BIG MEDIA set and shape the agenda of information parceled out to the American public.

"In Panax, we intend to join the battle of ideas, to insure that our readers have facts they need to make complete and effective choices. Some may call it heresy to imagine that community newspapers can or should play such a large role in public affairs. I think not. I think that we will discover that our readers will welcome the fresh and vital insights we can bring to them."

The Washington Conference was organized with painstaking detail. Every minute was to be invested, not spent, not wasted.

Enjoyed? Yes, but productive, useful, stimulating. The corporate staff and Michigan editors traveled in the company-owned, converted Greyhound bus with the interior altered to combine the comforts of an executive lounge, mobile office and small group conference center-on-wheels.

Leaving the Lansing headquarters on Tuesday at 8:00 A.M. with a fifteen minute stop at the Detroit Metropolitan Airport to pick up outstate and Detroit area editors, the bus was scheduled to arrive in Washington at 8:00 P.M.

During the daylong travel, Jay Behuncik, a Congressional Fellow in national security affairs with the Heritage Foundation and Foreign Policy and Defense Advisor to the U.S. Senate Steering Committee, was on board to conduct small group conferences on National Security and National Defense, using position papers as the reference source for discussion.

Beginning on Wednesday, sessions started early each morning, continued until late each night, including speakers at lunch and dinner. Subjects covered Soviet Military Capabilities and Intentions, Congressional Trends and Issues, Status of Armed Forces, C.I.A., Salt II Risks, Shape and Mission of the U.S. Navy, The White House Press, followed by the Daily Media briefing by the President's Press Secretary.

Traveling from place to place by the Panax bus, sessions were held on site, prefaced or followed by tours of the facilities: The National Press Club, The State Department, The Old Executive Office, The White House, The Russell Senate Building, C.I.A. Headquarters, The Pentagon.

The program glittered with talent from distinguished national leaders: a former Ambassador to Russia and Professor of International Studies at the University of Miami's Center for International Studies, Consultant to the Department of State, Chairman of the Joint Chiefs of Staff, The C.I.A. Director, Chairman of the Advisory Council of John Hopkins School of Advanced International Studies, Representative of the Secretary of Defense at the Strategic Arms Limitation talks with the Soviet Union, a prestigious former Secretary of the Navy. Others of similar rank met with the visitors.

The week swept by, swift-winged as the winter winds across the western plains. These small town and suburban daily and weekly editors were not passive listeners anesthetized by the glamor of the occasion. Skeptical of platitudes as competent editors should be, they probed for the concrete, the specificities, the supporting evidence.

They returned to their jobs with a newly piqued interest and a fuller knowledge of the implications of fast-breaking world events. The participative educational experience withered their reluctance to relate these issues to their local community readers. Almost without exception, articles, columns, commentaries appeared as a direct result of this conference.

Post-conference evaluation by the conferees was "excellent", with a high percentage requesting a more balanced program to give conflicting points of view.

The Annual Editors' Conferences, usually four day sessions, became a treasured tradition. Held at some isolated resort area, these conferences were designed to inform, to educate, to motivate, to inspire and to weld a sense of unity and pride in the company. Publishers (General Managers), editors, corporate staff, State and National bureau chiefs attended. Nationally recognized specialists, authorities, scholars and leaders in all spheres of newspaper publishing served as speakers, discussion leaders, and resource counselors.

The Seventh Annual Editorial Conference at the Shanty Creek Conference and Resort Center in Bellaire, Michigan was representative of the quality of the programs. The theme, "You Make the Difference" was reminiscent of McGoff's early day pleas to investors. In his introduction to the conference he said, "A month ago the men and women who direct the editorial destinies of Panax newspapers gathered in Washington for a high level seminar on national security.

"We have asked you to join us in this beautiful Michigan setting for still another learning experience, this one devoted to the eternal issues and advances of our profession.

"Both of these conferences in their separate ways reflect the commitment of your company to your growth as professionals. We do this because the notions that people make the difference are far more than mere words at Panax. They are the essence of our management style and purposes."

With fifty-five editors and managers present and a dozen outside guest speakers, sessions covered such subjects as editorial management by objectives, dealing with labor unions, electronics, technology, First Amendment rights, human resources development/planning, circulation, photo-journalism, graphics. The Chief Editorial Writer for Hearst Newspapers talked on the subject, "What Makes a Newspaper Great?" This conference featured a series of critiques consisting of four concurrent sessions, one for Panax dailies and three for individual groups of non-dailies. The findings of each group were discussed at a plenary session. This was a highlight of the conference, providing new ideas and insights as editors and publishers saw their product as others viewed them.

To be effective, conferences must be planned to meet the needs of the participants, not to inflate the ego of the planner. Favorable reaction to the variety of conferences for Panax employees was the most dramatic testimony of adherence to that tenet by planners.

Enlightened management recognizes the multiple values of participation in decision making, not just in meetings. It is one of the inducements to higher morale and increased productivity. Individuals need that feeling of importance, that sense of belonging, so essential to self-esteem and pride of performance. It instills a desire for personal growth requisite to achievement of excellence.

To encourage a more participative systematic approach to management, Panax initiated a fully integrated Management by Objectives program in the 77-78 period.

It brought participating managers into goal-setting, planning, measurement and review.

Quarterly Performance Review and appraisal followed logically to link planning cycles after periods of implementation. Both individual performance and practicality of goals and methods of reaching the goals were reviewed. Everybody involved was able to understand the results.

The Management Inventory Program was the third phase of the basic tools, consisting of an annual performance review rating and an individual development plan. Holding management inventory meetings at each location, appropriate corporate and local staff appraised the performance of each management team, inventory management potential, plan for growth, promotion and succession within the organization.

Panax had been a dynamic company for twenty years. Since its inception, most of its properties had been located in competitive markets. Efficient utilization of human resources and a steady flow of leadership, ready to assume greater responsibilities, were imperative to this type company.

Providing opportunities and motivation for self-development as an integrated budgetary requirement throughout this growth period was the cornerstone of its success. Prime concern for each individual human being on the job primed each individual to stand for excellence. It paid dividends in the form of a quality staff, prerequisite to a quality product.

Hiring and holding a quality staff dictated material inducements commensurate with performance expectations. Panax employee compensation included generous fringe and retirement benefits.

These internal policies were not recognized by readers. They saw only the paper that came to their door. McGoff wanted quality because he wanted to influence people. He believed firmly, as Disraeli observed, that with words we govern people. To McGoff, publishing newspapers was more than running just another business.

Competition for advertising and readership was a part of the business, but not all of the business. Competition of ideas, competition for minds, competition in shaping public opinion on major issues of the day queued up with profits in his self-assigned mission as a publisher.

James Whelan, Panax Vice President/Editorial Director and later editor of McGoff's privately owned Sacramento Union said, "McGoff infused Panax papers with a purpose and mission unique in American journalism.

"Foremost," said Whelan, "McGoff broke new ground for community newspapers. Traditionally community newspapers, the weeklies and other non-dailies, so often lumped indiscriminately with 'shoppers', operated on the assumption that world and national affairs were beyond their editorial purview. Part of the reason was that commentary on these questions was available through other media.

"Their place in the market was to be uniquely and utterly local. Another part of the reasoning was that these papers lacked the sheer sophistication to do a conscientious job of commentary of such transcendental issues. In this there may have been a measure of realism although not much more so than there would be for small dailies.

"But John McGoff infused Panax papers with another notion—

the *right* and responsibility of small weeklies to add thoughtful voice to such non-local issues. He held that it was good business for us to do so. . . . We gave our readers an alternate point of view. The result was that Panax newspapers, uniquely among so-called 'community' newspaper groups in America, projected a coherent, forceful and consistent vision of world, national and regional concerns. But this was done without retreating one iota from our awareness and commitmant to leadership, the essence of responsibility to those communities. The mechanical device for achieving this was to run not only an editorial page devoted to local issues, but also an op-edit page devoted to non-local commentary. That was almost without precedent in operation of smaller newspapers."

Whelan continued on another unique contribution that McGoff made to American journalism:

"In further extension of this principle, McGoff established his conviction that there is nothing immoral about a publisher assuming access to the pages of his newspaper, to express his convictions on issues. In this, he ran counter to the fashionable orthodoxy in much of the business that the level of wisdom in newspapering ends at the level of the highest paid hired hand in editorial.

"He insisted that a publisher is not merely the owner or manager of a business, but the custodian of a responsibility that includes intellectual and idealogical commitments. Nor did any of this mean that he underestimated the value or integrity of his editor. He believed in quality editorial matters."

McGoff, Shepherd, Whelan, the three top executives of Panax, spoke of excellence, quality of product, high standard of performance with evangelistic fervor, not just as ghost words for rhetorical embellishment or stylistic effect. They conceded that such words in themselves were not susceptible to quantification; that connotations varied with different people due to disparate personal standards or divergence in assignment of distinctive marks of measurement. Such perfumed phrases defied precise definition unless clarified with fixed criteria for application.

Each executive defined what he meant and expected in practical, pointed, resolute terms. McGoff amplified his personal expectancies for excellence in seven basic categories:

(1) THE NEWS SHOULD BE PUBLISHED FACTUALLY, FULLY AND WITHOUT EDITORIAL TILT.

"Our founding fathers perceived the indispensible role of communication in a democratic, self-governing society. Their First Amendment guaranteed a free press. It said that Congress shall make no law to abridge that freedom. Although there is no guarantee of a responsible press, I think that freedom of the press, like all our freedoms, demands responsibility. The purpose of the news is to inform, to give facts on events as they occur, not as a reporter or publisher would like for them to be. The news should be factual, fair, informative and objective.

"Of course no one newspaper, TV or media station can report everything that happens in these cataclysmic times. But when we do publish, it should be news, not personal opinion of what happened."

2) THE NEWSPAPER SHOULD HAVE A STRONG EDITORIAL AND OPINION SECTION CLEARLY IDENTIFIED TO DISTINGUISH IT FROM THE NEWS.

"Every newspaper has a right, a privilege, a duty to take a position on public issues that influence our freedoms, our businesses, our personal lives. A newspaper publisher has a right to a mission, an opinion, a voice in what is happening in this turbulent world. These opinions should be marked as such, not disguised as news. That is the purpose of editorial pages and byline commentaries.

"Panax subscribes to some of the leading columnists in the nation and numerous syndicated feature services. We use the services of the North American Newspaper Enterprise Association, respected economists, analysts and special single interest features on a wide variety of interests.

"These writers come at a high price. In addition to our own staff writers, their opinions are thought-provoking. They are intended to influence public opinion. That is why they are published."

3) THE NEWSPAPER EXECUTIVES SHOUlD PARTICIPATE ACTIVELY IN COMMUNITY AFFAIRS WHEREVER THEY OPERATE.

"Panax is a part of any community where we publish. Our economic well-being is dependent on a sound economy in that community. Our executives are encouraged to be active citizens in the civic, the business and the organizational activities that are designed to develop and protect the interest of its citizens. I believe these men and women can be active participants in community life without losing their objectivity in coverage of news events or in articulating an editorial policy on community developments. The press has the privilege of attacking anything it thinks is wrong in community affairs. It has a duty to support what it thinks is right.

"Because of their special training and experience, newspaper executives usually make sound leaders. By assuming leadership roles, we identify with the community and demonstrate our willingness to contribute to its progress. It is good business, good for business, good for the community, the state, the nation. It is good citizenship. We expect to be good corporate citizens and expect our people to be active in citizenship affairs."

(4) THE NEWSPAPER SHOULD COMMUNICATE THE CONCEPTS OF FREE ENTERPRISE.

"Newspaper publishing is a private enterprise operation. We are controlled in the marketplace by consumers who buy our product. We are subject to the risks of a free market economy. We exist only as long as our business is profitable.

"I believe that a newspaper publisher has a responsibility to support the free enterprise system, to explain it, to interpret it, to promote it, to strengthen it. This does not imply defense of the offenders of some ethical practice or overlooking the relatively few who attempt to cheat or foist shoddy products on their customers with false claims. Unethical, illegal practices should be exposed. The bad examples are no excuse to condemn an entire system which has enabled so many people to enjoy high standards of living.

"Misunderstanding, misconceptions, economic ignorance are the reasons so many people make senseless attacks on free enterprise. I believe a publisher has a selfish right as well as a public duty to use his editorial and opinion pages to create an understanding of our economic system."

(5) THE NEWSPAPER PUBLISHER SHOULD EXERCISE SELF RESTRAINT AND VOLUNTARY PROFESSIONAL STANDARDS TO PRESERVE THE FREEDOM OF THE PRESS.

"Freedom of the press grants awesome powers to publishers. It is time for the press to come up with an initiative of its own to help solve the problems created by its great and growing power. At the present time, the media fall short of uniform professional standards. Professions provide procedures and standards for qualifying their practitioners. Lawyers, doctors and all other professionals meet a level of training and learning before they are admitted.

"There is no universally accepted standard of professional ethics to guide and judge the behavior of newsmen, editors or publishers. There is no procedure external or internal to condemn those who do not live up to a pattern of responsible conduct.

"Of course, I recognize that it is not a matter of training, qualification, examination, restriction of entrance into the publishing business. It is a business—a competitive business—an integral part of free enterprise. Publishing is not a profession, although the term is used loosely in referring to it. The difference from other business enterprises is the special privileges and freedoms granted by the Constitution. This presents a challenge to adopt standards of practice adapted to the realities of a free society. Abuse of the privilege can lead to governmental restrictions."

(6) THE NEWSPAPER SHOULD BE PROFITABLE.

"As a historian and an individual deeply involved in the business of news, I spend a great deal of time analyzing the role of the press. It is obvious that our responsibilities as communicators to the citizens of this nation and the business community under the First Amendment of the Constitution are great indeed. What is often misunderstood is that in order for us to fully exercise our First Amendment responsibilities, we must be profitable. We would fail in our responsibilities to our fellow citizens, to the business community and to ourselves if we are remiss in our ability to make a profit. For it is in being profitable that we maintain our independence and critical, unbiased posture as guardians of the Constitution. Were we not profitable, were we subsidized or controlled by some method or agency other than the profit motive, our claim to independence would have a hollow ring to it."

(7) THE NEWSPAPER OWNER SHOULD PROVIDE THE BEST QUALIFIED STAFF HE CAN FIND WITH THE BEST EQUIPMENT AVAILABLE TO ASSURE EFFICIENT PRODUCTION AND AN ATTRACTIVE, EASY-TO-READ PUBLICATION FOR THE READERS.

"The advances in production of print journalism require up-to-date equipment. With the operation of our new $6 million production center in Mt. Clemens, all of our papers will be printed with the most technologically advanced machinery available. Centralization of printing into centers is not only economically sound, it enables well-trained staff to observe their creative efforts produced in an attractive form. Finally, the product we issue is for the benefit of the reader who is the prime beneficiary of this consolidated production program."

McGoff talked in broad, idealistic terms. He recognized that perfection was a worthy goal but impossible to reach. Few, if any, Panax papers met those aims consistently, but just as navigators set their course by the stars though they never reach them, striving for lofty goals resulted in a better product.

Frank Shepherd was responsible for the primary day-to-day operations. He was concerned with lines of advertising, circulation growth, budgets, revenues, personnel problems, supplies, costs, inflation, maintenance of equipment, sales efficiency, productive results. Asked about excellence, Shepherd illustrated his idea in less than euphemistic, but understandable language.

Said Shepherd, "If the market in a given area increases ten percent a year and lineage and circulation go up fifteen percent, I rate that as an excellent performance. If the market potential improves ten percent, and lineage and circulation remain static or decrease, that is a crappy performance and I don't give a damn what the excuses may be."

Stressing teamwork among general managers, editors, production managers, sales staff, corporate staff, Shepherd said, "Good editorial content brings readers. Readers bring ads. Ads bring profits. Profits mean capital for expansion. It's a matter of teamwork. In order to remain independent, we are interdependent. We must get things done ourselves, not wait around like pigeons for somebody to drop popcorn. High editorial rating is meaningless unless somebody reads it and there is enough advertising to pay for it. Editors are at the very center of the fifth estate. Their conduct is directly related to the future of our company. That does not downgrade the importance of the production, advertising or circulation staff. Each has an equally responsible role. One cannot do without the other.

"It would be simple to put out a paper with a prize-winning editorial rating if we had a few million dollars to lose every year. Losing money is not our business. Publishing quality papers while

102

making money is our business. We can do that if each person in the company accepts that old axiom that the whole is only as good as the parts. Each employee must think, believe and act, 'I make the difference.' Each separately and all collectively do make the difference in success or failure—in profit or loss—in the satisfaction of achievement or the frustration of defeat."

Like evangelists preaching the same basic message of salvation over a period of years, these Panax leaders repeated the same ideas time after time. The words changed. The illustrations varied. The charts, figures, tables, were updated. They conveyed the same concepts, ideas, goals, standards, phi!osophical outlooks and day-to-day practical demands. Seeping through the entire Panax structure, these ideas created high expectancies by Board members, corporate staff, editors, production managers, sales managers. The largest dailies and the smallest non-dailies in obscure areas were expected to aim high. All of them did not attain the same heights. All kept trying to reach new ascending levels.

Persistent preachments for quality standards befitted a community newspaper chain with widely dispersed operating units in relatively small communities of disparate natures. Such a policy was unusual for ownership of community and suburban newspapers. Continual spurring was needed to assure consistent performance. The rhythm of the business was not obedient to metronomic regularity.

Meeting deadlines did not at all times allow for sober deliberation needed for the most intelligible treatment of a sensitive story although this was more applicable to a daily than a non-daily community paper. Space limitation could restrict coverage to a paragraph where a column would have been preferable. Inexplicable mechanical breakdowns seemed to occur at discommodious times. Gremlins seemed to be omnipresent in the press room.

Embarrassing typographical errors sneaked by proofreaders. Misplaced or omitted sentences disrupted the continuity of a story or even changed its intended meaning. Inevitable delivery delays irritated subscribers. Editorial positions prompted complaints from readers. Economic conditions clipped advertising and circulation revenues. Internal union activity, strikes, friction between line employees and departmental supervisors abducted time from pursuit of quality production. Excess paper and plate spoilage escalated costs. Political pressures, corporate office demands, a dozen other unscheduled vexations tested the concentration and patience of the most dedicated staff. A sustained effort to excel was required just to keep pace with the galloping deterrents.

A battery of corporate awards proffered incentives. Each year a corps d'elite was selected in twenty-five separate categories to encourage both fiscal and editorial excellence.

John P. McGoff Awards were bestowed on winners in five classifications: display advertising, classified advertising, circulation, commercial printing and top producers for daily and non-daily publications.

Additional awards for business promotion included Circulation Excellency Award, Best-in-Paper Promotion-Best Carrier Promotion, Advertising excellence, Best Classified layout, and Best Sales presentation in Commercial Printing.

About seventy-five percent weight was given to objective factors such as lineage, circulation and total revenue increases over the previous year. Subjective judgment of the judges, McGoff and Shepherd, took into consideration other personal, non-quantitative elements.

Whelan joined the other judges for the Editorial Excellence Awards for Special Section, Feature Pictures, News Story, Front Page, News Photo, Sports, Feature Story, Column, Editorial, and Investigative Reporting.

An Editor of the Year received recognition from the recommendations by local publishers and a Publisher of the Year was selected by the three judges.

Was the attention and expense of the corporate office to conferences, training sessions, self-renewal and incentive awards justified? Did the cost in time and money pay commensurate dividends? One measurement was the long string of awards conferred on Panax papers annually by various associations, most of them comprising peers and hence competitors. An assemblage of all the awards would cover the wall of a sizeable exhibition hall.

Cherished awards came from many organizations dedicated to the improvement of journalism, such as The Michigan Press Association, The Florida Press Association, The Detroit Press Club Foundation, The League of Home Dailies, The National Editorial Foundation, The Association of Classified Advertising Managers, The Associated Press and United Press International. Numerous non-newspaper associations made special awards for special services. Excellence awards were received from The Michigan Tourist Council, Keep Michigan Beautiful, American Bowling Congress and many others. The type of awards covered all categories from year to year: Editorial Page Content, General Advertising Excellence, Coverage of Local Government Affairs, Coverage of Environmental Issues, Best Weekly in the State, Advertising Idea of the Year, and dozens of other categories, all eagerly sought by all newspapers. Prizes were well distributed from the smallest weekly to the Macomb Daily. In 1976, for example, the Macomb Daily won eleven top wire service awards—seven from Associated Press and four from U.P.I. Competing with all the large papers in the state, these awards for writing and photography went to a paper with a circulation of less than 60,000 and a total editorial staff of 31 people. The Detroit Free Press won only nine awards; the Detroit News received only eight.

So it went. Each year blazoned new honors. Evidence piled up for the efficacy of unceasing emphasis on a better product, better performance, more dedicated effort. Never mind last year's success. Past laurels did not excuse tapering off or future failures. Last year's achievements signalled this year's minimal standard. That was McGoff's attitude.

It was the same attitude expressed by Andrew Carnegie. On one occasion when away from his office he received a telegram from Charles Schwab, his General Manager, which said, "Broke all production records yesterday." Carnegie wired back, "What did you do today?"

Achievement in any business depends on the individual and collective efforts of many people. It cannot be attained by conferences, impassioned speeches, orders from headquarters, or even superior talents. Motivation is the basic ingredient for all-out performance.

John Gardner, author of the excellent book entitled "Excellence", writes about "discipline and tenacity of purpose" as prerequisites to excellence. All of these meetings, goals, incentives at Panax were directed toward building a desire to strive for the superlative. In the quest for excellence, the process of motivation was never-ending, requiring all the "discipline and tenacity" that had been displayed by McGoff from the beginning of his business career.

105

Chapter 8

Opinions Have Consequences

"If you chop wood, chips will fall."

. . Yiddish Proverb

In the process of building a suburban and small community newspaper chain and acquiring half ownership of one of the world's leading television news gathering agencies, John McGoff did not endear himself to many of his contemporaries in the communications business.

Still Lilliputian in size compared to chains such as Gannett, Knight-Ridder, Washington Post-Newsweek, Time/Life or the T.V. Networks he operated in relative obscurity until he bid for the financially ailing Washington Star in 1974. This thrust him into the critical glare of the powerful national media. When he made disparaging remarks about the liberal Eastern Establishment, the aggressively liberal Washington Post and the T.V. Networks' news policies, he exposed himself to their microscopic scrutiny. National visualization set him up as a target. He became a news maker, not just a news dispenser. Never again would his actions enjoy privacy.

An ardent advocate of a conservative press, an acidulous critic of the termite-like intrusion of the federal bureaucracy into private business operations, his bluntly expressed views agitated questions.

Who is this unknown small town midwest interloper? What hidden special interest does he represent? Where does he get that kind of money? Who does he think he is, disturbing our liberal

106

complacency? His response to questions about reasons for wanting the Washington Star did nothing to pacify the skeptics.

Speaking on the record, he said, "I see the Star as a means to counter the liberal elitist bureaucrats and journalists in Washington who still believe in the new deal, big government and socialization of America." He left no doubt that he wanted to provide an alternate view to the Washington Post. "We *need* another *voice* in Washington, not an echo," he said, saying clearly that he considered the editorial policies of the Post as antithetical to free enterprise principles and traditional political institutions.

McGoff had been speaking in this angry tone for years. Outside his own local areas of operation primarily in Michigan, nobody thought him newsworthy. He and his news chain had grown up unnoticed. Now as a potential competitive threat, the words carried authority.

In 1974, while negotiating for the Star, he spoke to the Alumni of Michigan State University School of Graduate Studies on the subject, "The Role of Media in a Fast Moving World". Excerpts from the speech disclose more of his scorn for his curious eastern press adversaries:

"We, in this country, have come to a state in the last ten years that even the most pessimistic sociologist would not have dared predict. Regrettably, those of us in the media have participated in the escalation of the crisis and confusion and anguish that every citizen must be experiencing . . .

". . . and yet perhaps the worst thing that has happened to all of us in these years is a loss of self-confidence, spawned by the media and continually fed upon by those who provide your news and commentary.

". . . Racial strife; a generation that we begot but that, in turn, turned its back upon us; a distant war that shook our foundations of patriotism and national service; a class B movie called 'Watergate' which television and the Eastern Press played beyond all proportions; a fleeting point in history that has been used to subvert our most urgent priority—the solution of our economic problems.

". . . We have watched one leader after another being chewed up by unfair and half-truth tactics in a seemingly concerted effort to destroy leadership wherever that leadership may be, in all segments of endeavor, on national, state and local levels.

". . . I am sure that many of my colleagues would disagree

107

with that analysis. But you, a part of the many publics that we serve, will have to make that judgment. We cannot continue to abuse the great freedom that we have as disseminators of information without someday losing that freedom because of those abuses . . ."

Later, speaking at the annual meeting of the Missouri Chamber of Commerce, his remarks continued the thrust.

". . . Much has been written and said about the mood of the country today. We are told that the traditional American sense of optimism has been replaced by doubt and gloom. I am not suggesting that we do not have troubles. We do. But we had troubles before without wallowing in cynicism and pessimism. Why is the future, in our eyes, not what it used to be?

"I am sorry to say that one reason is the omnipresence of the media, a profession of which I am a part. Any dispassionate assessment would have to conclude that in many ways our journalists are better than they have ever been. Often we offer a better product than we have ever offered before. But one indisputable fact stares us in the face. The profession as a whole lacks a sense of history which is essential to balance of perspective and to optimism.

"We cannot continue to receive the day-to-day stentorian lectures on national television news and the constant barrage from the New York Times Service and the Washington Post News Service that appears in your local papers without getting some negative fallout."

Appearing before the Civitan Club in Lansing, he lashed out at a new force in shaping public opinion.

"The new force of so-called advocacy journalism operates in the belief that the role of the press is no longer to try to dig out the truth fairly and present all sides of an issue. The new role is seen as taking sides in public debate and emphasizing in the news coverage whichever side you are aligned with while downplaying or totally overlooking the other side . . .

"We are seeing it in the reporting of the proposal by the Navy to put an extremely low frequency communications system—Project Seafarer—in Michigan's Upper Peninsula. The system will permit us to maintain contact with our undersurface craft no matter how far or deep they are. The advocacy journalists have decided it is bad. They frantically wave every bit of evidence, real or imagined, to convince us the project was conceived by Satan himself.

"The worst example of this has been the work of the left wing Detroit Free Press. It has consistently emphasized every word the opponents utter and glamorized those who opposed the project while ignoring those who feel it may have some merit. They have judged it and confused the public with their ill-formed and ill-conceived information even before all the studies are complete . . ."

Hitting close to home, this could have been considered a dig at a competitor in the Detroit area where Panax published one daily and more than twenty-five weeklies circling Detroit. Actually, the remarks reflected ideological differences. Economics were unrelated to his dislike for the Free Press. His papers in S.E. Michigan at the time carried about one million dollars in advertising, but he had disdained economic impact of his opinions on numerous other occasions.

When the recipients of his pointed barbs had a chance, they struck back with force, in an equally uncomplimentary form.

In 1975, a feature article in the Free Press Sunday Magazine supplement, *Detroit*, by David Johnston, at that time a Michigan Capitol Correspondent, was entitled, "John P. McGoff, Michigan Baron of Free Enterprise Journalism". Setting the tone in the opening sentence, he wrote, "John P. McGoff is the Colonel Sanders of the media world with his own secret recipe for success: Buy failing newspapers cheap, run them like a chain discount department store and turn them into politically conservative community boosters."

Giving him a left-handed boost as a "master promoter", Johnston proceeded to itemize flaws in his "right wing view!" He wrote, "But McGoff is a complex man of many paradoxes. For example, he belongs to the National Association for the Advancement of Colored People, although he does not list the affiliation in his official biography. He is also a major apologist for the white supremist government in South Africa where a Panax subsidiary, Xanap (Panax spelled backwards), trains blacks in operating press equipment and publishes about fifty black periodicals ranging from comic books to women's magazines . . ."

Referring to McGoff's political philosophy, Johnston mentioned another paradox as he wrote, "While those views may seem rather right wing, McGoff holds other views which are akin to theories expressed by radical economists and political scientists. For example, some radical thinkers see the world evolving into three major interest groups: the technologically competent, the adolescent and the superfluous, with the educated elites in the first group, the blue collar workers in the second and the illiterate and unintelligent in the last group.

McGoff: "No longer are we in a world of haves and have nots, but of producers and non-producers. An amazingly large proportion of people in the world are no longer producing."

This lengthy feature article paid McGoff the compliment of limited financial success but belittled his views, questioned his motives and cast a negative conclusion.

Competition, the essence of private enterprise, is essential to a free market economy. Competition is the adhesive that binds consumer, producer and public interest. Competition in the newspaper business can be, and usually is, bitterly personal. Rivals are competing not only for the advertisers' dollar, but for the readers' minds. In this backyard battle of words between Panax and the Detroit Free Press, ideological differences took precedence over markets.

McGoff did not seem bothered by the counter-attacks. He expected them. It kept the adrenalin flowing. Robert Refior, a Panax director at the time, said, "John, like most of us, is happiest as a victor. But as we all know, he enjoys a scrap almost as much as winning. When the opponent is the (make it ten bleeps) Eastern media conspiracy composed of the Washington Post, C.B.S., N.B.C., New York Times or the Detroit Free Press, he really revels in beating them at their own one-upmanship."

McGoff did become aroused when the National News Council denounced him. When aroused, and with his flash-flood temper he arouses easily, he is as difficult to restrain as an erupting volcano. An impavid in-fighter, he is unawed by the stature of his antagonist. The bigger they come, the more tenacious he becomes.

This unexpected attack started innocently enough. McGoff was in Europe on June 6, 1977, when Frank Shepherd, the Executive Vice President, sent a memorandum to all editors enclosing four byline articles by George Bernard, Panax New York Bureau Chief, a new service established by the corporate office a few weeks before the memo was written.

The first article listed in Shepherd's memo was the result of an interview with Dr. Peter Bourne, a psychiatrist at the White House with the title of Special Assistant to the President for Health Issues. Over seven closely typed pages in length, a major part of the story related to Bourne's close relationship with President Carter, his role in convincing Carter in running for the Presidency, his duties at the White House and his association with Mrs. Carter in establishing Georgia's first drug abuse program.

Considerable attention was given to Bourne's political background as a Vietnam War dissident and other activist connections as well as to similar protest group activities of Mary Bourne, the doctor's wife, also a federal employee on Carter's staff.

Bernard's opening lines established the thrust of the article:

"President James Earl Carter condones promiscuity—affairs with other women—for the male staffers who work for him. This startling fact came to light in an exclusive interview with the one man in America who knows him best and who is responsible for influencing the former Governor of Georgia to become a candidate for the Presidency of the United States."

This lead came from what seemed to be a rather casual comment by Bourne when he said, "One of the interesting things about him," continued Bourne on Carter, "is that he's a man who believes very strongly in his own beliefs and values. He is extremely non-judgmental about others. And this includes women. Even though his own relationship is monogamous, he's never held anything against people in his organization who were involved with other women."

"When you say,'other people's women', you're talking Doctor, about promiscuity?" Bourne was asked.

"Yes," the psychiatrist responded emphatically.

"If he knows about it, does it bother him?" the psychiatrist was queried.

"Well, he just accepts that as other people's business and does not impose his values on them."

The second article was a critical commentary on Roslynn Carter's assignment to represent President Carter on a mission to seven Latin American countries. Bernard, commenting on President Carter's pledge to exercise leadership in the White House wrote, "And indeed he has. For the First Lady's current two-week, twelve thousand mile swing through seven countries, Mr. Carter has assigned a role to wife Roslynn that is truly unequaled in

111

magnitude and scope. In fact, Eleanor Roosevelt, Lady Bird Johnson and even Betty Ford never were entrusted with the responsibilities accorded Roslynn Carter.

"While the White House promoted Roslynn's trip as a major diplomatic effort at interpreting the President's Latin American policy, others viewed the good will overture as a task Mr. Carter himself should have personally handled."

One of the people expressing an opinion to George Bernard, quoted widely in his article, was William Van Precht, Ph.D., a New York psychologist. Among numerous other comments, Dr. Van Precht said, "Therefore, my careful analysis says that Jimmy Carter is grooming wife Roslynn for the Vice Presidency in 1984." Further quoting Van Precht, Bernard wrote, "If Walter Mondale's health does not hold out through the ominous year of 'Big Brother', Mr. Carter will push his bride to become Vice President of the United States."

Dr. Leonard Bachelis, Executive Director of the Behavior Therapy Center in New York City, expressed further views on the likelihood of Roslynn's increasing decision-making role.

Another Bernard article related to the Human Fly, then climbing buildings in New York. Finally, the last of Bernard's stories attempted to analyze the New York Yankees.

For the first two articles, Shepherd's memo said, "Release Wednesday. This could be an explosive story...run front page if possible. Mail tear sheets to John McGoff a.s.a.p." Such memos were issued by the corporate office, usually referring to some feature byline commentary or Panax editorial concerning state, national or international affairs.

The corporate office did not keep a tally sheet to check compliance with such requests. In general, editors exercised their judgment depending on space available, relevance to local interests, timing and various local factors at the time.

As a policy, local editors had total authority over news and editorials related to local interests.

Upon receipt of the Shepherd memorandum and the accompanying Bernard articles, David A. Rood, Editor of the Escanaba Press for eight years, rejected forthwith the Bernard stories. In a memorandum to Ralph Kaziateck, Vice President responsible for the Upper Peninsula papers, Rood documented his reasons with point blank lucidity, stressing his firm belief and practice of a policy enumerated by John McGoff when the U.P. papers were acquired in 1966. That policy: local and area news should receive priority attention, followed by state and then national, international news and special features.

Rood asserted that during the period of the few weeks after George Bernard's appointment as the Panax New York Bureau Chief, the local papers had been deluged with irrelevant material of no interest to the local community; that the stories were poorly written and full of innuendo and slanted conclusions unencumbered by fact. He branded Bernard's articles as advocacy journalism at its worst.

Rood, with no attempt to disguise his disgust, expressed the opinion that other lengthy articles forced on the local editors were a departure from McGoff's publicly stated policy of decentralization of editorial control. His prime objections, however, were aimed at the quality and content of the Bernard discourses.

Robert Skuggen, Editor of the Marquette Mining Journal, rewrote one of the Bernard stories, did not use the others, and protested verbally to Ralph Kaziateck, basically reiterating complaints about quality of Bernard's material being inconsistent with Panax standards.

In Europe at the time the contention surfaced, McGoff was briefed on developments. He called a conference for June 10. McGoff had employed Bernard after meeting him through a fellow board member of an insurance company. McGoff liked Bernard's political views, was impressed by his uncanny ability to get interviews, his swashbuckling reputation. Literary style was not considered. As a national-minded publisher, he wanted his papers to crusade on major public issues. He had come to the firm conviction that many national policies were supported, or passively accepted, because people were uninformed or misinformed. His zeal for his causes dictated an obligation to give more coverage to the issues that bothered him.

Some of his editors were willing to follow his lead but bucked the volume coming from the corporate office. Others disagreed and either ignored much of the material or rewrote it to fit the local situation.

Now two editors were challenging his judgment. He did not relish second guessing. Anyway, these editors did not know Bernard. Bring them together for a face to face, albeit officially sponsored, discussion. Bernard would break down suspicions and the editors could orient him to the local interests in Michigan's U.P. The whole matter could be settled in a couple of hours. Tensions would be eased, or so he reasoned. Who would attend?

Frank Shepherd's memo ignited the flare-up. So he was a key participant. Brisk, impatient with anything he considered trivial, fast talking, action impelled, Frank operated on the management theory that problems should be faced directly when they occur and then get on with the business. On one occasion, he said that an effective organization needed a dreamer, a schemer and a reamer. He viewed his role as that of the reamer.

Tom Ochiltree, Chief of the Washington Bureau was invited. He was not involved in the incident in any respect. With more than forty years experience, he had joined Panax in 1972 after spending twenty-three years with the Associated Press, including fifteen years overseas as a diplomatic correspondent, covering international conferences, wars, revolutions and new emerging nations of the countries of Europe, the Middle East and Africa. His byline columns were used by the local papers. They were relatively short, usually related to activities of legislation or events with a bearing on the respective regions.

Tom Ochiltree did not cherish involvement in the conference. He knew that Bernard could be tough. Calm, tactful, respected, Ochiltree's presence was expected to exert a mitigating influence on a heated situation. Or so McGoff and Shepherd thought.

Skuggen was selected by the U.P. editors to represent them. As editor of the largest paper in the Upper Peninsula, he was articulate, direct, sometimes blunt, rated as a good editor by the corporate office. He enjoyed sound working relations with Kaziateck. He seemed to be the logical spokesman.

Living in the small communities as neighbors and personal acquaintances of many of the readers, these editors identified with their communities, believing sincerely that they reflected the interests better than the corporate office. They were reluctant to impose too many ultra-conservative Republican-slanted features in these overwhelmingly Democrat areas. They thought it was not economically or journalistically sound to force-feed readers with material that was distasteful to them.

Few, if any, of those provincials in the Upper Peninsula communities gave a damn about what happened to New York City—

and they hoped it would. So Bob Skuggen came to the conference primed to let the big city sophisticate know that the small town folks had no appreciation at all for his interminable essays.

Ralph Kaziateck, the field executive in the chain of command, lived in the area. He wanted to get rid of the tempest in the editors' offices. He recognized the resentment to the pressure from the Lansing office for use of the Bernard features. He hoped the conference would clear the air.

The wrangle centered around burly, deep-voiced George Bernard. Born and bred in New York City, aggressively competitive, self-motivated, a probing interviewer, skilled in the subtle techniques of getting people to talk, the former undercover reporter for the National Enquirer was no stranger to controversy. At the age of thirty-eight, his career had been studded with more controvertible developments than a dozen journalists combined would experience in a lifetime.

As a new Panax associate, his writing motives, even his integrity, were under attack by two small community editors. Having wriggled out of more tight situations than an escape artist during his adventurous career, Bernard went to the meeting with full confidence in his ability to convince everybody of his merits.

The rationale for the meeting was logical. The chemistry was explosive. As Bobby Burns observed, the best laid plans can go astray. This plan was no exception. It did not work. The session degenerated into an acrimonious debate, with no winner.

Everybody, except observer Ochiltree, had something to defend. Harsh words stiffened differences of journalistic philosophy. Emotions reigned. Reason retreated. Bruised egos begot discourtesies. Even post-meeting versions of the session differed. McGoff and Shepherd blamed Skuggen for rudeness and belligerence. Skuggen saw no wrong in venting deeply felt convictions that Bernard's brand of writing violated Panax standards. Ochiltree saw little to choose between behavior of Skuggen and Bernard. Nobody was happy with this Friday fiasco.

On the following Monday, June 13, McGoff wrote to Skuggen expressing disappointment at what he termed bad manners, abuse and arrogance. Other issues unrelated to the meeting were mentioned. The letter could be interpreted as nothing short of a reprimand, although written in a sort of avuncular tone.

On Tuesday, June 14, Skuggen answered, offering apologies if such apologies were necessary. In defense of whatever may have been said, Skuggen stated he was unaware of doing anything more than speaking firmly on what he thought was a departure from McGoff's own expectations. He recognized that his neck was out but stated that it was for preservation of the integrity of the Mining Journal and Panax, not for any personal advantage.

Skuggen acknowledged McGoff's prerogative to cover subjects of his choosing or to make ultimate decisions on what should be published. He put forth hope that he, as editor, would be allowed to protest if, in his judgment, the news or feature was below the quality they both demanded.

The tone of the letter was conciliatory, rational, free of arrogance that McGoff accused him of displaying. Three days later he resigned, giving as the reason, philosophical differences with the President.

In the meantime, Dave Rood renewed his dialogue with Ralph Kaziateck. The subject was Bernard's stories, but it was obvious that the underlying issue was conflict over authority of publisher and editor. Rood insisted that he would exercise final judgment on suitability of any copy as long as his name appeared on the masthead as editor. Panax policy gave the editor full authority for local news and editorial policy, but reserved the privilege of distributing whatever copy McGoff deemed appropriate.

When questions of final authority clashed at the intersection of publishers' responsibility and editors' rights, McGoff had the right of way.

Rood was adamant. He refused to accept the policy; refused to resign. He was released for insubordination.

The corporate office adjudged the departure of the two editors as the close of an internal personnel problem arising from an unpleasant incident. None of the other fifty senior editors had been involved, although by this time it was known that a score or more editors had set aside the contestible articles or had edited them if used at all.

No publicity was given to the developments.

However, Dave Rood did not go gently. After eight years as editor of a grass roots paper in a community of fifteen thousand population, he was well-known. Word of his dismissal spread like a brush fire in a drought-stricken forest. A Committee for Responsible Journalism arose with the dawn. Advertising and subscription boycotts were advocated. Another committee sprang up in Marquette. After the whole affair died down, only a combined total of fifty subscriptions and one ad were cancelled temporarily. The groups clamored loudly, but numbered few.

Financial loss to Panax was insignificant but the noise made locally did not escape the attention of three of McGoff's more caustic critics. On June 25, the fate of the two editors received prominent coverage by the Detroit Free Press, the New York Times and the Washington Star. Subsequently, various papers throughout the nation picked up the account.

Seething at the condemnatory slant of the news coverage and what Panax officials considered one-sided treatment, Panax issued a statement for publication in its papers entitled "A Declaration of Interdependence".

This document of more than a thousand words summarized what was identified as "original and necessary policies which have made this Michigan based corporation a growing and healthy concern." It placed the publicized incident of the two editors in perspective.

In clarifying the respective responsibilities of the editor and publisher, it was stated, "Adequate coverage of state, regional, national and world news is an on-going responsibiltiy of any publisher while the timing and manner in which the news is presented is the prerogative of the editor. Harry Truman simplified the discourse of authority with a small sign placed strategically on the front of his White House desk reading, 'The buck stops here.'

"Panax applies that philosophy and believes it is the only way to insure a better understanding of where responsibility finally rests. John McGoff not only has the privilege, but is accorded the right, as principal stockholder, President and Chief Executive Officer, to distribute whatever news copy he deems appropriate and to demand that such copy be printed. Rarely has the authority been used and never has it been abused. In the case of the two Upper Peninsula editors, the factor which dictated dismissal was pure and simple insubordination."

The news stories evoked the interest of staff at the National News Council with headquarters in New York City. According to its own descriptive pamphlets, the National News Council was organized in 1973 as a non-profit organization for the purpose of reviewing complaints about inaccuracy or unethical conduct by a news organization. Eighteen members representing various shades of opinion pass judgment on practices. Advisors and paid staff work with the Council members.

The Council has no power, authority or control over any news organization. It cannot regulate or impose penalties. Once it passes judgment or adopts a resolution, it depends on publicity as its force to influence actions of any operating news agency.

Claiming major financial support from foundations, supplemented by contributions from news organizations and individuals, the Council refused to release a list of supporters to Panax when it was requested.

It is not supported by numerous publishers including the New York Times and the Detroit Free Press. When it was organized, John Knight, respected head of the powerful Knight-Ridder chain, said, "Any self-respecting editor who submits to bar association guidelines or subscribes to meddling by the National News Council is simply eroding his own freedoms. Editors are responsible to their readers, not to a group of self-appointed busybodies with time on their hands."

In 1972, the American Society of Newspaper Editors voted 257 to 196 against the establishment of a news council-type organization.

It was organized anyway.

When the Council invited itself to intrude into Panax operating practices, Norman Isaacs, Editor in Residence, Graduate School of Journalism at Columbia University, was Council Chairman. William B. Arthur, former Editor of Look Magazine served as full time paid Executive Director, assisted by Ned Schnurman, Associate Director.

Retired Editor of the Escanaba Daily Press, Jean Worth, observed, "The Council has a journalism school aura of divorce from reality." A chronology of events in handling the Panax affair illustrates how it operated in that particular situation.

Accepting credit or blame, depending on the point of view, for initiating inquiries into the Panax editors' dispute as a result of articles published nationally, Council staff forwarded copies of news stories and what it classified as "other information" to Council members in early July. The Council refused to specify "other information." Presumably, it included summary of conversations with the two editors and others.

118

On the week of July fourth, Chairman Isaacs talked with some of the Council members by telephone, seeking approval for a resolution denouncing John McGoff and Panax Corporation. After the holiday weekend, Ned Schnurman held two lengthy telephone conversations with Jerry Schiappa, Panax Vice President and Director of Public Affairs. Schiappa furnished both official record and off the record details about the terminations.

On July 9, a document entitled "Statement on John P. McGoff and Panax Corporation Policy" was approved by a twelve to one telephone poll, conducted by Chairman Isaacs. The dissenting vote was cast by William Rusher, publisher of the National Review. He dispatched a copy of his opinion to McGoff.

On July 11 the Council released a news story to all news media announcing the decision. The brief news story was accompanied by an eight paragraph summary of the case, concluding with: "To the Council, the central issue is the relationship of chain ownership to news control. Mr. McGoff has highlighted one of the underlying public fears about newspaper chains—that what the public reads is directed from afar by autocratic ownership........

"The National News Council finds Mr. McGoff's policies regressive—a throwback to crass episodes that marked journalism of a by-gone era—and is a gross disservice to accepted American journalistic standards."

William Rusher's dissent said: "I respectfully dissent from the conclusion of my colleagues. If newspaper publishers are to be held responsible for the contents of their publications—and they most certainly are and ought to be—then I do not see how we can deny a publisher the right to determine in the last analysis, what that content shall be.

"When Mr. McGoff orders that a particular news story must be carried in his papers, he is assuming *pro tento* the prerogatives of editorship. But what is wrong with that? Henry Luce, though in fact the owner, reserved the prerogatives and even the title of editor on every magazine he published.

"No doubt most publishers do—I assume Mr. McGoff himself does—ordinarily leave questions of editorial judgment to the editors of his respective newspapers but the nature and responsibilities of ownership certainly entitle him to override a particular editor if in Mr. McGoff's own judgment it is appropriate to do so. That, as far as I can see, is all he has done in this case, unless and until the

119

Council undertakes to study the particular articles in question and formally holds that they do indeed transgress what this Council has always held to be the very broad units of editorial discretion and judgment. I can see no reason for condemning Mr. McGoff."

The press swooped down on the Council action with falconlike alacrity. Many of the publishers had no special regard for the News Council but controversial Mr. McGoff was news. Sprouted as an internal personnel squabble, the affair of the two obscure editors mushroomed into a national issue. Suddenly Panax was branded as an example of the evils of chain ownership. Shocked, stung to rage, McGoff's response mirrors his bulldog tenacity when he thinks he has been maligned. During the shouting stages of verbal hostilities, charges and counter-charges exploded like grenades at the outburst of an insurrection.

On July 12, McGoff fired off a letter to each member of the Council, protesting the position. He enclosed a copy of the Panax Declaration of Interdependence since the Council had singled out just one sentence of the entire document to object to the policy. Informed that the vote had been taken by telephone and that members had not seen the release or the attendant documentation prepared by Council staff, he enclosed a copy of each with a request for a hearing.

An open hearing was set for August 16. To prepare for this confrontation, he requested from the Council a dozen different items.

Chairman Isaacs sent back the by-laws, rules of procedure and a brief brochure. In an icy tone, he informed McGoff that no written complaints were made and that none of the other requested information was available to McGoff.

On August 11, a lengthy legalistic document with fifteen separate exhibits was transmitted to the Council by Gregory L. Curtner of the law firm, Miller, Canfield, Paddock and Stone. Placing in chronological order all developments since early July, he accused Isaacs and staff of numerous violations of by-laws and procedures, specifying each in detail. He claimed that Panax had been denied fundamental fairness. He cited major factual inaccuracies in the denunciatory statement.

Further, Counselor Curtner contended the Council was guilty of precipitous action without justification. Mr. Isaacs had exhibited bias and unfair treatment in refusing to provide details previously requested and should be disqualified from participating in the hearing except in his capacity as admitted complainant. He then demanded that the Council rescind prior denunciations and that the hearing proceed according to written procedures.

Response to this letter was delayed until September 26. It was addressed to McGoff, not Curtner. Isaacs brushed off the attorney's chronology as "an exercise in obfuscation".

Isaacs took the position that the rules of procedure did not apply to the Panax decision because it was not the result of a complaint and, anyway, the rules were flexible. "Even if the by-laws," he rationalized, "were construed so as to accord with the reading given by the Panax attorney, past practice of the Council had operated to amend the by-laws."

He advised McGoff that the Council at a meeting on September 20 had scheduled another public hearing for October 19, that he had invited the Citizens Protest Committee to be present and the discussion would be limited to:

"1. Whether John McGoff has a policy of mandating that editors run in the news columns of the papers they edit, certain articles sent from Panax Corporation headquarters and if so, under what circumstances such a policy is invoked.

"2. Whether the interests of reading audiences and their access to a full and free flow of news is better served through the delegation of authority to resident editors of chain-owned newspapers or whether headquarters control over news columns are proper and/or desirable."

The request that Isaacs be disqualified for participating as Council Chairman had been rejected by the Council at the September 20 meeting.

A major portion of that meeting had been devoted to Mr. Curtner's charges. It was obvious that the Council was vulnerable to attack by the Panax attorneys and wanted no part of the adverse publicity that would ensue.

In the meantime, the procedural precautions were rendered academic when Panax attorneys notified the Council that Panax had been advised to seek a different forum if it wanted a fair hearing. Panax did not show. In the absence of Panax representatives, the Council reaffirmed its July statement. However, this time several

121

members dissented and one concurring member filed a separate opinion with serious reservations.

William Rusher filed another dissent more biting and penetrating than his first objection in July.

Loren Ghiglione, Editor and Publisher of the Evening News, Southbridge, Massachusetts, wrote a strong dissenting opinion to the October 19 decision to reaffirm the July 8 statement:

"Based on the October 19 hearing, my reading of the articles in question, and my understanding of John McGoff's conduct, I believe that his behavior was not in accordance with the highest ethical standards of the profession. I believe Mr. McGoff has the right to be wrong and that he was wrong.

"But, that said, I cannot reaffirm the Council's decision of July 8, a decision in which I participated. The Council asks journalists to publicly admit their errors, giving corrections as much prominence as their initial mistakes. In line with that principle, I must acknowledge that I feel the Council's original decision—again my decision—was flawed in two respects, one procedural, the other substantive....."

He went on to outline a series of reasons why he, as an editor and owner of a newspaper, concluded that the original decision was hasty and too broad.

Richard S. Salant, President, C.B.S. News, dissented in the reaffirmation hearing. He agreed generally with Mr. Ghiglione's opinion. He stated, "The absolutely never decision bites off more than I can chew... I believe the Council should be particularly restrained and careful in rulings which deal with internal relationship in news organizations lest it find itself as arbitrator of employer-employee relationships." He concluded that his dissent was made in spite of McGoff's personal attack on him, not because of the attack.

One additional separate opinion was filed by Ralph Renick, Vice President/News Director, WTVJ, Miami. He agreed with the majority opinion but made specific reservations to the scope of the decision.

These dissentions placed the issue of publisher/owner responsibility and editor rights in focus. The press had highlighted the Panax condemnation with floodlight visibility but gave no coverage to the opposing opinions of the three Council members. It developed that the Council planned it that way. As a matter of record, the Council did not release the dissentions until December, 1977. Even then the release was limited to one publication, The Columbia Journalism Review.

Learning of the coverup by the Council by coincidence, Editor and Publisher featured a condemnatory editorial in the December 10, 1977 issue. It said:

"The action of the National News Council in handling news of its complaint against Panax Corporation has caused it to lose stature, in our opinion.

"Almost simultaneously with the departure of two editors in July, the Council denounced John McGoff, President of Panax, in what was almost knee jerk reaction.

"At a meeting in mid-October the Council 'reaffirmed' its July decision. It wasn't until this week that Editor and Publisher learned there were three dissenting opinions to that decision. They are significant because two of the three represent reversals of original votes after hearing further evidence.

"Text of those opinions were given to the Columbia Journalism Review more than two weeks ago but they were not revealed to anyone else.

"This is a strange way for a supposedly unbiased arbiter of newspaper ethics to behave."

A review of the Council's intrusion into a Panax personnel affair reveals strange behavior from the outset. According to the Council's own claim, no one made a complaint, not even the two editors. The Council raced into the case with the same urgency of a doctor rushing a patient with a hot appendix to the hospital. Norman Isaacs, Chairman of the Council, resorted to a hurried telephone poll to get approval of a hastily drawn denunciation of John McGoff without producing evidence from the accused. The desperate effort to grab maximum publicity before Panax was advised of the action reflects dubious motives.

Rather than justifying the precipitous action, the Council's excuses for the haste and closed door tactics confirmed John Knight's reference to "a group of self-appointed busybodies with time on their hands."

Having rejected the Council's last invitation to appear before what he classified as a "kangaroo court", McGoff addressed an open letter to his fellow publishers with a double spread ad in Editor and Publisher magazine.

As the News Council polemics stretched over the months, a side skirmish with CBS escalated into a major encounter rivaling the main event. A series of uncoordinated approaches by separate departments at CBS were interpreted by Panax as a continuation of harrassment by a member of the Council, Richard Salant, President of CBS News, in spite of Mr. Salant's denial.

On July 11, Betty Ann Bowser taped an extended interview with McGoff in his office, covering the case of the two editors. It was spot news. The interview had been preceded by interviews with the contending parties in the Upper Peninsula. Miss Bowser asked the hard questions, recorded the unexpurgated answers. The mood was friendly, matter-of-fact, non-contentious. Segments were scheduled for use in the Walter Cronkite newscast on the following evening. No mention was made of the incident then or later by Cronkite, other breaking news items taking priority.

About the middle of August, Ms. Galovic, identifying herself as a researcher for Morley Safer of the CBS Sixty Minutes Program, called James Whelan, newly appointed Panax Vice President and Editorial Director. She requested copies of the Bernard article about Roslynn Carter. Whelan asked that the request be confirmed in writing. No further request came.

On August 22, Irena Posner, a CBS producer wrote to McGoff announcing plans for a news special on the future of newspapers with emphasis on the business of journalism. She wrote, "We will be looking at monopolies, group ownership, cross-ownership, conglomerate growth and the fascinating change in newspapers as the new technology makes its impact." Ms. Posner explained that the dispute involving the two editors would be covered. She requested an interview with McGoff.

Suspicious of motives, defensive, angered, McGoff related this letter to Ms. Galovic's telephone inquiry and to the earlier interview by Betty Ann Bowser. So it was referred to Counsel, Richard Jones, for answer. Jones dispatched a letter to Richard Salant complaining about what he defined as "questionable methods" and indicating a conflict of interest because of Salant's personal participation in the News Council attack of Panax.

Responding promptly, Salant acknowledged that the separate approaches could create confusion to someone on the outside but refuted the conclusions He explained in order.

1. The Bowser interview was intended for the Cronkite Evening

News but was crowded out by more pressing news of the day. No future use of the interview was planned.

2. Ms. Galovic, secretary-researcher for Morley Safer, had been collecting previous articles about Mrs. Carter strictly as background material for Safer in preparation for his Sixty Minutes Program. She recalled a news story about the Bernard articles and called to get copies. It was not important since she had more than adequate material without it, so no follow-up was made.

3. Ms. Posner, indeed, was just beginning production for a feature about the newspaper business. It had no relation to the other requests. All parties were working independently on different projects.

Salant categorically denied any conflict of interest between his official duties and his News Council volunteer work. Testily, he suggested that any further communications on the subject be from the journalists at Panax, not its lawyers.

In a business bureaucracy as widespread as CBS, it is not unusual for various departments to work on the same issue without knowing others are involved. This reality of big business notwithstanding, McGoff accepted the challenge for direct contact with an astringent letter to Salant reiterating the indictment of conflict of interest, doubting his capacity to present an objective view in the planned feature and questioning motives of using a relatively miniscule newspaper group such as Panax for a major hatchet job. Dripping with vitriol, the letter exchange manifested about as much cordiality as a Begin-Arafat relationship.

In December, Panax purchased an eight page pull-out section in Editor and Publisher reproducing copies of the correspondence and warning fellow publishers of the forthcoming news special. It was designed to preemptorally safeguard Panax from anticipated impugnment.

All the contending parties lapsed into relative silence for the next seven months. Isaacs made exculpatory speeches to academic and newspaper audiences. He gave so much time to the subject at a national conference of editorial directors that the general evaluation was "Me thinks he protesteth too much". In his speeches, McGoff blasted both the News Council and CBS.

Then all hell broke loose again on July 14, 1978. Hughes Rudd anchored the CBS Special called "The Business of Newspapers".

Nine minutes of the hour-long program featured the Panax controversy. Nothing of the company side was included. Instead, Hughes Rudd gravelled, "Neither Panax nor its President, John McGoff, would discuss the issue with me."

During the interview with Betty Ann Bowser, she had said to McGoff, "Well, I thought we would show you that we were really sincere in coming here; that we really want both sides of the story; that maybe you would agree. I think it is best to deal with someone in person than over the telephone. I'm just really relieved that you sat down and talked with us, because it puts me in a position of either saying you didn't want to do it, which always makes somebody look bad. You know it really does." Really, that is what she said. (Taken from tape recording of the interview.)

So McGoff and his associates waxed indignant at what they deemed a deliberate attempt to make them look bad. Documenting the case from the beginning, McGoff requested that the Federal Communications Commission publicly admonish the network to present its news specials fairly and accurately in the future. He asked that the Commission impose appropriate sanctions. Nothing happened.

A full page open letter to Mr. Salant from Mr. McGoff, published as a paid ad in Editor and Publisher, climaxed the public phase of the year-long enmities.

An inescapable irony stares back at an uninvolved observer reviewing these sequential developments for the first time several years after the conflict burst forth. From the beginning, these communications specialists, masters of their trade, failed to communicate. As business executives and professional communicators, the adversaries had shaped successful careers in the communications business. Yet they did not use the knowledge acquired in their respective careers to communicate understanding of their positions.

They corresponded—reams of it. They publicized their disagreements—volumes of it. They exchanged bitter words—an abundance of them. None of this constituted communication.

Communication has three basic elements: A sender—a message—a receiver. Any breakdown in one of these elements stifles communication. Everybody sent messages. Nobody received the messages. Communication is the art of creating understanding, credibility, belief. Derived from the Latin word, *Communis*, the

126

function of communication is to create a common understanding. In this case, from the time the first memo was sent all the basic elements of communication disappeared in an atmosphere surcharged with clashing opinions, fretted egos, bureaucratic channels. In the contagion of anger, nobody came out of this embroilment crowned with glory. Individuals involved and the organizations they represented suffered inerasable scars. As Benedict said to Don Pedro in Shakespeare's "Much Ado About Nothing", "In a false quarrel, there is no true valour."

Precognition is less unerring than retrocognition. Looking back, it is simple to perceive how a routine personnel problem within the confines of the Panax structure veered off course, gathering velocity like a capricious hurricane. The company should have retained control. Mindless meddling by the Council turned an ordinary internal disagreement into a national muddle.

None of the original cast in the drama had the perception to identify the underlying cause of the tensions that prompted the two editors to rebel. The Bernard incident was the bursting point of a festering boil of dissatisfaction that had been tumefying slowly over a period of time with these two editors. They used the Bernard articles as an excuse to air pent up grievances. The articles were not a basic cause of their disgruntlement. That became evident in comments made subsequent to the termination.

What would have happened if one of the editors had called John McGoff to express concern over some problems and requested a private conference? Or to speculate further, suppose John McGoff had called Bob Skuggen and Dave Rood and said, "Listen, I understand you are unhappy about certain policies. Why not sit on them for a few days and come into the office? Let's talk it over."

It is possible, and probable, under the circumstances, that they would have agreed to disagree anyway. The ultimate decision for terminations could have been the same. It is doubtful if the separation would have been nationalized.

McGoff has a reputation for rigidity in his opinions after he has committed himself publicly. He can be reasonable, flexible and amenable to suggestions when approached before his decision becomes engraved in stone. Back in the early entrepreneurial days when he had an informal, more intimate relationship with all the employees, the direct private discussion would have been the logical and probable course of action.

But as the business had grown, layers of supervision separated him from the intricate details of daily operations. Corporate policies established reporting channels. His personal contacts with local staff diminished in proportion to the degree of bureaucratization. A sensitive but solvable problem became insoluble in the presence of various levels of authority.

This moved new uninvited characters, outside the Panax performers, to center stage. The same cold, adversative, channeled formality prevailed. During all the long months of contention, the major disputants did not talk face to face. They expressed their opinions of the issue, and of one another, in written form.

In his Pulitzer Prize-winning book, "Present at the Creation", Dean Acheson wrote that President Harry Truman never allowed his ego to interfere with the momentously difficult decisions living history forced him to make. In the future, history will look kindly on the man and the events.

If history should bother to glance at the Panax/National News Council/CBS events, it will smile sardonically as it views the actions of these proud, strong-minded, opinionated men. They were successful in the business of communication. They refused to communicate. Egos blocked the way.

Chapter 9

Passion for Action

"The margin between that which men naturally do, and that which they can do is so great that a system which urges men on to action and develops individual enterprise and initiative is preferable, in spite of the wastes that necessarily attend the process."

. . Justice Louis Brandeis

In the customary chief executive officers' message to stockholders in one of the annual reports, John McGoff wrote, "We are pleased to report that in 1971, Panax grew in size without sacrificing any of its bold and adventurous spirit and without retreating from its dedication to report the news accurately and impartially in the communities which it serves."

Later in the same message, he told stockholders, "By borrowing, buying, selling, merging and building, your company has emerged as a viable, growing and profitable publishing organization."

These few words portray the classic entrepreneur: succinct, candid, uninhibited, on the move. In just two sentences, McGoff expressed the spirit of entrepreneurship. At the same time he explained the policy, the process, the fervor for action that characterized his own method of operation as an entrepreneur. These words enlivened the charts, the graphs, the statistical tables used to depict the financial condition of the company at the close of the year.

Although not intended to be auto-laudatory, these parts of the message described McGoff, the entrepreneur, in action—bold, adventurous, buying, selling, merging, building, making a profit. To him, doing business was more than a cold, statistical, impersonal transaction to make money. Each venture was an adventure with all the excitement, suspense, plot and climax of a drama. Full of paradoxes as a business executive, he was a dreamer and a reamer, an instigator and an activator. As an entrepreneur, he never waited for things to happen. He made them happen. As the business grew and management responsibilities increased, pursuit of new ventures was essential to add zest to the daily management routine.

McGoff's present and former associates picture him as action-oriented, a man in perpetual motion, frequently pleased but never satisfied with the status quo, an idealist who has the flexibility to temper his idealism with realism. He is happiest when the action is most spirited. Although not happy with unfavorable results of some of the action, he would be less pleased if no action had occurred at all.

Don Layman, Vice President and Controller of the company and a C.P.A. by training, mentioned, "John McGoff turned the organization chart upside down. He started this company from scratch. In the beginning he was the company. He built up from him; on top of him. He showed the capacity to select good staff. He delegates responsibility, outlines objectives and expectancies. He wants to be kept advised on developments. He does not like to be surprised.

"He can be democratic, diplomatic and casually communicative in his relations with associates but when he does not agree, he is not hesitant to overrule all of us. That one vote by the President outweighs all the rest.

"He selected and held an active, capable, high level Board of Directors all these years, but he was the spark that set the fire. He respects the Board members. They respect him. The combination of McGoff's zeal and the conservative Board's cautious deliberation provide a responsible balance to decisions."

Frank Shepherd, in charge of day-to-day operations, phrased similar thoughts in different words: "John establishes the goals and working structure. He gives you complete freedom to operate within that framework. He does not want to be bothered with details. Never does he look over your shoulder to see how you do your work. He holds you accountable for results. He insists on regular progress reports.

"I try to keep him up to date daily when our respective schedules permit. I make certain that I tell it as it is. I don't try to surprise him. He does not want sugar-coated reports. He has total recall, particularly on financial matters. He remembers what you say. You had better be sure you give it right the first time and stick to your story. He believes in action, thrives on action and enjoys a challenge. He supports you come hell, fire and brimstone if he thinks you are right. He can come down on you hard if he thinks you are wrong. He expects loyalty and an honest open relationship because that is what he gives."

Joe Gross, Vice President, Personnel, until his retirement in 1978, said, "John McGoff is a man of high morals. He has deep religious roots but he does not wear it on his sleeve. He practices what he preaches. Associates, employees, all twelve hundred people at Panax have been his primary concern. He believes in the principle, 'quality begins with me' and tries to set the best example by hard work. He is committed to high standards. I know of no company more dedicated to quality, to consideration for staff, to providing opportunities for self-improvement. His support for my efforts and his appreciation for ideals in business were a source of inspiration to me."

James Brown served almost a decade as a Vice President, working in a variety of assignments. After leaving Panax he observed, "Suggest to John that he buy the Taj Mahal and he would ask, 'What are the terms?'" Jim Brown, an admirer of McGoff, meant it as a compliment, not a criticism. He divulged the keystone to McGoff's operations.

Much of the growth of Panax had occurred by his celerity in sensing opportunity from such casual remarks. He pursued a suggestion until some practical result had been attained, positive or negative. From 1959 until 1974 he devoted all his time, energy and entrepreneurial effort to building Panax. The names Panax and McGoff became synonomous, as inseparable as Sears and Roebuck. From gross revenues of $12,000 in his first year of operations, Panax had net revenues of $25.5 million for fiscal 1973. From one small FM radio station the business had expanded to thirty-six weekly and eight daily newspapers, several major commercial printing plants and a few media-related operations.

In 1974, he entered a new phase of his business career by founding another corporation, first known as Star Newspaper Publishing Company but later changed to Global Communications. He was, and is, the sole owner of this holding company, engaged in publishing, the travel business, and multi-investments. The two parts of this dual role were related but separate, comingled, though independent.

This new phase of his business career was conceived and born by the same kind of cursory suggestion noted by Jim Brown. Early in 1974, McGoff was having dinner with Tom Ochiltree, his Washington Bureau Chief and Tom's wife, Jewel. During the conversation Tom remarked, "John, why don't you buy the Washington Star?" His response was, "Well, why not buy the Washington Star? What do you know about the situation?"

Jewel, a real estate specialist of no mean success in her own right, and Tom gave him the benefit of their collective knowledge of Washington journalism, the market prospects and merits and demerits of the Washington Star as they saw them.

For years the Star was Washington's leading newspaper. It dominated the area for several decades up to the late fifties. Owned by the Kauffmann and Noyes families, the Star epitomized the elite of pre-World War II Washington society. The Kauffmann/Noyes families had prospered and proliferated over the years with each new generation joining the newspaper payroll. The paper dominated the local political and economic power structure. The owners failed to recognize, or chose to ignore, post-war changes in Washington. As cataclysmic social changes, new political influences and new economic forces emerged, the Star continued to publish for the upper classes, not the insurgent masses. The Star's inbred leadership and outdated policies provided feeble competition to the Washington Post, under the aggressive leadership of Phil Graham, son-in-law of the owner, Eugene Meyers.

In 1959 the Post passed the Star in circulation. Advertising followed readership. Political power shifted to the Post. At the time the Ochiltrees talked to McGoff, the Post was acclaimed as one of the nation's two most influential and profitable papers. The Star was floundering in the murky waters of financial deficits, kept afloat only by the lifesaving profits of the company's radio and television stations.

132

Tom and Jewel Ochiltree were convinced that the family owners were desperate to unload the paper. They were confident that the city could support two major papers, particularly if they offered different philosophical approaches to the critical local, national and international issues.

Of course, they recognized that it would be an uphill battle. The Post had resources to employ the best management and professional staff extant. It could afford to spend liberally to retain its prestigious rating.

This did not intimidate McGoff. It inspired him. The conversation planted a seed. It germinated instantly. The Ochiltrees could not have contemplated the excitement their suggestion induced.

McGoff's mind was whirling before the last course was served. He could picture himself as a publisher in Washington, the seat of world power; the source of world-shaking news by the hour; the nation's decision capital where the press provided the fulcrum and the lever to exert its weight in this decision-making process.

The mere thought of the power of the liberal press in shaping the bulk of these federal decisions raised his well-developed capacity for outrage to stratospheric heights. Nothing propelled him into paroxysms of indignation more than the thought of infringement on individual and corporate life of galloping government and the consequent burden to taxpayers to support its rampant power.

Before he reached the hotel room, he visualized the opportunity to exert a conservative influence on these national decisions. He thrilled at the idea of competing head-on against the ultra-liberal Post. By the time he returned to his office in East Lansing, the fire in his heart was blazing with the luminosity of sulfurous gas.

Although dedicated to a progressive growth pattern and sympathetic to McGoff's intentness to expand into the big city market, the Panax Board of Directors was faced with financial realities. At the end of 1973, Panax net earnings were slightly less than $600,000. Long term debt was in excess of $4 million. Fixed rental commitments for non-cancellable leases added $2.5 million. Plans to convert two Upper Peninsula dailies to the photo composition system from hot metal in 1974 and short term notes would cost a few hundred thousand dollars.

It was impractical to consider going into debt for $25 million or more, even if banks would make the loans. However, the Board offered no objection to McGoff's personal pursuit of the paper if he thought he could get sufficient financing without committing Panax to any obligation and without neglecting Panax interests. He incorporated the Star Newspaper Publishing Company in March, 1974. He was on his own in a new venture.

Numerous conferences with Washington Star officials, attorneys, bankers, private financiers and brokers devoured swift-footed time for nine months. He engaged a Detroit broker and a New York public relations firm to bolster his efforts.

Joe Albritton, a Texas millionaire was bidding for the newspaper, radio and television properties. McGoff sought the newspaper only, in spite of its heavy losses over a period of years. He made no effort to get the profitable broadcasting stations, believing that FCC would disallow new ownership of newspaper and broadcasting operations in the same market area. Albritton's efforts were rewarded with success in the fall of 1974. He purchased all the Star's properties for a reported $40 million. After the transaction, Godfrey Kauffmann, Treasurer of the Star during the negotiations period, claimed McGoff's bid was not given more serious consideration because their examination of Panax financial reports confirmed suspicions that the company was not in the "publishing major leagues". He was quoted in the press as saying, "It was sort of like Jonah swallowing the whale."

Then, when McGoff continued his personal efforts for his newly organized Star Newspaper Publishing Company, Kauffmann and his associates were not convinced of his capacity to complete the deal, even though McGoff's Detroit broker and others supported contentions that he was ready to purchase at a price of $25 million. Kauffmann, in retrospect, stated, "I think if we had been given a letter from some reputable financial institution saying, 'We have in escrow XYZ dollars,' we probably would have been satisfied. As it was, there was too little cash, too many notes and too many conditions attached to the offer." Kauffmann paid McGoff the compliment of being "a conservative, unabashedly so, and a very interesting man. He is not an unpleasant man to deal with and he comes across very persuasively."

Newbold Noyes insisted that McGoff resisted disclosure of the source of his funds and therefore the company dismissed his offers. Noyes avowed the eventual sale of all properties to Albritton was, in his opinion, a better deal for the stockholders. Never mentioned by the Star officials or the press, another factor could have been decisive. McGoff had been emphatic about his intentions to implant his own management team if he acquired the paper. He asserted, privately and publicly, his belief that one reason for the decline of the Star was a payroll overloaded with high-salaried relatives in non-productive executive positions. He won no internal family votes with such allegations

After Albritton assumed control, McGoff filed a complaint with the Federal Communications Commission requesting that the sale be voided because of multi-media ownership in the same market area. FCC took no action.

The case was closed. Many of McGoff's friends believed his failure to acquire the Star was a blessing in disguise. Albritton continued to pour millions into the operations to make it competitive and profitable. Its losses pyramided into 1979 when he sold it to Time Inc. for $20 million. In the meantime, he had sold the radio properties for $35 million and the TV stations for $65 million. So his investment in 1974 paid rich dividends.

McGoff holds stubbornly that his proposal would have been more advantageous because he could have made the paper into a profit maker. He is about the only one harboring such ideas.

In 1981, the Washington Star folded. After losing millions, Time, Inc., with all its resources and talent, could not turn the downward trend of the paper. This confirmed the ideas of both McGoff's friends and foes that his luckiest break was losing out in the bid for the paper.

Although the negotiations were closed in 1974, four years later, unproven allegations about South African funds as a part of McGoff's bid would surface.

Soon after the Washington Star effort, Ed George, retired President of Detroit Edison and a Panax Board member, returned from a visit with his daughter in California. Talking to McGoff about the visit, he said, "By the way, John, while I was there I heard that the Sacramento Union is ceasing operations at the end of the year unless it finds a buyer. Some people think it could be bought as a bargain. You may be interested."

No sooner said than McGoff was off and flying like a fighter squadron in a scramble exercise. Facts were gathered with the speed of a computer. Copley Press, Inc., owned the Sacramento Union. Losses had accumulated each year, reported to be approx-

135

imately $25 million over a decade. In 1973 alone the loss was $1.8 million. The Copley family had announced plans to terminate operations on December 1, 1974, unless suitable terms could be reached with a buyer. The real estate was estimated to be worth about $18 million. Zoning laws permitted addition of twelve additional stories to the building. Equipment was in first class condition. In an effort to be competitive with the dominant newspaper in the Sacramento Metropolitan area, the Sacramento Bee, Copley interests had invested heavily in modern, up-to-date, sophisticated printing machinery. McGoff estimated an excess of four large presses. Elaborately furnished private offices, executive dining rooms and private facilities occupied the upper floors.

With such security, financing presented no problem. He was assured of loans to cover the entire purchase. Aside from considerable savings in executive and administrative costs, his studies revealed seventy-five to eighty surplus production employees in what he considered boondoggling jobs, accumulated over a period of years in labor negotiations. So he conferred with the labor leaders involved and made these points:

- The business was scheduled to close within a week unless a new owner took over.
- Readiness to purchase the paper, take immediate ownership and keep it operating with no cessation of publication.
- Analysis of operations by management and production specialists indicated potential for profitable operations. However, to be profitable, union cooperation was necessary.
- Translated into practical terms, this meant release of seventy-five to eighty union production workers that were surplus for the new operation.
- A management team would select the workers to be dismissed. No promises were made to rehire them. These featherbedding jobs were syphoning off money that contributed to the bankrupt condition of the present owners.
- The alternative: Four hundred and fifty well-paid workers would be jobless, the productive facilities would be dismantled, the jobs would be irreplaceable.
- The deal could be consummated within the next forty-eight hours. Unless the union agreed to this proposal, there would be no deal.

Union officials delivered the signed agreement on the next day, December 25, 1974. All the papers were signed, sealed and recorded on December 27, 1974. The check for $7.75 million was delivered on December 31, 1974. The Sacramento Union Corporation, a wholly owned subsidiary of The Star Newspaper Publishing Company assumed control immediately. The name of the holding company was changed to Global Communications in 1976.

Actuated by an appetence to fill key positions with tried and trusted individuals imbued with his own spirit and philosophy, he appointed Don Hoenshell to the editorship of the new paper. At the time of the appointment, serving as Panax Editorial Director and previously Michigan Capital City Bureau Chief, Hoenshell took to the new assignment broad reportorial and editorial experience including service with the Alpena News, the Midland Daily News, the Lansing State Journal and the Detroit News, all in Michigan. McGoff retained the top business executive until 1977 when he installed his own chief executive.

A few months after taking over, McGoff sold four surplus presses for $4 million. Converting the top floors to office space, he leased them to state and private agencies. This brought in about $300,000 a year. Elimination of the production employee overload saved $1.5 million annually in payroll costs. The paper operated in the black from the first month. Profits increased each year.

About six months after purchase of the Sacramento Union, McGoff acquired twelve weekly newspapers in the area with a voluntary pay circulation of approximately 135,000. His investment was $400,000. Three California corporations were created. The Sacramento Union Corporation published the Sacramento Union. Sacramento Suburban Newspapers, Inc., published ten affiliated weekly papers in the metropolitan area. Two of the weeklies were published by the Telegraph News Publications, Inc., a wholly owned subsidiary of Suburban Publications, Inc. All the California corporations were owned by Global Communications.

The Sacramento Standard Metropolitan Statistical Area, late in the decade of the seventies consisted of Sacramento, Placer and Yolo Counties, boasting a population of close to one million people, retail sales of almost $3 billion, and claiming a place in the top forty retail markets in the nation. Spreading urbanization melded the metropolitan areas of Sacramento, Fresno and Modesto into one general market area, sometimes identified as the Inland

Central Valley of California. It includes the cities and suburbs of Sacramento, Stockton, Modesto, Merced, Madera, Fresno, Red Bluff, Chico and Redding..

The dominant newspaper in this rich market for several decades had been the California Bee, owned by McClatchey Newspapers. In addition, the company published the Fresno Bee, the Modesto Bee, and owned several radio and TV stations in this same market. McClatchey sales promotion identified the market as "The Valley of the Bees".

Recognizing the Union under the new, aggressive leadership as a serious competitor, the Bee initiated a new weekly free circulation newspaper in 1975 called the Bee Liner. It was delivered in the Sacramento Metropolitan area to households not subscribing to the Bee. It was discontinued at the end of 1976. The battle lines were drawn. The bare knuckled brawl for circulation, advertising and editorial acceptance was no place for the faint-hearted. No timidity was displayed by either of the rugged competitors.

Meanwhile, another serendipitous conversation put McGoff in the international communications business. In January, 1975, Dusty Rhodes was having lunch with Rodney Beaton, President of United Press International. Beaton mentioned that Paramount Pictures wanted to dispose of its interest in United Press Independent Television News, a London based news gathering agency. UPI held twenty-five percent of the stock, Independent Television Network, an English company, owned twenty-five percent and Paramount held the other fifty percent. Suggesting that Panax might be interested, Beaton referred Rhodes to Peter Kuyper, Vice President of Paramount.

Originally, Paramount had purchased interest in the company thinking that it would provide an international outlet for entertainment films. It failed to work that way. A news gathering agency selling its product to stations and networks, it had no controlled network of its own, only independent customers. So Paramount wanted out.

McGoff recommended that Panax buy Paramount's shares. Panax Board members rejected the proposal, but again gave McGoff their blessing and moral support if he chose to follow the lead as an individual.

Agreeing to terms with Paramount and already endorsed as a desirable partner by UPI, it was then prudent to confer with the

ITN partners in London. Each of the three partners had a thirty day option to match any outside offer if any one of the partners desired to sell. The visit was arranged for late February, 1975. Accompanying McGoff and Rhodes were attorney Richard Jones and Robert Leipprandt, Vice President of Global Communications.

With the exception of William Hodgson, ITN General Manager, the British officials were courteous, gracious and cautious. They seemed somewhat formal to the Americans, accustomed to the casual banter of their own conferences.

All were dressed in the wonted dark suits and white shirts with conservative ties except McGoff and Leipprandt. This was unusual for McGoff. He seldom wore sports clothes back home but on this occasion he chose to dress modestly casual. Leipprandt could have been going to the races with his flashy sports jacket. This may have offended the bristly proper Hodgson. At least it did not assauge his resentment.

He lost no time in letting the Global intruders know that he could see no advantage or prestige which owners of a provincial paper in a remote western state could bring to UPITN. The gist of his disaffection was, "Just what can you do for the company?" Rhodes, realizing that he would be the new president if this proposal went through, tried to reassure him. He suggested that one of the first goals would be to go after the U.S. TV networks.

"And what, my dear fellow, makes you think you can do that? You know, of course, we have been working on that for several years to no avail. Is it not presumptuous to infer that your presence would be more productive?"

Countered Rhodes, "Well, a fresh look, new approaches, new ideas, new personalities may be just what is needed!"

So the sparring went for a shaky start. Dignified, gentlemanly Sir Geoffrey Cox and the personable, able editor, Nigel Ryan, diplomatically shifted the conversation to more general subjects. McGoff made it emphatic that he understood the options of the partners to match or better his offer, but he was ready to complete the transaction on the deadline of March 25 and would expect to assume his share of the responsibility. The initial session closed on a friendly optimistic tone.

Going back to the hotel in an ITN chauffeur-driven limousine, the American delegation exchanged opinions of the new prospective partners. They had been amused more than annoyed by Hodgson's churlishness. Some of their remarks were complimentary, some were caustic. All comments were light, jocular, casual. Uninhibited by the chauffeur's presence, it did not occur to them that he was an attentive listener with a cultivated capacity for retention of what he heard and a skilled raconteur back at the executive suite. As an English career chauffeur, he was loyal to his employers and exchanged confidences with them. His report was detailed and accurate. He was doing his duty as any good man in service would do. Of course, Dusty learned of this long after he had assumed his new duties in London.

It had no discernible effect. Although ITN approached the ABC network and others, the deadline passed with no takers. Global Communications acquired the fifty percent ownership on April 20, 1975. McGoff and Cox were elected Co-Chairmen. Rhodes was selected as President, full time executive officer and Board member. Jones and Leipprandt assumed the two additional seats allotted to Global. Cox and Nigel Ryan represented ITN. Robert Beaton and Frank Freymane of U.P.I. completed the eight member Board.

Dusty Rhodes lost no time in demonstrating promised action. UPITN aired a profit for May, 1975. In July, 1975, Rhodes signed a contract with ABC network. In March, 1976, NBC was added as a client. At the end of the first year's operations, UPITN reaped a sizeable profit. Any skepticism faded in the sheen of black ink. The Board worked compatibly. Rhodes was given freedom to operate within the general policies established by the Board.

During the first four years, Rhodes recounts that about the only thing resembling an argument occurred between McGoff and Nigel Ryan over how and what to order for dinner after one of the Board meetings. Prior to McGoff's entry as a partner, Board meetings had been held in London. McGoff, the inveterate traveler, suggested that Board meetings be held in different countries, particularly where they could meet and get closer to major clients. It made sense, even to the English who thought the center of the world was London and the rest of the world revolved around it. Future meetings were scheduled for Paris, Vienna, Frankfort, Rome, Miami.

In Paris, it was agreed to schedule dinner at Maxim's. In accordance with American business custom, McGoff was ready to order a standard meal for all fourteen participants. As a steak and potatoes devotee, he had difficulty in understanding why that would not be acceptable to anyone in any place. Ryan, possessing more refined epicurean tastes, could see no reason to select the exclusive Maxim's if such plebian fare was to be forced on them. After considerable bandying, each individual ordered from the menu. Leipprandt was stuck with the check. The staid British partners were beginning to see merit in McGoff's repeated reminder, "When business ceases to be fun, it's time to get the hell out." As it developed a few years later, this remark was prophetic.

With one hundred and twenty clients serving two hundred stations in seventy countries at the time, UPITN offered a complete television news service with a network of editorial offices in New York, Washington, London, Rome, Beirut, Salisbury, and Hong Kong. Forty staff camera crews of a multitude of nationalities covered the breaking news, backed by five hundred freelance photographers subject to a moment's call. No reporters or regular correspondents were assigned to the field. Editing, commentary, preparation of special features occurred in the editorial offices. Camera crews filmed news events in international sound, which included all the natural noises at the scene: shouts, gunfire, traffic, voices. UPITN special coverage to any client was available at a fee for events of particular interest. With the main servicing center in London, stories were fed to clients by satellite (since 1977), microwave and landline links.

Film libraries were maintained in London and New York with films and videotapes of world events going back to 1955 and some as far back as 1898. It was rated the world's most comprehensive television library.

Beginning in 1967, a Roving Report documentary film program was produced weekly with in-depth coverage of the critical news stories of international significance. In addition to news analysis, coverage was given to science, arts, religion, sports as they reflected life and news in remote areas of the world. Thirty-five clients in twenty English speaking countries subscribed to this service. It was available with a written script to allow commentary in any language.

UPITN Productions specialized in commercial and industrial films on order and operated on an interational scale.

To assure that events were reported without national slant, bias or favor, a news committee consisting of top level professional journalists worked in accordance with high ethical standards. Sensing a crisis on feverishly sensitive issues of worldwide interest, the committee would arrange interviews with leaders of the nation involved. On one occasion Dusty Rhodes personally interviewed John Vorster, South Africa's Prime Minister during a critical stage of the Angolan civil war. Vorster agreed to the interview because he had confidence in UPITN's fairness and reputation for independence, objectivity, and credibility.

"This was no puff job for Vorster," assured Rhodes. "The News Committee drew up twenty-eight hardnosed questions. I followed the script to the letter." Vorster gave candid answers. In this interview he accused the United States of reneging on a commitment of support in Angola. It attracted worldwide coverage.

So UPITN prospered, gaining new accounts and prestige. No transplanted mid-western yankee enjoyed his London experience more than Dusty Rhodes. He adapted easily to the London rhythm of living; the slower pace, the calmer outlook, the stoical approach, the unflappable reaction to crisis. He was happy in his work, pleased with the measurable success of operations and wore the success well. He was thrilled at the opportunity to travel, visiting about fifty countries during his four years in the leadership position. Fascinated by the history of the older countries, the entire continent became a living museum for the family. The theatre, the arts, the music, the cultural life afforded an endless source of joy and enlightenment.

In 1976, McGoff bought fourteen suburban papers in the Houston, Texas area. Losing money fast when he acquired them, he sent a management team from Panax to reorganize the operations. Within six months the papers were showing a profit, although an effort to expand too soon resulted in later losses. Beginning with his California purchase, he made an arrangement with Panax for use of certain key executives on a fee basis. When Panax staff was assigned to a special consulting project for Global, all expenses were absorbed by Global, including travel, salary and incidentals plus a twenty-five percent of the total as a fee. This had an advantage for Panax and Global. In 1978, Panax bought the Texas papers after appraisal by an independent consultant. At the time of McGoff's original purchase, Panax was given first option to purchase.

"Tomorrow is D-Day for most of us. The day to determine for ourselves whether we wish a change of leadership in the country or whether we are willing to be satisifed with the style and form and progress of President Gerald Ford."

These were the opening words of John McGoff before the Women's Forum of Sacramento on election eve, 1976. With characteristic candor, he warmed to his subject as he continued, "Many times we hear the pundits say that the American voter, in most cases, makes the right decision in behalf of his fellow citizens when he enters the voting booth. That is a lot of nonsense because the fact of the matter is that he or she has in most cases entered the booth uninformed and ill-prepared on the issues and voted for disastrous proposals and many dunderheads.

"Many of those who have been elected to Congress of the United States over the past forty years have been just that— dunderheads who have heaped this nation with a debt that we shall never get out from under; who have taken us down the dead end road of socialization, perhaps hoping that we'll go the same road as Great Britain. And Great Britain is now in the middle stage of bankruptcy unless the International Monetary Fund bails them out. That fund is funded by your taxes and my taxes."

Taking his customary dig at the liberal press, mentioning in particular his Sacramento competition, he continued, "Also, I am perplexed that there are so many in my profession who wear their brains in their feet or perhaps some other part of the anatomy. This particular election has become a media war and a war of the polls. There have been so many distortions and leaks of untrue news stories in this campaign that the public is having a difficult time discerning what is and what is not true.

"Last week the Sacramento Bee endorsed Jimmy Carter. They said, 'He stands out as the candidate with the leadership qualities to rouse the country from its stagnation and restore its standing among its own people, and the nations of the world.' Now that's a lot of nonsense. The Editor should have defined those leadership qualities. If he, the candidate, has any then he must have gained them running his peanut farm or perhaps as Governor during a mediocre administration of one of the lesser states in the United States. And too, I believe the American people are becoming weary of self-recrimination. I don't believe we have to restore our standing among our own people or the nations of the world. As an

143

American, I am proud of our role on the world stage and I am disappointed in the editors who write that kind of trivia because they know it is not true."

This was not the first time he had disparaged the policies of his area competitor. The political stands of the two papers were separated by an unbridgeable chasm, offering a clear-cut choice between liberal-Democrat and conservative-Republican. This presented a healthy balance for the readers in this fiercely competitive market.

Although each paper vigorously pursued its editorial views, this idealogical cleavage had no bearing on legal actions instigated against the McClatchey papers in January, 1977. These actions reflected economic warfare.

Filed in the District Court for the Northern District of California, the complaint for damages and injunctive relief under the antitrust laws of the United States was brought by Sacramento Union Corporation, Suburban Newspapers, Inc., and Telegraph News Publications, Inc.

Stripped of legalistic minutia, the lawsuit contended that McClatchey Newspapers resorted to a variety of illegal actions in the competition for circulation and advertising to maintain a dominant position in the areas served by both papers. The suit sought damages of forty-three million dollars, trebled, and asked for reasonable fees and costs of the suit and discontinuance of the alleged illegal practices.

In March, McClatchey Newspapers filed answers, denied all charges and filed counter charges against McGoff and all his corporations, including Global Communications, Panax Corporation and UPITN. The countersuit, among other broad charges, accused the McGoff controlled publications and services of similar, though not identical, illegal tactics and actions in competition for an increased share of the market and requested unascertained damages.

This type of highly technical, intricately involved corporate finger pointing is not unusual in a tensely competitive situation in this litigiously prone society. It is rare for competing newspapers accustomed to cutthroat competition.

As the litigation dragged through the protracted processes of the court for more than thirty months, the competition continued unabated but with a perceptible effort to be certain that nothing

144

could be interpreted to support charges under court review. Both companies continued to operate with increasing profits. At no time did the McGoff or McClatchey papers operate at a loss during the extended court hearings, but it was alleged that profits would have been much better if the competition had not intentionally instituted certain actions that they claimed were in violation of certain provisions in the Sherman Act.

At a critical period of the court proceedings in the fall of 1979, McGoff's attorneys claimed that irrelevant material was being demanded relating to sources of McGoff's financial backing when he bought the California papers. Soon after, by mutual agreement of the litigants, both suits were dropped.

Back in the middle seventies McGoff met two men who were to exert a beneficent influence on his independent business career. He became a friend of J. William Middendorf II, Secretary of the Navy from 1974 to 1977, as a result of a series of briefing sessions at the Pentagon. Middendorf wanted to inform opinion leaders and media executives of the merits of the Navy's proposed submarine communications system called Project Seafarer. The project, later to be renamed ELF (for Extremely Low Frequency), involved installation of an advanced low frequency radio communications system to permit direct contact with submerged submarines any place in the world. At that time, submarines were required to surface for transmission or acceptance of long range messages. Under the high technology of modern warfare with its air, sea, ground capabilities, U.S. submarines were placed at a distinct disadvantage.

The Navy had originally examined sites for the operations in several states in the West, Southwest, Southeast and Midwest. By the mid-seventies, after exhaustive studies including tests in the small experimental laboratory at Clam Lake, Wisconsin, the Navy selected Michigan's Upper Peninsula as the location for the installation.

With knee jerk reaction, environmental groups opposed the project. Politicians, eager to hold the support of the environmentalists, raised their own din with resolutions denouncing the proposal. Michigan's Governor and the U.S. Representative from the selected district, both captives of the hyper-environmental fringe, joined in the clamor of protest. The press in Michigan, with the exception of Panax papers, allotted disproportionate space to the opposition and made little effort to explain the Navy's answers. Hence, the sessions in Washington.

McGoff endorsed the project enthusiastically. He gave strong editorial support, urging that final judgment on alleged hazards await results of scientific studies, pleading for national interest over undocumented local objections, denouncing the emotionalism of the opponents, praising the patriotism of the supporters. As a charged-up one-man lobby, he talked to the Governor and public office holders, arranged for appearance of high ranking Navy officers to speak before leading business groups in an attempt to counterbalance the political pressures against the project.

Robert Ferneau, one of Middendorf's top deputies said, "John McGoff, more than any other person, kept the project alive."

At another meeting in Washington, McGoff met Richard Scaife, heir of the fabulous Mellon banking fortunes. Among his multifarious holdings, Scaife owns the Pittsburgh Magazine and the Greensburg Pennsylvania Tribune Review. These two Pittsburgh progenies from the opposite sides of the tracks sensed an affinity of interests at the outset. They had a number of common traits. Both are conservative. Both are unrestrained hawks on national defense. Each of them have supported conservative candidates and causes. Each is a non-conformist, independent, plainspoken. A free and easy relationship materialized from these Washington meetings and other politically related associations. The friendship evolved into a business relationship in 1977.

Scaife wanted to expand his media holdings. In mid 1977 he agreed to join McGoff in a bid for the Oakland Tribune, owned by the family of former U.S. Senator William Knowland. Handling the negotiations, McGoff made an offer of $18 million. Unsuccessful in this effort, Scaife then bought half interest in McGoff's California papers for $10.8 million.

In less than three years from the initial purchase of the Sacramento Union, and the twelve suburban papers for a total cost of slightly more than $8 million, McGoff had realized $4 million from sale of surplus equipment, $10,8 million for one half ownership, reaped a profit on the operations each year and still owned fifty percent of the total business.

When the Carter administration took office in January, 1977, Bill Middendorf returned to his Washington banking business as President, Financial General Bankshares, a bank holding company with banks in Washington, Virginia, Tennessee and New York. In 1978, after Bert Lance left the Carter Administration, he was associated with certain Arab interests who tried to gain control of Financial Bankshares. Publicity of the ploy and uncertainty of the future of the holding company dropped the value of the stock. Recognizing problems for his friend, McGoff purchased a sizeable block of stock. When the showdown came on the sale and the proposal was submitted to the stockholders for a vote, McGoff's shares provided the decisive vote needed to rebuff the takeover. Stock prices shot up as the matter was settled. He sold at a good gain about a year later.

Bob Ferneau, a Vice President of the holding company stated, "We would tear down walls for John McGoff. He saved our Seafarer project and he stuck with us on the critical vote to hold on to our business. He could have made more money by selling much earlier than he did.

"He is an unusually keen businessman," concluded Ferneau, "who never forgets his friends. His sense of loyalty and his willingness to stick his neck out in spite of any criticism sets him apart. Bill Middendorf and I would do anything to help him."

Ask McGoff about his uncanny knack to make money on his personal investments and he is likely to answer, "I guess I am lucky," or "Somebody up there looks after me." Insurance executive, C. Jon Holmes, says, "It takes more than luck to make extraordinary gains as consistently as John McGoff. He has a sense of timing, seems to know when to get into something and when to get out to his advantage. Much of John's personal wealth is due to his capacity to select ordinary ventures that pay those extraordinary gains."

On occasion he will invest some of his personal funds on nothing more than a visceral tingle and come out smelling like a bank vault. In midsummer of 1978, when his ship docked at Sarnia, Canada, to clear customs before going into Canadian waters for a leisurely cruise, Don Lee, a Canadian businessman and personal friend boarded during the half hour clearance routine. Among other things, Lee sells pipe used for oil drilling. As he came aboard, one of McGoff's guests was musing about the St. Clair Inn, visible across the St. Clair River on the Michigan side. Knowing that Lee traded with oil interests and frequently met customers at the Inn, Lee was asked, "Say Don, several years ago when there

147

was a mini-boom in oil exploration over near Port Huron, a very talented entertainer at the St. Clair Inn during the summer plunged rather heavily in land hoping to strike oil. Did you know her?"

"Sure, I knew her well—a beautiful girl from New York with a marvelous singing voice. Her name was Toni. She hoped to strike it rich and retire in Michigan."

"What happened to her oil land?"

"Toni had a dry hole," replied Lee.

After a hearty laugh, Don Lee turned to McGoff and said, "That reminds me, John, my luck has been a little better than that. I have been selling a lot of pipe to several exploration companies in Tennessee. Some of them are doing well. Most of them are small. They start out with limited funds. I have been able to get a piece of a couple of companies for $5000, the limit any one person can invest because these fellows are independent and don't want to lose control of their operations. My son took a chance on a couple of others. All of them so far are paying off much quicker and better than we expected."

"Can anyone get in?" asked McGoff.

"Well, I don't know about anyone. I doubt it. I sell to them and have a pretty close relationship with them. They offered me the chance to be a limited partner.

"Suppose I give you a check for $50,000. Do you think you could place it where it would do the same for me?" asked McGoff.

Lee gasped, "$50,000? My God, John, what are you saying? Are you joking?" After catching his breath, he explained.

"Look, John, I was not trying to sell you anything. I was just telling you of my experience in recent months. There is nothing guaranteed. You could lose every dime on these exploration deals. Some of them go broke fast. I would not want the responsibility for that amount of money from you with no assurance that you would get any of it back."

McGoff responded, "Of course, Don, I would not hold you responsible for any losses. I am willing to take a chance. I know how conservative you and your son are. Tell you what I'll do. Take a check for $15,000. If you can't make a deal that looks satisfactory to you, return the check. If it works, fine. If not, I took the risk and we are still friends."

Over a period of the next month, Lee did invest the money for McGoff. Several months later some of the wells began to pump oil.

Eventually, all of them did. Earnings on the $15,000 have been far beyond expectations and more than he could have earned in the money market even with the high interest rates. Subsequently, he invested heavily in seven different oil wells. They are paying off handsomely.

Serendipity again? The visit aboard ship was unscheduled. The mention of the Tennessee connection was unplanned. The spur of the moment action was unexpected. Don Lee saw the Global Star passing his riverfront home along the St. Clair River. Since he lived about ten minutes away, he thought it would be an appropriate time to discuss further details about tying up McGoff's ship for the winter at Lee's private dock. If the subject of the singer had not been broached, it is unlikely Lee would have thought of the Tennessee experience.

To McGoff's critics, this instant decision after a few minutes conversation on an unknown issue would be called reckless, impulsive, shooting from the hip. Actually, McGoff's reasoning was logical. He knew Don Lee as a man of unimpeachable character with a cautious approach to any investment of any size. He was not a man to waste his money on risky deals. McGoff hedged his risk with confidence and trust in the judgment of his friend. He was rewarded with an extraordinary gain from an ordinary source under uncommon circumstances.

Most of his private ventures have been deliberately planned, thoroughly investigated, sagely advised by expert counsel. Acquisition of Furlow Tours in mid-1979 fo!lowed that course. The attempt to launch Panax on the waters of the cruise business was aborted by an accident. Still, his zeal for capitalizing on some phase of the leisure trade was not dulled. Alfred Neugebauer had been employed to head the short life of the Panax Leisure Division. The division died. The idea lived. Al Neugebauer had a long, successful history in the travel industry. In June, 1979, Watersedge, Inc., a wholly owned subsidiary of Global Communications, acquired Furlow Tours, one of the largest wholesale tour companies in the nation.

Initially a motorcoach tour operator when founded in 1935, it had expanded into offering complete air-land-wholesale tours with executive offices in Oakbrook, Illinois and sales and service offices in South Bend, Indiana.

Furlow Tours packages all expense trips by bus and bus/air

from various locations in the nation. All expenses are included in the cost of each tour: transportation, sightseeing admission fees, tour escorts, guide fees, all lodging, baggage handling, service tips, meals as outlined in each tour package. Travel agencies retail the tours, charging a commission to the wholesaler. As soon as a travel agency sells the excursion, Furlow assumes full responsibility for all further details.

Short regional and national tours emanate from different locations, as well as longer tours to Hawaii, Canada, Mexico and a host of other attractive vacation and historic sites. Originally a midwestern tour company, it has become international under the expansion plans of Watersedge ownership, with Al Neugebauer as President. The company owns outright retail travel agencies in Illinois, Indiana and Florida.

McGoff's management methods at Panax and his various privately owned companies through his holding company, Global Communications, present an engrossing study of contrasts. Management of Panax papers had been centralized with the corporate office exercising tight control and supervision, requiring a sizeable corporate staff. Global Communications operations are decentralized loosely. Broad policies are established by McGoff. He reserves the right of ultimate control but remains aloof from operational details.

In retrospect, McGoff endorses lean corporate staff, elimination of the trappings of bureaucratic power, assignment of authority with responsibility at the day-to-day operational level, minimization of layers of supervision above the "hands-on" activities.

From the time McGoff sought the Washington Star in 1974, critics, skeptics and some friends made conjectures on the source of his financing. His answer was simple and direct. It had been necessary to build the Panax Corporation from scratch with borrowed money from personal backers and banks. His credit rating was high. He had a personal reputation in these circles for integrity, reliability, ingenuity. He learned early in his business career that assets offered as collateral/security and valued in excess of the loan, put financial institutions in competition for the business. In building Panax, he had made many friends in high places in the world of finance. They trusted him. They liked to do business with him.

The Washington Star bid came at a time when his personal

reserves came from salary and bonus from Panax, personal investments in stocks and stock earnings from Panax. All of them seemed piddling when speaking of a twenty-five million dollar deal. Some of his friends lifted eyebrows but expressed complete confidence in his ability to raise the necessary money because of his past enterprising successes. Critics engaged in prejudicial speculation, hinting that he was fronting for a coalition of big business firms. By innuendo, others related his outspoken support of South Africa to possible loans. Joe Albritton's acquisition of the Star quenched the rumors for the time. When he obtained the California papers and continued to increase his personal holdings, no questions were raised. It was taken for granted that he knew how to raise money for his enterprises. It was assumed that he would continue to borrow, buy, sell, merge and build. His blazing passion for action would allow no less.

Chapter 10

The South African Connection

*"I do not regret having braved public opinion
when I knew it was wrong and was sure it would
be merciless."*

. . Horace Greeley

John McGoff's connecting link with South Africa was fused in
1968. He was invited to be a guest of the government for a three
weeks all expenses paid tour of the nation. He accepted eagerly.
His knowledge of the country was limited at the time. He had been
enchanted with all parts of Africa since his landing at Fedala,
French Morocco in World War II. As a history major, his memory
clung to a few accounts that seemed significant. He recalled from
his studies that back in the fifteenth century, a Portuguese navigator
named Bartholomew Diaz had discovered what was eventually
named the Cape of Good Hope, after his predecessors had
searched the uncharted seas of Africa for three-quarters of a
century. Then a decade after Diaz's first voyage around the Cape,
Vasco de Gama passed the furthest point that Diaz had reached and
sailed through the Malabar coast to India to open rich trade
between the two countries. At that time, South Africa was
unexplored.

He was aware of the strategic importance of this major shipping
lane to the United States, cutting the length of sea routes between
New York and the Persian Gulf by five thousand miles. With our
growing dependence on the Persian Gulf region for oil supplies it
took no profundity to recognize the importance of this area.

A few references to his previous studies soon brought back knowledge of South Africa's importance to us, with the world's largest deposits of gold, platinum, vanadium, chromite, manganese and fluorspar, plus rich quantities of coal, asbestos, antimony, diamonds, iron ore, lead, nickel, titanium, uranium, zinc, and other critical minerals so vital to the U.S. economy and national defense.

These factors weighed heavily in his desire to learn more of this southern tip of Africa.

Although he had not been involved in any meaningful manner on either side of the turbulent civil rights movement and its ascendency in the sixties to political power, he knew that South Africa was under heavy bombardment in the United States for apartheid policies. In fact, L.E.S. De Villiers, the South African Information Officer stationed in Washington, was candid about the purpose of the visit when he issued the invitation. He pointed out that press attacks on South Africa had a detrimental impact on the country's relations with the U.S. government. He insisted the Western World could not afford to allow this one issue to endanger its security. Therefore, the Information Department was inviting thought leaders to inspect the country hoping that personal observation of conditions would create a better understanding of reasons for the racial policies and would build public support for a covenant of cooperation between the two countries in the battle against communism. He explained that newspaper publishers, writers, columnists, business leaders, preachers, politicians, and other leaders that may have some influence on public opinion were being invited from various nations, particularly U.S., West Germany, France, England, Japan, Israel, Holland.

McGoff accepted the invitation with an open mind and no commitments on anything. This first trip was revelatory. It opened a whole new world of interest. He was amazed at the modernity of the cities, the beauty of the countryside, the advancement of the free enterprise economy, the advanced stage of industry. He was impressed by the tremendous investments in the country by American, German, Japanese, Dutch, French industry. He marveled at the vast mineral resources, the enlightened attention to the performing arts, the applied arts, the art galleries, the museums, the sciences.

Nothing swayed him more than the implacable hostility to

153

communism and the visibly harrowing fear of the metastatic effect of this virulent malignancy throughout the body politic of the African continent.

The racial policy was discussed by various officials but little was observed of the actual conditions of the blacks, coloreds and Indians, the three classifications of all non-whites. In the presentations by government and private officials, justification for the apartheid policy was emphasized. A mass of facts and figures were available to show the relatively high economic status of the non-whites in South Africa compared to any other African country.

Back home, McGoff became an advocate for close relations with South Africa. He visited the Embassy when in Washington. He recommended associates and friends to the Information Department for invitations to visit the country. Over the period of the next decade, he returned to the country one or two times annually, at his own expense. Through Eschel Rhoodie, who had moved up to the top position in the Information Department, he met the Minister of Information, Cornelius Mulder, Prime Minister B.J. Vorster and numerous other cabinet members as well as high echelon business leaders.

In 1971, he joined Mulder, Rhoodie, De Villiers and four other South Africa acquaintances in the purchase of six hundred and forty acres of prime land in the secluded area of the country near the Kruger National Park, one of the world's largest wild game preserves. From the purchased property, a clear view is afforded of Mozambique. Each of the associates in the purchase invested $13,000 for the land. With full consent of the partners later, McGoff built a house on the site. He used the dwelling for his own vacation and made it available to numerous friends in the United States and South Africa.

As his newspaper chain grew in the seventies, he arranged trips for his Washington Bureau Chief and other members of his staff. Observations were published in some of the Panax papers. On one occasion, he wrote a series of articles accenting the strategic importance and the economic opportunities for American business. Although relatively objective, they were favorable. No mention was made of the racial policies. He opposed with characteristic vigor, the proposals to reduce, sever or in any way restrict private American investments in South Africa. In 1976, he testified before the Sub-Committee on African Affairs of the United States Senate

Committee on Foreign Relations. His testimony reflected the tone and content of various speeches on the subject:

..... As I understand it, this subcommittee is considering what policy should be followed regarding American private investments in the Republic of South Africa."

"Depending on their own experience, I have found that people with the best of motives generally find themselves divided into one of three camps when this subject is discussed.

"First, there are those who feel American investments and business enterprises should be withdrawn completely from South Africa and the Republic placed under a strict economic embargo until Prime Minister John Vorster's government changes the racial policies there.

"Second, there are people in a middle position who would not disturb existing American investments but who favor stopping any further capital investment as a sign to the world that the United States strongly disapproves of apartheid.

"Third, there is the group, to which I associate myself, which feels a policy based on either of the first two approaches would be a tragic mistake on diplomatic and especially on humanitarian grounds.

"At the outset, I want to make it clear that I am speaking as an American businessman with holdings in South Africa. I am not here to defend, even by implication, the racial policies of the South African government—policies which I feel constitute a tragic mistake for all the races of South Africa and serve as a block to that country's fuller development."

McGoff proceeded to relate in detail his experience in South Africa and to present his reasons for opposing any measures that would choke off American investments to South Africa. He expressed the opinion that a wiser policy would be to encourage the use of more American capital and production techniques, not only to South Africa, but to the new African nations. The basic points made, with supporting data were:

- The government development agency that encouraged, and sponsored, such businesses to locate in South Africa required that a majority of blacks be employed and trained in all phases of the work.

155

- South Africa was an excellent example of free enterprise working at its best.
- Wages and salaries paid were ten times the average in other parts of the continent.
- American business firms tended to dilute apartheid restrictions. The American influence, over and above the economic values, carried a humane dividend.
- Since the considerations for restrictions were prompted by concern for the blacks, they would be the first to be hurt and would suffer the most from the policy.
- Extreme economic pressure in the form of cutting off trade and development restrictions would strengthen, not weaken, the hand of whites resisting racial reform.

By the time that he made these remarks before the Senate Committee, he had acquired a reputation here and abroad as one of South Africa's best friends. He disclaimed support of apartheid, but the press was merciless in its criticism, branding him a front and spokesman for South Africa.

McGoff was not a front for anybody. He spoke for himself only. An activist, a patriot, a non-conformist, he spoke publicly on this issue because of firm personal convictions that it was strategically advantageous to the United States to maintain cooperative relations with a nation located at a pivotal point in an explosive part of the world. We needed friends. He made no secret of his personal friendships there. He recognized the consequences of defying popular public opinion. He had the courage of these consequences. He did not and could not at the time anticipate the ultimate impact of his actions. He resented misinterpretation of his motives by the news media. He refused to be silenced on this sensitive subject, bad press or no bad press.

In his testimony he had said, "I want to make it clear that I am speaking as an American businessman with holdings in South Africa. I am not here to defend, even by implication, the racial policies of the South African government-policies which I feel constitute a tragic mistake for all races of South Africa and serve as a block to that country's fuller development." He had made comments to this effect on numerous occasions but little, if any, attention was given to this rejection by press coverage of his speeches. Frequently he was identified as an apologist for the policy.

His denunciation of apartheid was not confined to this country. In March, 1978, he spoke to the American Men's Club Luncheon in Johannesburg about the Carter Administration's policy on South Africa. Warning that relations with South Africa would be critical under Carter he said, "As long as those oafs are running our country, you are going to have serious problems."

In a question period, he was asked, "What should South Africa do to increase its rating and support in the United States?"

Answering instantly and with ringing clarity, he exclaimed, "The apartheid policy must be eliminated absolutely. Then acceptance into the international community certainly must come."

He went on to express hope that South Africa would eradicate apartheid on its own initiative and take away the opportunity for the Carter Administration to say, "We made them do it!"

In his speech he advised South Africans to accept and work for evolutionary change, stating, "Change is inevitable because that is what life is all about."

In the bastion of apartheid, both the Afrikanner and English language papers reported his remarks with screaming headlines, and they editorialized copiously on his unequivocal rejection of apartheid. The Rand Daily Mail, no friend of McGoff because of the close relations with the Nationalist Party leaders, captioned its editorial, "Friendly Advise for South Africa." In part it read, "American publisher John McGoff had long been regarded as a friend of the South African government—a tough conservative who sees things the Nationalist way.

"That being so, we hope the advice he offered to this country in his luncheon speech in Johannesburg on Monday will be given close attention.

"South Africans, he said, must eliminate apartheid and they must take the initiative themselves in doing so. In order to regain international acceptance, South Africa must eliminate apartheid absolutely....

"If such a man believes South Africa should abandon apartheid, how can it be ignored? What possible motive could John McGoff have for saying the things he did? The only possible answer is that he believes them to be in the interests of South Africa."

157

Here, in his own country, the press was atypically wordless when he mentioned his position on the race issue in South Africa.

His criticism of South Africa policy was not limited to apartheid. In a speech in Chicago before a South Africa and American audience he deplored the crackdown of the Nationalist government on the press when he said, "I am not here to preach to South Africans about their internal policies since they have a right to control their destiny just as we have controlled ours; that is, until recently. As a friend, however, I am concerned about recent moves in South Africa concerning the banning of the press and certain individuals. As a publisher, I cannot accept the muffling of dissent as a healthy solution to their problems."

In the same speech he elaborated on his favorite theme: a damnation of the proposals to boycott American companies operating in South Africa and the pressures on universities and individuals to dispose of stocks of these companies.

A decade after his first visit to South Africa, McGoff was recognized as one of the better informed businessmen on the subject of trade with South Africa. Requests to speak on that and other subjects increased in proportion to his ascendency in the publishing business world and his growing reputation as a polemicist. That made him an attraction. He did not solicit the invitations. He accepted when his business schedule permitted.

With the evangelistic fervor of a circuit revivalist trying to save souls, he besought a powerful America, economic power, military power, intellectual power, bargaining power at the tables of international assemblies.

He opposed frenetically what he branded "hypocritical government policies" that condemned such countries as South Africa for its apartheid practices while exhibiting fawning sufferance of dictator and communist regimes, avowed enemies of the United States and guilty of fiendish inhumanities to their subjects that made South Africa a fanciful model of brotherhood and fellowship by comparison. He opposed apartheid but thought that was a puerile excuse, not a logical reason, for condemnation of South Africa. He contended that U.S. investments in South Africa served to ameliorate and could eventually be a catalytic agent for its elimination.

It would have taken an act of Congress to keep him from

expressing his opinion in his public utterances and in his opinion column of his newspapers.

When McGoff made his first trip to South Africa in 1968, Panax was still in the process of converting from broadcasting to newspaper publishing. The newspaper chain had fourteen papers with a combined circulation of 125,000; several radio stations, sold pending approval of FCC; a printing plant; and a printing machinery company. Gross revenues from operations amounted to about $6 million and profits from operations and sale of radio properties were approximately $1.5 million.

A decade later, Panax was at the crest of its growth, publishing six daily and sixty-one weekly newspapers with circulation approaching one million. Revenues were in excess of $36 million. McGoff's privately owned Global Communications reached almost as many readers. The worldwide news gathering organization touched untold millions.

McGoff was riding high on the waves of success. Speaking and writing bluntly on major national issues, documenting his assertions with conclusive evidence, bruising official egos with scathing censure, he made many friends in business circles and gathered numerous antagonists in federal officialdom.

An outspoken iconoclast, he dared to challenge certain practices of his fellow publishers with biting criticism. His reward was a hostile press.

Wary federal bureaucrats, an unfriendly press, a well established reputation for controversy plus his South African connections combined to set the stage for the next, and most harried, period of his business career

In 1978, internal party conflicts in South Africa over the expenditure of secret funds allocated for propaganda programs actuated a series of speculations hinting misuse of the funds. Originally set up to divert attention from the racial issue and to build a more favorable image abroad by stressing the economic and strategic values of the country to the Western nations, news reports revealed questionable practices by some leaders directly or indirectly involved in administration of the program.

Eventually, this resulted in appointment of a Commission of Inquiry into alleged irregularities. Conducted by Judge Anton Mosert, the first investigation made certain charges against South

Africa leaders. Judge Mosert was relieved of his Commission responsibility "for exceeding his brief" when he released to the press testimony implicating Prime Minister Vorster and Minister of Information, Cornelius Mulder.

Justice Rudolf P. Erasmus was appointed to head a second commission. Logically, it became know as the Erasmus Commission. Findings were released piecemeal beginning in December, 1978. The final report was published and made public in May, 1979.

In October, 1978, news stories in the Rand Daily Mail of Johannesburg and the Johannesburg Express published allegations that John McGoff had borrowed money from South Africa in his unsuccessful bid for the Washington Star: had used some of the money later to purchase the Sacramento Union and in 1975 had received an additional loan to acquire fifty percent interest in United Press Independent Television News with headquarters in London.

Suddenly appreciating how Marie Antoinette must have felt when the guillotine started its descent, McGoff denied the allegations. He said, "The allegations made by the Rand Daily Daily, an implacable and frequently rabidly irresponsible enemy of its own government, are not only utterly false but wantonly crude. They are lacking in any kind of substantiation or documentation as to cast severe doubt on the seriousness and integrity of publications which reproduce them. And these allegations, so recklessly repeated are so crude as to err by two full years in the timetable of my actual involvement in negotiations to acquire the Washington Star.

"Responsible journalism, it seems to me, would direct its investigative energies and curiosity to a newspaper which would publish such flimsy charges rather than to the victim of such charges."

Although reference to McGoff was a miniscule portion of multifold allegations relating to South Africa officials, the American and London press lunged hungrily at the McGoff connection like circling buzzards dipping for newly discovered carrion. Subsequently these news stories set him up as a target for investigation by the U.S. Justice Department, the Federal Communications Commission and the Securities and Exchange Commission.

The sole witness mentioning McGoff's name before the Erasmus Commission was his erstwhile friend, L.E.S. De Villiers, one

160

of the South African officials testifying because of his duties as a high ranking officer in the Department of Information. The official statement in the Supplementary Report of the Commission of Inquiry into Alleged Irregularities in the Former Department of Information read: "Apart from De Villiers' evidence and the documents (otherwise unidentified) handed to the Commission by Mr. Kemp (otherwise unidentified) in connection with the Star project, there was no other witness who gave evidence before the Commission in this connection."

The De Villiers testimony was published verbatim in the Erasmus supplementary report. In summary form it said:

- In 1974, McGoff requested and received a loan of ten million dollars to be used as part of the financing for purchase of the Washington Star.
- The money was taken from the Special Defense Account of the Department of Defense.
- The loan was made because the South African officials thought that a newspaper in the heart of Washington could help South Africa if it had a positive attitude toward the Republic.
- Failing to acquire the Washington Star, McGoff used part of the loan to purchase the Sacramento Union.
- An additional $1.35 million was advanced to McGoff in 1975 to buy fifty percent ownership of United Press Independent Television Network.
- McGoff paid back $4.97 million. The balance was arbitrarily reduced to $1 million and later settled for $30,000.

The Commission did not find the statements by De Villiers true or false, made no charges against McGoff, did not accuse him of doing anything illegal and made no demands on him. In the final summation of the episode the Commission said no more than, "The Commission finds it incredible" that the allegations could have happened.

L.E.S. De Villiers was the Deputy Secretary, Planning, for the Department of Information. He handled some of the secret projects. He was questioned by the Erasmus Commission on many aspects of the operation, not just the testimony he offered about McGoff.

161

The Commission's supplementary report in which De Villiers' statements were included was critical of De Villiers, and in some comments, outright dubious of De Villiers as a witness.

The reference to McGoff and the South Africa officials allegedly associated with what was captioned "The Star Project" filled less than three and one-half pages of the seventy-two page Supplementary Report. These few pages, scanty as they were in content and documentation, became veritable Holy Scriptures for quotation by newspapers and magazines. Febrile speculations flowed, seriatim, on what laws McGoff may have broken, what penalties could be imposed, what action the federal government might take. The magnet of scandal was too powerful to quiet "the arts babblative and scribblative" to use the words of Robert Southey.

Then a new source for news stories opened. The United States Justice Department evolved into a fountainhead of quotation for publication despite a formal policy established by Attorney General Griffin Bell in January, 1978 which made provision for establishment of certain procedures in sensitive investigations to avoid embarrassment and disclosure of information.

Apparently, unnamed individuals in the Justice Department accepted the gallimaufry of repetitive news articles as Divine Revelations even before the Erasmus Report was published in its entirety. As early as November, 1978, the Johannesburg Rand Daily Mail wrote, "Mid-West Publisher, Mr. John McGoff, is under federal investigation following South Africa information disclosures. United States Justice Department officials confirmed probing possible violations of the Foreign Agent Act, which requires Americans active on behalf of foreign powers to register and report their activities."

This bred a second generation of spectacular stories in papers in the U.S., England and South Africa. News tidbits continued to drip from the Justice Department sieve. No matter whether they were passed on to reporters surreptitiously or inadvertently, the information was just as quotable. Scandal mongering headlines were just as juicy.

In December, 1978 a story in the Miami Herald read, "McGoff reportedly is under investigation by the U.S. Justice Department for failure to register as a foreign agent."

In March, 1979 a Detroit Free Press headline shrieked, "U.S.

Probing Ties of Panax Publisher with South Africa." It went on to report a Justice Department spokesman had announced, "The Department is looking into the possibility that (McGoff's) dealings with the South African Government violated Federal law. The spokesman said the Department is interested in whether McGoff violated the Foreign Agents Registration Act. . ."

In April, 1979 the Los Angeles Times News Service circulated a story to its subscribers which said, "Department of Justice officials said they were awaiting State Department cables from South Africa to assess the basis for the findings by the special investigating commission. Therefore, they declined to call their inquiry an investigation." They also noted that the South African commission had not cited McGoff in its report.

In September, 1979 the Lansing State Journal reported, "The Justice Department said Friday it has authorized a Grand Jury investigation into possible illegal activities with the United States by the government of South Africa.

"The focus of the probe is believed to be John P. McGoff, a Michigan publisher who has been accused of unsuccessfully trying to purchase the Washington Star with South African funds and by using South African funds to buy the Sacramento Union in California . . ."

On or near these dates, other papers from coast to coast used various versions of these same releases, including Panax and Global papers. From the time of the initial denial, John McGoff had made no statement. In July, 1979 he broke his silence with a lengthy response to the allegations and editorial attacks. Used in full in Panax and Global papers, it received wide coverage in the national press. In brief, he covered the following points:

He admitted to being a man with strong views. He had fought against big government and for a strong America. His criticism of government policies had been blunt and harsh. They had rankled the Eastern Establishment Press. He resented the allegations of the competitive paper in California in claiming that his paper, the Sacramento Union, was owned or controlled by a foreign government and the tactics of sending reporters to pry into his personal affairs among his friends, neighbors and business associates. He outlined eight points in refutation to press speculations:

1. No foreign government had ever had any financial interest in

any media entity with which he had been associated.
2. No outside individual or organization had any voice in news policy or content of any newspapers with which he was in any way associated.
3. No foreign country had ever controlled, directed or influenced policies, practices or procedures of any media entity in which he had an interest.
4. If any such attempts had been made, the answer would be, "Go to hell."
5. He was not, nor never had been, an agent or front for any foreign government, including South Africa.
6. Every purchase of any newspaper or other business had been based on his own judgment.
7. His views in any of his publications had been his own and had been so identified.
8. He was not a bigot and deplored the kind of journalism that made it necessary to make such a statement.

He went on to accuse the federal government of trying to muzzle him as an outspoken publisher. He stated that he would not be silenced.

As other federal agencies leaped into the case, adverse publicity snowballed. In June, 1979 the Securities and Exchange Commission instituted action to gain access to all written records relating to McGoff's interest and dealings in South Africa. The subpeonas applied to the Panax Corporation, Global Communications, Sacramento Publishing Company. The latter two companies are private corporations not under the purview of S.E.C. The sweeping demand covered a nine year period. In addition, subpeonas were issued to the legal counsel for McGoff, Panax, Global and Sacramento and to another director and officer of Global. S.E.C. claimed right to examine all records to determine whether McGoff had used South Africa money to purchase Panax stock in the name of Global and Sacramento without disclosure to stockholders of Panax, as required by law.

McGoff's attorneys charged that the S.E.C. action was "apparently designed to intimidate John McGoff——from exercising his constitutional rights including the right to freedom of the press and associational rights guaranteed by the First Amendment."

Claiming the action violated his First Amendment, Fourth Amendment and Fifth Amendment rights and further appeared to reflect a concerted effort "to harass and intimidate a vocal critic of the administration", the attorneys asked that the subpoenas be squashed. Calling attention to numerous occasions that McGoff had been critical of governmental policies, the brief said, "We submit that these subpoenas must be examined with particular care by the court to ensure against the awesome power of the government being utilized singly or in concert with other devices as an instrument of repression, retribution or harassment against media entities or publishers who sharply criticize the government in power."

In December, 1979 U.S. District Judge Gerrard A. Gessell upheld the subpoenas in part, stipulating that only documents relating to possible financial, political or other "connections" with South Africa be furnished. He prohibited seizure of material relating to news stories. He ordered immediate compliance.

The decision was appealed. The U.S. Circuit Court of Appeals issued a temporary stay. The Appeals Court failed to take any action before the February 19, 1980 deadline to turn over records. Supreme Court Chief Justice, Warren Burger, was asked to stay the subpeonas pending completion of the appeal process. Burger granted further temporary postponement and requested S.E.C. to show why McGoff should be required to comply with S.E.C demand.

In March, Chief Justice Burger referred the case to the full Supreme Court. The court ruled that it was necessary to complete the appeal still to be considered by the U.S. Appeals Court before the Supreme Court could act. Attorney Raymond Larocca, representing McGoff commented, "I am disappointed that confidential documents dealing with the publishing activities and decisions of a vocal critic of the administration may have to be disclosed to the government even before his appeal can be heard. The Supreme Court, of course, expressed no view as to the merits of Mr. McGoff's First Amendment claims. Neither has the Court of Appeals where his appeal is still pending."

Indifferent to the deadline hanging over McGoff's head like the Damoclean sword, the Appeals Court dawdled, for unexplained reasons. As though fearful of a court decision that would block the action, S.E.C. insisted that the records be submitted immediately. In April, 1980 the intricate process of assembling and yielding the information began.

Back in July, 1979, the Federal Communications Commission exacted its pound of flesh. Noting the Justice Department publicity about a Grand Jury investigation of McGoff, the FCC, in an unparalleled exercise of autocratic power, set aside approval of the Panax purchase of television properties approved by its Broadcast Bureau.

With mountains of business problems screaming for attention, the mounting pressures of three powerful federal agency investigations, the plethora of damnatory news stories and feature articles, it was a credit to his strength of character that he was not reduced to emotional jelly. Possessing a pachydermatous skin, he shook off ordinary criticism as easily as a politician shrugging off campaign promises. But these were not ordinary circumstances. He was not immunized against assaults on his integrity, his motives, his loyalty to his country. When these events broke, his first reactions were natural for any normal person—shock, disgust, disappointment, resentment, wrath. Nevertheless, with the same fatalistic outlook that sustained him at Anzio, he refused to wobble under duress. He went about business as usual, kept his emotions under control, retained his sense of humor, displayed the same compulsive drive, presented a serenity that reenforced the confidence of his associates and bewildered his assailants. If indeed the federal agencies, separately or collectively hoped to mute his rebukes, as he proclaimed, the ploy miscarried.

His column, In My View, had been written irregularly. It became a weekly feature in all his publications. His views were more flinty, more strident, more cutting. In a column in November, 1979, about the Iranian hostage situation, he wrote:

"Across the shame-stained land of ours, ordinary Americans are reacting to the desecration of American honor in Iran. They are doing so with a spontaneous dignity which our government in Washington has not now—nor has it ever since that plague was visited upon us thirty-four months ago—been able to master . . . . . Meanwhile in Washington, D.C. our nitwit President said there would be no follow-up session of the National Security Council, Wednesday—as the crisis deepened—because none was needed."

At the end of the column he suggested positive options:

1. That the United States organize an immediate boycott of Iranian oil (Iranian oil purchases to U.S. was prohibited about a week later.)
2. That James Earl Carter resign. Now, he said, "This nation can no longer afford the luxury of even fourteen more months of this moralistic montebank."

In a later column, he continued the onslaught:

"Who, if not we, the people of the United States, all the people, are the real hostages.

"Hostages without hope of escape for at least another nine months, sure to be fraught with new perils at home and abroad, months which will doubtless witness even more follies perpetrated by a man who, increasingly, has sealed himself off from the world around him..."

On the CIA he wrote: "The first thing to remember is that the CIA, under Jimmy Carter's classmate, Stansfield Turner, has been strictly a tame tabby.

"In fact under Turner, it has not only been gutless, it has been gutted. Turner, history should record, was the man who forced out into the cold around eight hundred of the CIA's top spies, all but decimating the agency's clandestine services . . ."

On Foreign Policy, he wrote, "One key to how we find ourselves in such a fix—thundering loudly while carrying a little stick—is because we have approached foreign policy with an Alice in Wonderland innocence.

"This simple minded approach to world affairs did not begin with Carter. But Carter has weakened it badly, not only our will but also removed many weapons and allies we would need to fight..."

Commenting on Ted Kennedy, he wrote: "I give you a word for our times. The word is demagogue. According to Webster's Unabridged Dictionary, demagogue is 'a person who tries to stir up the people by appeals to emotions, prejudices, etc. in order to become a leader and achieve selfish ends.'

"I give you a demagogue. Edward M. Kennedy! . . . . ."

On the Palestine Problem:

"The Palestinian question is an American matter because American honor is at stake, the honor of our promises (to Israel). It is an American matter because the American sense of fair play and

167

justice for the underdog can have it no other way.

"It is no good to talk about what might have been in Palestine, or anywhere else on the face of the earth, once wars or plagues or nature have erased boundaries and swallowed up or diluted whole populations. In the case of Palestine these 'might have beens' go all the way back to the Thirteenth Century, B.C. when the Egyptians permitted the Israelites to settle Palestine and thus change the course of history."

As the threat to Free Enterprise he listed "propaganda and government" as the twin dragons threatening to devour and destroy free enterprise.

On Congressional spending (before the 1980 election), quoting some of the seventy-two recommendations of the Congressional Budget Office study on how Congress had ignored them he wrote, "Two things, it seems to me, are plain and urgent. One, we must abandon the notion that the federal government owes us a living, while we still can.

"The second reality we must face urgently. Nothing can or will happen until we clean out of Congress—ruthlessly, decisively— every last one of the big spenders who put us in this fix, who keep us in this fix . . ."

And so he expressed his opinions with a torrent of harsh words on subjects running the gamut of national and international concerns: welfare, education, the myth of liberal concern for the poor, illiteracy, sex education in the schools, energy, Iran, the draft, NATO, the evils of social engineering, Jane Fonda, Jesse Jackson, Mike Wallace, The Civil Liberties Union. He condemned what he did not like—a Westbrook Pegler of the seventies.

Yet, underlying all the upbraiding of individuals, public policies, bureaucratic practices that he considered abuses of the American system, was a reverence for the nation, its institutions, its traditions, goals.

Defying the politicians and bureaucrats with rude, disrespectful, sometimes shrill imprecations, he included the highest elective official in the land. He was the first to make it clear that his barbed remarks were directed at the individual in the office, not the office itself.

In his columns and speeches, all his attention was not aimed at governmental foibles. His running feud with some members of the newspaper and broadcasting industries dawned before even innuendoes were made of any South Africa connection. As unsparing publicity on the investigations proliferated, his general observations of press shortcomings hardened. His tone roughened. Whereas his criticisms before had been on the intellectual level, now they were more personal, more emotionally stabbing. In objecting to the publication of secret information about the hydrogen bomb he wrote:

"Invariably, those who argue for the publication of such information fall back on the First Amendment. In my view, they fall flat on their prats. First, because I fail altogether to see how this information serves any good or necessary purpose of any kind whatsoever for the survival of this ar any other civilization.

"Secondly, because I fail to see altogether what this sort of story has to do with the First Amendment, an amendment which in recent times has been used as a shield to license everything from sin to sedition in this country ...."

In a speech to the Warren, Michigan Chamber of Commerce Annual Meeting he devoted his remarks exclusively to his attitude on the press:

"Freedom of the press is essential to political liberty. A society of self-governing people is possible only if the people are informed; thus the right to exchange and print words. Where the people cannot freely convey their thoughts to one another, no freedom is secure. But what if freedom is used in a vulgar, cynical, immoral, dishonest, libelous, obscene or seditious manner? Is it not true that no man is free if he can be terrorized by his neighbor? Is it not possible words as well as swords do terrorize? Furthermore, can a citizen be truly safe if falsehoods come masqueraded as truths? Is is not true that abused liberty can destroy liberty? And is a democratic society unable to defend itself against these kinds of threats to its internal welfare and society?"

The entire speech was a critical examination of attempts to get sensational scoops, unrestrained power, advocacy journalism and the failure to exercise self-restraint. The press from Detroit and nearby papers was present in abundance. Reporters, feature writers, editorial specialists who seldom covered such meetings occupied several tables. They paid little attention to the talk. They were present to interview McGoff who had refused to meet reporters or talk with them on the telephone for many months. A new Public Relations Director for the Chamber scheduled a news conference because he knew it would attract these writers. He had worked for a chain in the Detroit area competitive with some of the Panax papers. McGoff did not want to appear but did not want to embarrass the new Chamber employee. It developed into an embarrassment for all concerned.

The first fourteen questions were pointed directly at the South African controversy. As he refused to answer each question, the reporters grew more personal, more accusatory, more belligerent, more antagonistic. He finally walked out. The ensuing stories in the papers gave little attention to his speech, but were condemnatory of his refusal to answer questions on his problems. The experience multiplied press carping, renewed the reporters' suspicions, reinforced McGoff's distrust.

Over a period of time his references to abuses by the press waxed into diatribes against his personal treatment. Finally, late in January, 1980, he had the opportunity to unload some of his pent up indignation before the Annual Meeting of the Michigan Press Association. In an orderly, surprisingly unemotional case by case recitation, he catalogued his experiences to illustrate the basic principles he had enunciated over the period of time as a publisher.

In opening, he acknowledged his discomfort because so many of the conferees knew him only from what they had read, or had written about him, and most of that was unfavorable. Referring to his problems with certain federal bureaucracies, he then personalized his relations with the press:

"More recently, however, I have become a target of the press. This concerns me more than petty actions against me by politicians and bureaucrats. I find myself consistently misquoted, my remarks distorted, facts dangerously manipulated. If I can be presented to the public as inaccurately and unfairly as I have been, then as a newspaper publisher concerned with the ethics and standards of fairness of the journalistic professions, I—and you—should be deeply concerned about the quality of reporting and editing of our nation's newspapers and magazines—and more importantly, about the quality of information our readers and viewers are subjected to on an almost hourly basis . . ."

Recognizing that his problems with federal authorities emanating from the South African question were uppermost in the minds of his audience, he faced it candidly.

"As you may know from press reports, I am under investigation by various agencies of the federal government. They have demanded that I and my companies turn over ten years worth of records dealing with our publishing decisions and associations. Power like that used against a publisher must be curbed if we are to survive as a free society. If the courts cannot do it—and that remains to be seen—the press is in deep trouble.

"Ironically, the press itself has helped to generate this particularly obnoxious piece of governmental muscle flexing against a publisher."

Mentioning South Africa one of the few times in any public statement since the incriminations, he explained his position:

"The development of my friendship with leaders around the world has been for one basic reason: the preservation of our way of life—the advancement of the interests of our country.

"Let's take my position on South Africa, since we are both controversial. South Africa is a country in deep distress. It is greatly misunderstood here—in great part because of press distortion."

He then outlined his reasons for supporting the country, using the same facts he had given many times in speeches. Then he said, "South Africa's problems are not the issue here. The issue is how my relationship with that country has been distorted by the press. For the record, it should be said that I oppose apartheid. The record shows I have testified against apartheid before the U.S. Senate Subcommittee. It is all on the record. I would like to say more. But since I am involved with the all-powerful government, I shall follow the recommendation of my lawyers to avoid topics which concern the investigations lest I jeopardize my position."

To place his remarks in perspective, McGoff clarified his reason for citing his experiences:

"It is not easy for me to stand here and explain my personal experience when such remarks could be construed as complaining. I am not complaining. I am reporting what happened in order to document what a miserably inadequate job our newspapers and the media generally do and the need for improved reporting and editing standards...When the press oppresses someone like me, it suppresses its own value. We need a free press. We need an honest and accurate press, a press which does not distort situations by omission of facts...

"The press is misusing its prestige. The press is misusing its power. It is failing in its responsibiltiy. It is haphazard in much of its reporting and editing. It is in danger of becoming something quite different from what we—the press—want it to be."

Some of the members of the press association had objected to McGoff's appearance before the group. One publisher of a weekly paper objected in a letter to the paid executive. In a column, he wrote, "I wonder how little it cost to buy the Michigan Press Association's Executive, Warren Hoyt. Hoyt, compared to other important people, is probably quite a cheap buy."

Dick Milliman, President of the MPA invited McGoff and introduced him. A personal friend and supporter of McGoff as a result of association with him for years, he answered the letter. The closing portion of his letter said, "If the MPA, or any press group...which thrives on openness, controversy, the right to dissent, the right to speak and the freedom of all to publish...were to close our platforms and our ears to the John McGoffs of this world, then we would be guilty ourselves of stubbornness, blindness and hypocrisy. And we would miss out on a lot of good information and a lot of good stories."

Although numerous feature articles, with a variety of speculative interpretations had been written about McGoff's South Africa connections, none galled him more than an article in the Columbia Journalism Review. Published by this major university, the Review had served as a self-appointed monitor of journalism ethics, standards and performance for almost two decades. Traditionally restrained and relatively objective, its criticism had become more grating under a new editor. Even so, it was out of character to publish such a scathing attack on an individual as the article entitled "The McGoff Grab", written by Karen Rothmyer. Her identification at the bottom of page one of the six and one-half page article read, "Karen Rothmyer, a former Wall Street Journal reporter, is currently a free lance writer in New York. The research on which this article was based was funded by the Center for Investigative Reporting."

Actually, the article disclosed little new information and nothing new of any significance. Development of his career in a sketchy fashion and the South Africa story had been published with monotonous repetition in dozens of articles. By placing various events in convenient sequence and sandwiching uncomplimentary quotes from others at the appropriate point, she was able to belittle his achievements, demean his motives, asperse his character and create a devious image of an individual trying to gain social status. It was a thorough hatchet job from beginning to end.

Aside from the baneful content of the article, McGoff's primary complaint was the failure of the Columbia Journalism Review to identify the author as an employee of this nation's largest anti-South Africa organization, the America Committee on Africa (ACOA). In an interview with Lester Kinsolving, Editor of the Washington Weekly, Karen Rothmyer admitted that she was employed as an associate research director of ACOA's Africa Fund at the time the article was written. She had written for the Africa Fund, a tax-exempt foundation, such pamphlets as "Fact Sheets of South Africa and The Krugerrand: Fact About South Africa Gold Coin".

Although she claimed to have left the employment of ACOA a month after writing the McGoff article, she continued as a writer for the anti-South Africa magazine, *Southern Africa*.

Staff member, Daniel Noyes, the Center for Investigative Reporting, told Lester Kinsolving that she had four donors of the ten thousand dollars, prompting the Center to sponsor her research. He did not identify donors. Rothmyer denied that she raised the ten thousand dollars. The source of the funds remains unsolved. Her admitted connection bedimmed objectivity as well as creditability of her article.

McGoff was not the only person outraged by the article. In trying to refute claims by several UPITN Board members that McGoff was in no position to influence UPITN news policy, Rothmyer wrote, "Clarence Rhodes, a Panax Director, and reportedly a member of the pro-South Africa group known as the Club of Ten (he denies this) was installed as UPITN President in London."

These allegations had been made originally by two British newspapers in 1976. He had never heard of the Club of Ten until that time. He sued for libel. In December, 1978 both the Guardian and Observer papers in London printed front page retractions and paid substantial damages to Rhodes. The Guardian issue of December 13, 1978 said, "In the issue of the Guardian on December 20, 1976, it was said that Mr. Clarence Rhodes, President of UPITN, a leading television news film agency, had been named a member of the Club of Ten, an organization which at the time was well known for publishing advertisements in the British Press in support of the South African government, including that of apartheid. The Guardian reported Mr. Rhode's denial but in a manner which left the reader in doubt as to whether the denial was believed.

"We recognize that there was no substance in the allegation and fully accept that Mr. Rhodes is not and never has been a member of the Club of Ten, and that he does not support the policy of apartheid. We apologize for any distress caused to Mr. Rhodes by the article and for any doubts that the allegation cast upon his professional independence and integrity.

"To mark the seriousness of these allegations a statement to this effect was made in open court yesterday and we agreed to pay Mr. Rhodes a substantial sum in damages."

After the article in the Columbia Journalism Review appeared, Rhodes exchanged considerable correspondence with officials at the magazine demanding "an apology and retraction, prominently displayed." The matter was not settled to Rhodes' satisfaction. The ultimate decision may be made by the courts.

Following release of reports of irregularities in the propaganda campaign by South Africa, the British media gave the same unrelenting news coverage of developments. Allegations included activities in the U.S., Israel, Europe, Asia and some black countries. As though taunted by a curse, McGoff was a feature of the coverage. As Co-Chairman of UPITN and a major stockholder, his name was newsworthy in London.

These ceaseless references annoyed the staid UPITN partners, particularly the members of the British company, ITN. At the UPITN Board meeting, held in Miami, Sir Geoffrey Cox, representing Independent Television Network, broached the subject. Emphatically refuting the charges, avouching innocence from illegal or improper conduct, McGoff seemed to allay any doubts lurking in Sir Geoffrey's mind.

Back home in England, Sir Geoffrey reported the disucssions to his ITN Board. George Bernard Shaw once observed, "England and America are two countries separated by the same language." Apparently something was lost in Sir Geoffrey's English translation of McGoff's Americanized explanation. Although the UPITN Board was willing to accept McGoff's verbal statement of no involvement, the Board representatives from ITN wanted a written assurance for the record. Chairman of the Board of ITN, John

Freeman, was authorized to request the written denial.

Rather than mailing the letter directly to McGoff, Dan Maloney, Chief Financial Officer took the letter to New York to seek the support of Rod Beaton, President of United Press International. He refused to be involved.

Upon receipt of the request, McGoff called Rhodes to unload his indignation at this insult and to question why Rhodes had not advised him of this development. Rhodes was just as shocked as McGoff. He had not been consulted or informed of the action. Shocked, bewildered, bypassed, this had the appearance of an internal conspiracy that infuriated McGoff even more.

If they did not trust him, they could go "sit in a tree" as far as he was concerned. He wanted no further association with them. He instructed his attorney to start immediate negotiations for sale of his stock. A ten day deadline was set for ITN to exercise its option to buy it. ITN agreed to buy at McGoff's price.

Rhodes was given notice of his release by the new majority owners. He was assured that his performance had been one hundred percent acceptable, beyond reproach in all respects. However, the new controlling interests explained that his long time identification with McGoff made it impolitic for his retention as Chief Executive Officer.

McGoff's South Africa relations had been affinitive for ten years, affording many intellectual, social, personal and business satisfactions. Now within a few months these relations had become afflictive, bespattering actions and efforts alien to any involvement with South Africa.

During all this time, no formal charges had been filed against McGoff. Only investigations and speculations. Unfortunately, some federal agencies are wont to start investigations with a flurry of public statements in given cases on the theory that the publicity will serve as deterrents to others. When nothing is found to justify further action, the agency remains silent. The subject of the federal agency attention is left in a purgatory of uncertainty.

A fusillade of predatory assumptions, criticisms and judgments break into print from time to time, unabated in tone though with less frequency. When appearing as riders to some routine announcement, each story recapitulates the South Africa sequences. Repetition, ad nauseam, gives credence to the allegations. In the absence of countervailing statements, public opinion is shaped by these news account. Even if other facts were available, the great mass of readers would not go through the tedious exertion necessary for the analysis to get a balanced view of the happenings. Generally the public accepts the negative by preference.

The newspaper industry learned at the beginning that most readers look for headlines promising the sensational, the catastrophic, the criminal, the frictional, the scandalous, the disastrous, the unusual. Individuals and institutions conducting their affairs within the behavioral norms of society do not make news. The newspaper business has a vested interest in scandal, hence the accent on the negative.

The media interpretations of the McGoff/South Africa case either overlooked or ignored certain significant factors. The Erasmus report served as the infallible source of reference. Yet the Erasmus report rendered no judgment, other than an ambiguous expression of incredulity that it could have happened. The report did no more than record, verbatim, assertions of one witness. That witness was vulnerable to charges. He needed to exculpate himself from suspicion of complicity in irregularities. By relating this testimony to other events that could prove to be more happenstantial than circumstantial, a convincing case was established against McGoff. Ironically, out of all the massive reports on the whole Erasmus study, only two individuals in South Africa were indicted. One was cleared immediately. The other was convicted on a charge that had no relation to the McGoff connection. On appeal, he was cleared of all charges.

As a result of the press interpretations, an unfavorable image was projected for McGoff. Whether schemed or misconstrued, the writers of the so-called in-depth features failed to recognize certain singular traits that separate him from the stereotypical business executive: the intensity of his convictions, the breadth of his beliefs, the depth of his patriotism, the proclivity to defy popular opinion on unpopular issues, the inner drives, the fire in his heart.

Omission of these qualities of character as forces that impel him to action with such unrelenting tenacity resulted in unsound premises for his motives, leading to erroneous conclusions for his actions.

The record shows that McGoff advocated closer relations with South Africa as long ago as 1968, long before any hints of any

176

financial deals. From the beginning of his contacts, he held deep convictions that it was to the broad, long range interest of the United States to cultivate South Africa as a working ally for national defense purposes, if not for survival. He pled for United States security, not for special favors to South Africa.

Attributing his reasons to avarice, egocentricity, vanity, self-aggrandizement, the feature stories shrouded him in a sheet of doubt, suspicion, conspiracy.

Years before any relationship of any kind with South Africa officials, the record portrays a zealous citizen willing to sacrifice public understanding and financial gain for his private beliefs, asserting his right and duty to propagate his views as a contribution to the national interest.

The feature stories pictured him as an ally of a foreign racist regime, trying to buy influence through clandestine connivances. To McGoff, this has been the unkindest cut of all. All the gold in gold-rich South Africa could not buy his disloyalty to his country. All the gold in the vaults at Fort Knox could not relax the intensity of his convictions or keep him from expressing them. He forms his own opinions. They are not for sale.

Granted that each story is written in the distinctive style of the individual writer, the features, identified as studies or profiles, reveal a curious similarity in content and slant, as though they came from the same galley proof. Each rotates sequence of events and developments to meet the theme but basically they are the same. Generally, the quotes are from the same pool of detractors. Final conclusions and interpretations of his actions are similar and frequently identical. With few exceptions of the dozens that were published, the assessments are uncomplimentary, derogative, iniquitous.

Seemingly, the conclusions were predetermined and material assembled to support them, a process of inductive reasoning. The end product is a disfigurement, asymetrical to the figure they purport to portray.

By refusing to grant interviews with all media representatives, McGoff contributed to the mangled version of his achievements and his public image. He contended that neither the tone nor the content would change, because he believed his remarks would be twisted to fit the preconceived pattern. The media representatives returned his distrust in kind.

McGoff denied any illegal, unethical, or improper conduct in his South Africa connection. Under our system of justice, he is entitled to an assumption of innocence until proven guilty. It is granted that he offered no definitive statement about other sources of loans for the initial acquisition of private holdings. Such a declaration would blot out all speculation. There is the question of the right to privacy in private transactions made in accordance with all legal requirements. At a staggering cost in money and reputation, he vowed to fight for this principle to the end. McGoff and his battery of attorneys are confident that the end will be a vindication of his stand.

Back in 1952 when McGoff was still a fledgling working for his Master's Degree at Michigan State University, the distinguished Justice, Learned Hand, spoke to the Convocation of the Board of Regents of the University of the State of New York. Expressing the same penetrating insight reflected in his brilliant judicial decisions, he said, "That community is already in the process of dissolution where each man begins to eye his neighbor as a possible enemy; where non-conformity with the accepted creed, political as well as religious, is a mark of disaffection; where denunciation without specification or backing takes the place of evidence; where orthodoxy chokes freedom of dissent; where faith in the eventual supremacy of reason has become so timid that we dare not enter our convictions in the open lists, win or lose."

Learned Hand spoke to the assembly. He spoke for the McGoffs of the world, who learn in their own way that the life of the maverick is never dull, the way of the maverick is never easy, the price the maverick pays for noncompliance is always high.

In this age of human homogeneity, conformity is expected, non-comformity is viewed with askance. The non-conformist receives great satisfaction for having the courage to stray from the herd. In his stand on South Africa, John McGoff chose the maverick way. He believed he was right. He refused to remain mute because his ideas were unpopular. Was it worth the trouble it brought?

Without the slightest hesitancy, McGoff answers, "Most emphatically, YES! Naturally, these inaccurate and vicious stories upset me personally as they would upset any human being. What troubles me more is the effect they have on my family, our five children and my wife, who have taken abuse and ridicule. If that is the price I must pay for having strong views about our country and for expressing them bluntly, so be it. I believe sincerely in the views and am confident that they are right and good for my country. I do not regret any of my actions in my relations with any country.''

Chapter 11

Responsible Citizenship

"This nation was not founded solely on the principle of citizen rights. Equally important—though too often not discussed—is the citizen's responsibility. For our privileges can be no greater than our obligations. The protection of our rights can endure no longer than the performance of our responsibilities. Each can be neglected only at the peril of the other."

. . John Fitzgerald Kennedy

John McGoff is proud of his Irish heritage. If he is asked about his ethnic origin he will answer with a pixie gleam in his eye, IRISH. He is wont to laugh off some of his foibles with reference to his Irish temper, his Irish obstinacy, his Irish propensity for controversy. His brother, Dan, claims Scotch-Irish descent, with emphasis on the Scotch. Sister Ruth delves deeper into family history by avowing Irish, Scotch, English and Welsh lineage. All of them acknowledge the story of an Indian princess in the family some several grandparents ago. Whether legendary or real, they only know what has been passed down through the family grapevine.

It does not matter. The ancestors arrived in this country so long ago that John's generation is as American as the Plymouth Rock and just as solid. The McGoffs have been responsible citizens from the beginning.

Citizenship responsibility means more than success in business, a profession or exemplary performance on an ordinary job. It

180

cannot be equated with accumulation of wealth. Not that these achievements are incompatible with citizenship responsibility. It is just that many citizens, of all walks of life, remain sideline citizens. They are the non-participants in public affairs—the political eunuchs of society who cannot get aroused about anything, limiting themselves to activities in their own sacred harems of self-interest.

Citizenship responsibility means that individuals exercise their rights and fight to protect the same rights for others. They accept the privileges of a free society and assume their share of the responsibility for keeping it free. They believe in representative government and devote a measurable part of their life to the political process that keeps it representative. They inform themselves on the billowy issues of the day and participate in actions to resolve the issues. Partisans of citizenship responsibility recognize that a democratic society is not self-perpetuating and that individual citizen participation is the blood that keeps it throbbing with life.

As a stripling in the poor boy days in Pittsburgh, these tenets were embedded indelibly in John McGoff's consciousness, not only by the cogent words, but the example of his father. To grow up as an activist was as natural as growing up. The dynamics of his penchant for public concerns has been directed into myriad channels, disclosing a striking complementarity between his business career and his participative interests in the civic, cultural, educational and political affairs of his community, his state, his nation.

At one period in his younger days, he aspired to a political career. His brothers discouraged him. Bob told him, "You are too honest, too blunt, too independent to be a politician. You could never hope to be the Governor of Michigan. With your temperament you would be telling off everybody so frequently that you could not get elected drain commissioner."

Probably, his brother's advice was less influential in soothing the political itch than his first fling at practical politics. A few years after leaving Michigan State University as an employee, he sought the Republican nomination for the University Board of Trustees. Michigan voters had approved the recommendations of a Constitutional Convention in 1961 to modernize the state constitution. One of the anachronisms retained was the system of election of the Boards of the three largest state universities, Michigan State,

Wayne State and the University of Michigan. An attempt was made to change the system at the convention but in the trade-offs made to disgorge other absurdities from the 1848 version, this one remained. The Governor had the power to appoint the board members of the other state institutions of higher learning.

Board members for the three larger universities are required to run on a statewide partisan ticket after being selected by the respective parties at the state convention. Internal party politics rather than intellectual capacity usually determines the nominations.

McGoff worked hard for the nomination. He thought his wide acquaintance with the alumni as a result of his four years at the Alumni Association would give him an advantage. He believed he had the backing of John Hannah, President of M.S.U. Others harbored the same thoughts. Although wielding power with the legislature to get appropriations in the drive to build a great university, acute discretion was used in any influence he might exert in the politics of selecting the candidates for his board. Numerous candidates imagined that they had his support when they went to the convention because he had not rejected them bluntly. Not that he did not have preferences, but he played it close to the vest. Frequently selectees gave him credit. Just as frequently, the unsuccessful aspirants blamed him for a double cross. Many times he deserved neither credit nor blame. At that time, a Republican was seldom elected to the board anyway.

In this first political undertaking, McGoff learned what it meant to be torpedoed. The old college try was not enough to get nominated. He did learn some things about the whimsies of raw politics from the experience. This led to a more active volunteer role with the Ingham County Republican Committee, first as a member of the committee and then as Chairman. During this period, the Republican party in Michigan was undergoing a change. For the full twelve year reign of liberal Democrat Governor Mennen Williams, the dormant Republican party had been controlled by the ultra-conservative wing, some distance to the right of Louis XIV.

George Romney's election as Governor marked the advent of the moderate wing in the leadership of the party. Ironically, John McGoff, often labeled today by the press as a right wing Republican, moved into a leadership role in the Ingham County

Committee when the moderates were ascending to dominancy. Dee Kinzel, an active party worker at the time says, "John provided strong leadership for the county organization that was split between the two wings at the time. He had the capacity to bring the conflicting elements together. He concentrated on building a strong financial base, an area where both factions could work in relative harmony. Once rapport was established, the factions saw the advantages of trying to win elections against the Democrats instead of killing off one another."

As a by-product of working with McGoff on the committee, a close family friendship flourished between the McGoffs and the Kinzels. Dee and her husband, Dr. Ray Kinzel, have shared interests with John and Marge in art, music and numerous community activities. Dee says, "John is supportive, both verbally and financially, in a variety of cultural and worthy community activities with no expectancy of publicity or credit. Although he has been criticized by some people for rigidity, we have observed his reasonableness and flexibility on numerous occasions. That applies to the political field as well as others. He has a broad range of interests. He is very generous in his support of these interests in time and money."

In 1964, Governor George Romney appointed McGoff to the Board of Control of Northern Michigan University.

At Northern Michigan, McGoff once again joined his M.S.U. friend and benefactor, Ed Harden, who had assumed the Presidency in 1956, the year that McGoff earned his Master's Degree at M.S.U. When Harden became President, the student enrollment was little more than one thousand. When he retired at the end of 1967, enrollment had increased to over seven thousand. Close to $27 million had gone into capital improvements. This period placed heavy demands on the Board, newly created by the new constitution. McGoff's appointment demanded a new relationship with Ed Harden, his former boss at M.S.U. Now McGoff was on the Board of Control, responsible for establishing policies during an unprecedented expansion period with all its growth pains coupled with the student turbulence of the sixties. There was no strain in these new roles. Back in the M.S.U. days, relations between Harden and McGoff had been firmly welded by the ligature of mutual respect. Harden says, "John was a welcome addition to the Board. He took his duties seriously and did his homework conscientiously. We did not always agree on everything. He was no rubber stamp. He had ideas of his own and was never bashful about expressing them. I think John McGoff and Ed George, then President of Detroit Edison, made the greatest contributions to the advancement of the University through their Board participation."

Ed Harden retired in 1967, returning to Lansing to accept the Presidency of Story Inc. McGoff was elected Chairman of the Board of Control, serving in that office through 1969.

In search of a President to succeed Harden, McGoff tapped the vast reservoir of intellectual and executive talent at Michigan State University, culminating in the selection of Dr. John X. Jamrich. Reflecting on the decision to accept the challenge, Dr. Jamrich says, "Although I knew of Mr. McGoff prior to 1968, I did not become personally acquainted with him until that year when I was considered as a candidate for the Presidency of Northern Michigan University.....At the time of our interview he was serving as Chairman of N.M.U. Board of Control. I was aware of his business interests in the Upper Peninsula and of his personal commitment to the area through organizations such as Operation Action UP.

"Some of the basic traits of John McGoff as a person and as a professional businessman and leader became apparent during my first discussions with him. It was evident that he was enthusiastic and totally engrossed with the work of the university, even though Board membership was not his major pursuit at the time. Board membership is a purely volunteer matter through an appointment by the Governor. He was enthusiastic about the prospects for the university and he was willing to commit of his time and energy for pursuit of the future good of the institution."

Dr. Jamrich wanted assurance of strong lay leadership. Presidents of universities moved into the hazardous occupations classification in the years of 1967-1968-1969. Student unrest, campus disorders, rebellion against the traditional disciplines, required firm policies. Unless the volunteer Board members were totally committed to the support of high professional standards, Jamrich believed the Chief Executive was in a precarious position. It was easy for volunteer Board members to bail out if the situation became too tough.

Jamrich says now, "Not so with John McGoff. He sensed the critical state of affairs facing higher education and the highly volatile environment which existed at Northern Michigan in the midst of turmoil generally and with two or three personnel and policy matters here at Northern.

"Mr. McGoff was all the more tenacious, all the more persistent and all the more persuasive in talking with me about the future of Northern and type of presidential leadership he felt we needed—an executive officer to the Board of Control."

McGoff's choice of John Jamrich, approved by the Board unanimously and spiritedly, chalked up a victory for N.M.U. A mathematician, a concert pianist, a meteorologist, Jamrich's scholarship and administrative efficiency supplementing McGoff's leadership style and philosophy of education homogenized into a synergistic relationship between Board and executive.

This happy combination led to establishment of firm policies that met, head on, the immediate challenge of campus turmoil, while simultaneously committing the university to significant long range programs and curricula. Jamrich and his fellow Board members at that time pay tribute to McGoff for his leadership in recognizing a practical working balance between liberal education and training for specific tasks in the world of work. Some of the durable decisions attributed to McGoff's leadership are:

- An outside consulting firm was employed to analyze the merits of a School of Business and Management, resulting in expansion of a relevant curriculum for individuals planning a future in the business world.
- Establishment of a Skill Center. Previously, piecemeal programs were funded by federal grants. The Skill Center became an integral part of the university curriculum. A $15.5 million facility was started and eventually became fully operational.
- Expanded the Continuing Education and extension programs to serve more adequately the educational needs of the youth, business, industry and schools of the area.
- Established an ROTC program even though the campus hysteria over the Vietnam War in the late sixites seemed untimely. The program was accepted without incident and continues to flourish.
- Initiated a nurses training program; one for practical nurses and one leading to a Baccalaureate degree.
- Opened an extension center in Iron Mountain, seventy-five

185

miles from the main campus, for the convenience of that area.

- Expanded a limited FM radio and television program to a 100,000 watt radio station and a full color television station to provide cultural and educational programs for the entire Upper Peninsula.
- Expedited completion of three new residence halls, the Learning Resources Center and Jamrich Hall.
- Adopted a new student government constitution.
- Formed a Human Rights Commission.

After finishing his two terms as Chairman, he remained on the Board until 1972. Completion of his Board service did not diminish his interest in the university. At present he is a member of the Board of Trustees of the University Development Fund and serves, with his wife, as a member of the President's Club. In 1976, he was awarded the Honorary Degree, Doctor of Laws. The Citation Read:

"A man devoted to his family, his church and his nation for which he bore arms in time of war, he embodies the traditional values of diligence, honesty, fair play and love of country."

His response was brief, simple, undramatic, straight from the heart: "I am at first grateful that I am an American. Although some freedoms are eroding, this is still the land of the free and I think going back to the home of the brave. The Upper Peninsula is a part of me. Thirty years ago, as a student at Michigan State University, I recognized the free spirit, friendliness and rugged individualism of the people of this part of the state. I am here with you forever.

"We, as businessmen, are concerned about the attitude toward business by young and old alike. I firmly believe that the free enterprise system is the only system that can bring the freedom they want." His response is significant. These few simple thoughts, woven into the fabric of his character at an early age have never become unraveled by time or circumstances.

Time, talent and personal effort on behalf of Northern Michigan were supplemented by three major gifts to the university in 1978. Presenting $300,000 to the university, the largest single contribution in its history, John and Marge McGoff established the McGoff Distinguished Lecture Series. Former President Gerald Ford initiated the series in November, 1978. Spending two days on the campus, he lectured to individual classes, to combined classes,

186

to faculty and staff, to public meetings for members of the local community and to high school students. By all evaluations, he made a unique and enduring impact by this first person reference to history in the making.

Recognized as one of the international authorities on problems of world hunger, Dr. John A. Hannah, President-Emeritus of Michigan State University, dignified the lecturer's rostrum for the second Distinguished Lecture Series in November, 1979. After retirement as President of M.S.U., Dr. Hannah served as head of the International Development Administration under Presidents Nixon and Ford and later as President of the World Food Council

A few weeks before his appearance, the specter of South Africa hovered menacingly over the event. It dissolved after a flurry of publicity.

In the middle of October, the bargaining unit of the N.M.U. Chapter of the American Association of University Professors voted to disassociate themselves from the lecture series. Of sixty members present, thirty voted for the resolution, seventeen were against it and the others abstained. In a subsequent mail vote by 335 members of the chapter, 114 voted to support the proposal, 101 voted to oppose it, 120 did not return the ballot.

The non-binding resolution questioned the use of funds contributed by McGoff and the allegations being investigated by the department of Justice. The resolution provided that the action would be rescinded if the school administration could give assurance that the series was not funded by monies from South Africa.

Oddly, the supporters of the resolution saw no violation of the principles of academic freedom in their action. They could wail like tortured banshees at any attempt to restrict their freedom but sensed no conflict in encouraging others to boycott the lecture series.

The university issued a statement announcing that the series would continue as scheduled. It was pointed out that the resolution vote by a minority of the faculty "confronts major issues of academic freedom, intellectual integrity and the matter of rendering judgment prior to formal findings."

A later statement said, "This University, as all institutions of higher education in a free society must be, is dedicated by statement and action to academic freedom. It is dedicated to freedom to explore and debate economic and political issues of the day."

Citing freedom as fundamental to the educational process, the statement concluded, "Continuing the McGoff Lecture Series is but one means of bringing to the campus for exposure to our students, national and international leaders from a broad spectrum of pursuits and accomplishments.

"These leaders will address significant issues and will engage students, faculty and staff in serious discussion of these issues. Lecturers of the stature of former President Ford and Dr. Hannah make a significant contribution to the University and the humanistic principle which underlies it."

Confirming the judgment of the administration, the stature of Dr. Hannah overwhelmed the posture of the professors. The union resolution had no noticeable impact. Students, faculty and the public flocked to the lectures. The second session was rated a gratifying success.

In 1979, chimes of two carillons, located near the center of the three hundred acre campus, rang out as a result of another $48,000 gift from Mr. and Mrs. McGoff. The towers were constructed partly of native Marquette sandstone salvaged from towers atop the main entrance of historic Kay Hall, which had been razed in 1972. The rest of each tower was made of masonry tiles designed to resemble the original sandstone. Surrounded by a paved court and rimmed with benches, floral plantings and other greenery, one of the towers is eighteen feet, the other twelve feet in height.

The third gift of enduring significance was donation of a lake ship, the Spruce Hill, for use as a research vessel on Lake Superior, adding another dimension to the University program.

During Dr. Jamrich's term of office, student enrollment had increased to more than ten thousand by 1978. Additional capital improvements exceeded $31 million. In reviewing his own record, Dr. Jamrich says, "My personal success, if there be any, as I have worked with the University, derives very significantly from the close working relationship I have enjoyed with Mr. McGoff. He has been an inspiration to me, personally and professionally. His is an example of integrity and persistence in the pursuit of goals carefully developed and consciously set. His has been a personal and professional life with a purpose; a purpose extending beyond, but deliberately and consciously, forging into the affairs and lives of others. His has been an example of dedicated participatory citizenship from the local to the national levels.

"For us at Northern, Mr. McGoff will be remembered for his role in the important changes which took place and the important and significant fundamental principles which were retained."

McGoff's contribution to the advancement of N.M.U. would be a notable public service even if he had limited his volunteer activities to that single purpose. His public interests were much broader. Serving as a Board member, a member of the Executive Committee and for some time as Co-Chairman of Operation Action U.P., he displayed the same devotion to achievement of that organization's goals.

Founded in the sixties to promote interests in the Upper Peninsula when it was classified as a depressed area, Operation Action U.P. drew together business leaders from Upper and Lower Michigan to assure a unified approach to problems peculiar to the U.P. Efforts were directed to increasing job opportunities through economic expansion and full utilization of public projects. In effect, it was a do-it-yourself project, based on the philosophy that economic development in the Upper Peninsula was dependent on the concerted action of the people living there. The organization brought high level leaders in business, education and community development from all parts of the state to share managerial experience and technological knowledge to enable the existing industries to expand as well as to encourage other companies to locate in the area. It served as a coordinating group for the U.P. It remained a basically volunteer group with no effort to build a large staff or financial base. The dedication of the volunteers produced the results.

In 1970, McGoff was asked to assume leadership of an important Task Force of the Michigan State Chamber of Commerce. The Chamber had assumed leadership of a drive to extend the Great Lakes shipping season. Traditionally, the lakes were fair weather shipping lanes. Though they handled eighty percent more cargo than the Panama Canal, the lakes had a shipping season limited to seven or eight months. Everything stopped during the winter freeze, starting in late November or early December and stretching into April.

At the time, Michigan was the second highest exporter in the nation, valued at over $2 billion each year. Studies showed that every $1 billion of exports supported eighty-nine thousand jobs.

189

The State Chamber was concerned that the cessation of operations for several months created steep increases in unemployment compensation. Further, these massive layoffs escalated costs of shipping and fostered inefficiency for all the industries involved, including fleet operators, dock installations and government operated installations. Customers dependent on lake shipping faced expensive, inefficient use of capital and land during the shortened season. To stockpile winter needs during the summer, valuable capital in raw materials, inventories and industrial land areas were tied up in providing space to store the materials.

Because of its world leadership in ice breaking, Finland was selected for a State Chamber-sponsored study mission for the purpose of observing that nation's success in maintaining navigation in a winter, ice-locked area with weather conditions more severe than the Great Lakes region.

Ironically, Finland gained this world leadership through an idea acquired in Michigan. In 1893, a Finnish engineer observed the ice-breaking car ferry, St. Ignace, on the Straits of Mackinac. His subsequent research and development opened the Baltic to winter navigation.

Since Panax Corporation used lake shipping for bringing its newsprint stock to Michigan, John McGoff was invited to serve as a member of the Finland study mission. Following the in-depth consultation in Finland in March, 1970, and a series of evaluation meetings by the business leaders, university specialists, and glaciologists, the State Chamber agreed to spearhead and coordinate the efforts of various private organizations concerned with keeping the Great Lakes open all year.

John McGoff was selected to serve as Chairman of a Season Extension Task Force. The Great Lakes Commission, the Great Lakes Task Force and the Industrial Users Group formed a team with the State Chamber of Commerce. The Michigan Department of Commerce cooperated in research.

For about a year, the State Chamber Task Force gathered facts about Michigan and the entire mid-continent region using the Great Lakes transportation system. This covered the twelve north central states and three provinces in Canada. Geographically, it covered nineteen percent of the North American land form. Demographically, it contained a population of more than seventy million people. Economically, it produced thirty-four percent of the gross product, thirty-three percent of capital investment and thirty percent of the combined personal incomes of the United States and Canada.

Armed with an arsenal of facts, the State Chamber served as luncheon host for the entire Congressional delegation from all the Great Lakes states in March, 1971, about one year after the study mission to Finland. Arranged by Congressman John Blatnik of Minnesota, a long time supporter of the season extension program, the meeting was a fitting triumph for him. For many years he had strived vainly for the same type program advocated by the State Chamber and its affiliated groups. Although small appropriations had been made from time to time, they were divided among eight different federal agencies, each jealous of its prerogatives, each working independently. With no coordination, no noticeable progress had occurred. There had been no outside pressure for the longer season. It was asssumed that Congressman Blatnik was fronting for the steel companies. This outside initiative was exactly what Blatnik needed to arouse the interest of his fellow Congressmen. They now had pressures and facts to justify their action with constituents.

After the luncheon meeting and a series of individual conferences with Senators by the Chamber Committee members, Congressman Blatnik, Chairman of the Public Works Committee, made specific proposals that culminated in a commitment of $6.5 million for a three year demonstration project. Of equal substance, a winter navigation board was created with the Department of Transportation designated as the authority to coordinate and expedite the project involving eight government agencies. A working committee with representatives from seven working groups brought together all the developments relating to ice formation, ice navigation, ice engineering, ice control, ice management, economic and environmental evaluation. Originally scheduled for three years, the demonstration was extended to five years with a $9.5 million appropriation.

When the State Chamber first proposed the demonstration in 1970, it was estimated that it would take ten years for all-year shipping. Eventually, this schedule was revised to 1976 as the target date. Actually, all-winter shipping without interruption occurred during the 1974-1975 season.

Leonard J. Goodsell, Chief Executive of the Great Lakes

Commission said, "To say that the pioneer efforts of the State Chamber and the proponents of improving the navigation and commerce picture for this waterway have been highly successful would be an understatement. Working with its associates and enlisting the aid of the Great Lakes Task Force, the U.S. Congress, state legislators and a multitude of federal agencies, the Chamber Season Extension Task Force has seen its grass roots efforts blossom into a dynamic program that for 1974-1975 shipping season brings to realization a full twelve months shipping season on the Western Great Lakes.

"There is no doubt that the navigation season will render extensive benefits to the region and nation. Preliminary figures show a benefit to cost ratio of about six to one."

In recognition of genuine leadership performance, McGoff was elected to the State Chamber Board of Directors in 1971, Vice Chairman of the Board in 1972 and Chairman of the Board in 1973. He completed two successive one-year terms in July, 1975. He was awarded a distinguished service plaque at the end of his term as Chairman.

Contrary to the impression left by some of the critical stories published suggesting that he sought to build a power base for private gain, McGoff did not seek these voluntary leadership roles. The offices sought him. He served with distinction, playing a low key, but effective, role. At no time did he use his volunteer offices for personal gain. Any peripheral business that may have transpired was the incidental result of meeting other business leaders with mutual interests. It gave him considerable prestige. The primary gain was his satisfaction of achievement.

Adhering to his role of presiding over a volunteer Board responsible for formulation of broad policies designed to reach the objectives of the respective organizations, he did not interject narrow ideologies into policies. Fully supportive of the chief executive officers, at no time did he interfere with operations. Although subject to a vigorous travel schedule for his business, he absorbed thoroughly the briefing materials sent to him; attended meetings well informed on the issues involved. Informal in mannerism, precise in execution, independent in thought, yet a team worker in organizational action, his leadership style was conducive to constructive results. The organizational achievements during his terms of office were a tribute to sound leadership.

One civic responsibility post led to more frustration than gratification, more contention than constructive action, more puzzlement than understanding. Elected to the Williamston Board of Education in 1971, he was removed from office in a recall election in 1974 along with another Board member, Agnes Emery.

McGoff had agreed to allow his name to be placed on the ballot at the persuasive insistence of friends in the community. Wanting to strengthen the Board, they believed that his proven leadership in other volunteer positions would be advantageous. One daughter and four sons dependent on the Williamston schools for their education gave him a powerful motivation to strive for a quality program directed to high pupil achievement.

McGoff, Carolyn Adams and John Smith were appointed to a three member Curriculum Committee. McGoff's travel schedule was heavy. The other two members were busy, too. Breakfast meetings were mutually convenient. They were happy to accept McGoff's invitation to meet at his home for working breakfast meetings.

On a seven member board elected from a broad cross section of the community, it would have been unrealistically idealistic to expect unanimity of opinion on all curriculum issues. In a era of permissiveness, lowered pupil achievement, frivolous educationist fads, teacher union dominance of school administration, McGoff held a hardnosed preference for major emphasis on basic education. He believed that once these subjects were learned thoroughly, individuals would develop an understanding of the learning process and pursue many related matters on their own. Then the schools could eliminate trivial subjects cluttering up the curriculum. He advocated a balance between a liberal education and skills training so that graduates would have saleable skills that would permit them to assume their rightful place as self-dependent citizens. He agreed with the school of thought that claims the purpose of education was to develop the intellect, not to amuse, entertain or occupy time between play periods. He favored tough testing programs with no promotions until requirements of achievement examinations were met satisfactorily. He considered strict discipline an integral part of the education process. He opposed many of the federal programs, including hot school lunches, because they brought federal controls.

Some of these ideas were not popular. Many of them were

unacceptable to the life-adjustment approach to education. These advocates fostered what they called real life experiences. They wanted emphasis on such subjects as how to take care of your health, how to use leisure time, how to adapt to change, how to get along with people, sex education, how to maintain compatible relations with other members of the family. Never mind that high school graduates could not read, write, spell, add, subtract, communicate intelligently or even fill out a job application form. The life-adjustment-in-six-easy-lessons advocates failed to see any ambivalence between their approach and the illiterate graduates who became maladjusted misfits when they entered the job market.

This difference of educational philosophy was not patented by the Williamston community. A nationwide discussion was going on at the time. It did not imply that two factions on the Williamston School Board were in eternal battle to impose one extremity at the expense of the other. As in various boards in the nation, the fads of the day influenced their thinking and consequently their actions as board members.

McGoff and those who agreed with him looked for development of the capacity to learn as essential to a lifetime process, no matter if the career was in plumbing or surgery. The cliches of some of the educationists stressed life values, lifestyles, letting the pupils do their own thing, permissive behavior. No school board escaped the national debate.

McGoff was not the only member of the Board to urge a return to basics and a tightening of controls that would give the taxpayers more education per dollar. As evidence, the Board unanimously approved appointment of a new school superintendent from Walled Lake because he was noted for his no-nonsense administration. He believed that policies should be made by the elected board, not by teachers' union pressures for continually reduced class size and more pay for less work. He enforced dress codes for pupils, was a disciplinarian and demanded high performances from teachers.

Some teachers and parents did not like his style. It was a change that disturbed the status quo. They looked for a scapegoat. McGoff was accused of holding secret meetings in his home in violation of laws that required all public bodies to hold open meetings. Actually, there was nothing illegal in holding private committee meetings. The Curriculum Committee had no authority to take independent action. It could make recommendations only. All proposals went to the Board for approval. The Board meetings were open to the public. Harping on his opposition to federal aid, particularly his stand on the federal school lunch program, branding the Superintendent as a controversial figure, McGoff was blamed for this appointment even though the decision of the Board was unanimous. At any time the Board was split on an issue, McGoff was the culprit in the press coverage of the meeting, even though he may have been on the side of the majority in the ultimate decision.

Eventually, the disgruntled parents and the teachers' union gathered petitions for a recall. Agnes Emery was included in the recall. She was a teacher in the adjoining school district of Okemos but lived in the Williamston District. She agreed with the tougher approach of the new Superintendent. She was in general agreement with McGoff's philosophy of education. Since both of them were articulate and spoke more forcefully in meetings, they became the targets of the recall campaign. That seems to be the conclusion of some of the people close to the situation at the time.

Both McGoff and Emery say today that they do not know why they were recalled. Many of the citizens in the area are just as vague on the issue five years later. Carolyn Adams, a Board member at the time and Chairman of the Board for two years says, "I can give no logical reason why John McGoff or Agnes Emery were treated so shabbily. In my opinion, they were both excellent board members. They were effective, loyal, hard workers. They both made many valuable contributions to the improvement of our school program.

"I think John's position on federal aid, and particularly the free lunch program, were greatly exaggerated. Of course, as he moved up in the business world rather rapidly, a lot of people were jealous of his success. Others disliked him for his strong, outspoken conservative positions on controversial issues.

"In my opinion, the recall was unnecessary, unjustified and unreasonable. I belive it was a distinct loss to the community."

Driven by a resolute sense of citizenship responsibility, McGoff has not been a professional joiner. Discriminating in allocation of his time and support to organizational effort, he has selected groups where he can contribute most effectively to advancement of freedom and opportunity, in the hope of arresting

195

some of the political, economic, and social hemorrhaging of the times. He has not been attracted to the country club, the luncheon club, the service club or the so-called "do-good" groups that manipulate so many business executives into a state of guileless inutility. He wants his efforts to count so he does not waste them on trivial treadmill activities.

He belongs to the professional associations relating to his business: the national and local press clubs, the press associations, the Detroit Economic Club. He has accepted appointment to several commissions by the Governor, such as the Committee on Citizenship, Morality and Value Education, the Governor's Blue Ribbon Committee on Higher Education, Michigan Committee for Jobs and Energy.

As Chairman of N.M.U. he was a member of the Association of Governing Boards of Universities and Colleges. He served as Deputy Chairman of Michigan Week for a one year term. These assignments required neither excessive time nor long range commitment.

When he has agreed to a leadership role in a voluntary organization he has served with the same commitment of purpose that he exhibits in his business life. He takes his assignment seriously but does not take himself too seriously. Thus his colleagues respond to his leadership. By restricting himself to selective groups, he avoids overcommitment. He devotes the time and energy necessary to perform with merit.

This is the type of performance that would be expected of an incurable addict. The etiology of his addiction has no relation to drugs. Forbid the thought. He is as implacable as a hungry barracuda on all matters relating to drug abuse. The only time he has been known to resort to physical protest was to vent his outrage at what he adjudged a farcical ruse to glorify the drug culture in the presence of impressible youths.

His addiction accents his intense devotion to socially acceptable activities such as work, family, country and causes related to them. He has been a work addict since his newsboy days. His business is an integral part of his life, not something to be tolerated as a source of livelihood. Work fascinates him, brings out his creativeness, fires his imagination, affords pleasures and satisfactions that many people seek from avocational pursuits. Work is integrated so thoroughly in his pattern of living that vocational, avocational, family, social, religious affairs blend smoothly as parts of one entity. In moving from one part to another there is no discontinuity in the rhythm of living.

As his career bespeaks, he is allegiantly high on America, turned on by the mere mention of national defense, down on anyone who squanders our national resources. He is hooked on the competitive enterprise system, stoned on the concept of freedom of opportunity, turned off by government intrusion into personal and business affairs. Nothing gives him a greater buzz than a cruise with his family on his ship, the Global Star.

Happily married, not just plodding wearily through a marriage, he enjoys a compatible family relationship, derives pleasure from being with them, delights in doing things together, luxuriates in the commonplace household small talk and routines. He shares in their everyday experiences, enthusiasms, disappointments, interests and problems. Though possessed of all the accouterments that affluence has brought, the family life is simple, full of affection, free of affectation. Naturally, he can become exasperated as anyone else when something goes wrong but it does not disturb the basic relationship.

As the youngest member of the family, Andy gets attention from all the others but is not pampered or spoiled. Pictures of John and Andy at the same stage of juvenescence reveal a remarkable physical resemblance. Andy has the same playful, teasing nature, smiles easily and gets along well with his brothers. He wants to do well in his studies, in games or anything else he attempts.

John loved to travel at an early age but was limited mostly to the streetcar trips in Pittsburgh. Andy, at age nine, has been to several foreign countries, including Spain, South Africa and Switzerland and to numerous sections of this country. At an early age he showed a capacity to get what he wanted with his charm and loving nature.

Steve, the second youngest, is quiet, serious, smart, less extroverted, frequently seems to be in deep thought. He has taken music lessons for several years, plays the organ at home and the trombone in the school band. He likes music but is not possessed by it. He has no aspirations to follow it as a career.

Dave's interests in his early adolescence are baseball, basketball, golf, singing in the school glee club and girls. Priorities can shift by the season. He has attended Bobby Knight's basketball clinic at Indiana University. He passed up a trip to Spain with the family to participate in the basketball clinic at Michigan State.

Tom, the oldest son, entered Northern Michigan University in 1979. He is studying communications, majoring in broadcasting. At the end of his junior year in high school, he worked in the office of U.S. Senator Donald W. Riegle as an intern. During his summer vacation at the end of his university freshman year, he worked in a lumberyard in Charlevoix, Michigan.

Susan is the oldest of the children. She was married to Steve Traisman on a sunny midsummer Sunday afternoon in August, 1978. The wedding was held at the thirty-eight room, fifty acre homesite, Spruce Hill, on the edge of Williamston.

Embowered by lush shrubbery, varicolored plants, flowers and venerable, stately trees, a tent seating four hundred invited guests was pitched to one side of the sculptured yard. Although within shouting distance of neighbors on all sides, preservation of the natural wooded growth created the illusion of luxurious isolation.

The wedding vows were exchanged in front of the tent under a chuppah, a canopy of greenery, exalting the beauty and serenity of the scene. Intermingling the old with the new, a friend of the bride and groom, Hobart Ford, composed an original wedding march and a folk song about Susan and Steve. He played the guitar and sang.

Rabbi Richard Hertz, Ph.D., D.D., of Temple Beth El, Birmingham, Michigan, officiated. Honoring Hebrew tradition, Susan and Steve drank wine during the ceremony. In keeping with ancient superstition, Steve then crushed the glass under his right heel. Two sounds are symbolic. The first shattering sound is supposed to scare off the devil and keep evil spirits away. The second crunching sound, signifying sadness, is to remind the couple of the destruction of the ancient temple in Jerusalem in 70 C.E., meaning Common Era, equivalent to A.D. Later, they broke a loaf of bread, called hamotzi, to thank God for bringing forth bread from the earth.

At the grand reception on the grounds immediately after the exchange of vows, tables girdled the area, fountains flowed continuously with a variety of liquid refreshments. A tastefully decorated self-service table, plenteously loaded with palatable food enabled the guests to dine at their leisure and depart when they desired. Elegance with simplicity marked the entire affair.

For a wedding present, John and Marge gave them a three

month trip to Israel. They lived in a kibbutz for two weeks.

The family picture would be incomplete without including Ben, Chester and Alex. Ben is a big, lovable sheepdog who loves to be loved. Aging, he responds to head rubs with grunts, moans and guttural expressions of appreciation. Chester is a young, bounding, sleek black labrador, acquired by Tom in Washington. Determined to get his share of attention, he jealously noses himself close to anyone petting either of the other two pets. Alex is a cat with that typical feline independence. Although declawed, he likes to roam the grounds looking for rabbits. He can cuff a rabbit into submissiveness. Obviously, the thrill of the chase is more important than the catch. He walks away, leaving the rabbit scared but unharmed.

All three pets wander in and out of the house at will, very much a part of the family scene.

Grateful for a system that has permitted him to thrive, he responds generously to numerous causes. Former President Gerald Ford says, "John McGoff has become a trusted and intimate friend. That friendship is sealed by mutual respect and common concern for public policies. He is a man who is not afraid to speak up and fight for his convictions. We need more business executives like John McGoff. He does not hedge his support in politics. He puts his money where his mouth is." Gerry Ford has spent most of his career in politics. His opinion of political participation by business leaders is worthy of special attention.

McGoff contributed liberally to President Ford's campaign, to the Ford Library at the University of Michigan and to various Ford interests. His charitable and cultural contributions average a quarter of a million dollars a year. His particular interests include such varied organizations as the Lansing Symphony, Special Commission of Art, Kendall School of Design, Citizens For Seafarers, American Cancer Society, Fraternal Order of Police, Charlevoix Area Hospital, Harvard Society of Law, Michigan Corrections Association, the Olympic Foundation, as well as numerous others. Private assistance is given to a host of individuals in need. He contributes because he believes in a cause. He seeks no recognition or publicity.

In 1979, McGoff agreed to give Michigan State a one million dollar gift over a four year period in a fund-raising drive led by former President, John Hannah. A friend suggested that the recital hall in the Michigan Center for the Performing Arts be named in honor of Margaret Evert McGoff in recognition of her contributions to the Performing Arts Center. Both Hannah and Ed Harden, still serving as President, endorsed the proposal. The first payment of $250,000 was made.

Before any action was taken by the University Board, a new President assumed leadership. Ed Harden, having completed his two year interim term, returned to his business interests.

For years, vocal anti-South Africa groups had demanded divestiture of stocks held by the University in companies with plants in South Africa. On several occasions in the past, McGoff had been the target for M.S.U. protest groups. Plans for a sizeable donation to the University several years previously had been cancelled when a blistering editorial in the Alumni magazine had pilloried him for his stand on South Africa. When the announcement was made proposing the honor for Marge McGoff, the ghastly demon of the South African affair arose to torment him again.

The numerically small, but vocally loud anti-South Africa groups protested. This was all that was needed to intimidate the Board. To several members of the Board, the name McGoff had been anethematized, anyway, by his friendship with South Africa officials. The Board neither rejected nor accepted the proposal. They ignored it. The Board Chairman stated, "To my knowledge, John McGoff has not made any donation." Dr. Hannah clarified that technical dodge. The fund drive had been made by the Foundation. The first payment was in the bank.

This was another embarrassment for all concerned. The donation was made in good faith. The motive was honorable. Both John and his wife were grateful for their pleasant relations and experiences at M.S.U., both as students and since graduation. They wanted to share their success in a material way so that others might have similar enjoyment from association with the University.

At the time Dr. Hannah and Dr. Harden solicited and accepted the gift, they did not anticipate any hassle, nor did McGoff expect the treatment that ensued. It was disappointing to all of them that the Board did not have the courage to defend the sincerity of purpose demonstrated by this gift.

In November, 1980, two new Board members were elected. In January, 1981, the recital hall in the Center for Performing Arts was named for Margaret Evert McGoff. The two new Board members made the difference in both count and attitude.

An old Chinese proverb says, "The gem cannot be polished without friction, nor man perfected without trial." This incident was one of several where McGoff was subjected to calumnies while trying to perform valuable citizenship responsibilities. Once again he stood tall in time of trial. He did not resort to the indignity of retalitative exchanges with his detractors. He did not lose his poise, his dignity, his perspective.

His behavior reflected character—character forged in the fires of controversy, strengthened by the trials of criticism, matured through the tribulations of success and failure, sustained by the test of time. His character proved stronger than the fictitious reputation that others stamped on him.

The McGoffs of the world know that possessing character is preferable to being a character. It is something that they develop themselves. It cannot be conferred. Others cannot take it away. It is their own, to have and to hold. It may or may not be related to reputation.

Reputation is the opinion of others. Reputation can be woven out of the fabric of rumor, gossip, misunderstanding, incorrect interpretation of motives, disagreement, prejudice, idle speculation, non-conformity to peer patterns. Or it can be gained by deeds, correctly or incorrectly construed.

Character leads. Reputation follows. Like a shadow, it can be distorted by the angle of the light.

Adjudged by character, by deed, by citizenship involvement, John McGoff is a responsible citizen. The nation needs such citizens if a free society is to survive. The nation cries for citizens who are aware of the swirl of world conflict surging violently ahead, threatening our liberties, our privileges, our opportunities. The nation thirsts for citizens willing to accept the penalties of leadership to resolve some of the volcanic uncertainties of the present and future.

The future of the nation depends on the actions of responsible citizens with the courage to take a stand and stand by it, un-affrighted by vilification from people who disagree with the stand. At a time when apathy is becoming axiomatic, the responsible citizens of the nation are the hope of the nation.

Chapter 12

The Way of the Entrepreneur

*"All is flex, nothing stands still. Nothing endures
but change."*

. . Heraclitus

On July 16, 1980, the Panax Board of Directors approved a Plan of Complete Liquidation. On August 28, 1980, the shareholders adopted the plan with a unanimous vote at a special meeting.

To all but a modicum of inside confidants, the announcement came as a surprise. Many of the employees expressed shock. An unsuspecting press was unprepared. No predictions had been made by any of McGoff's media antipathists. Nothing foreshadowed the action.

On July 16, 1980, a total of 1,171,727 shares of common stock, five dollar par value, was held by aproximately 554 shareholders of record. Directors of the company owned or controlled eighty-two percent of the outstanding shares of common stock. Holding forty-two and two-tenths percent of the common stock, directly or indirectly through his solely owned companies, Global Communications and Sacramento Publishing Company, John McGoff exercised effective control of the company.

At the shareholders' meeting, they also approved an agreement for the initial sale of the three daily and two weekly papers comprising the Upper Peninsula properties. Thomson Newspapers Publishing Company had agreed to purchase this group of papers for approximately $21.5 million, subject to certain adjustments to be made at the closing date. These adjustments included such items as inventories, prepaid insurance, social security, rentals and similar components. The final adjusted sales price, completed in September, was $23.8 million.

In order to assure the new owners that McGoff would not enter into competition with them, he agreed to become a consultant to the Thomson Company in consideration of $100,000 per year for a ten year period.

Thomson Newspaper Publishing Company is a subsidiary of Thomson Newspapers Ltd., Toronto, Canada, founded by Lord Thomson of Fleet. At the time of the sale, McGoff said that it was his long and affectionate friendship with Lord Thomson of Fleet which led to the sale to Thomson Newspapers, saying, "Lord Thomson was an inspiration to me from the early days of formation of our newspaper operation. I am immensely pleased that the future of the daily newspapers in Marquette, Escanaba and Iron Mountain and the weekly Houghton newspaper are going to be under the stewardship of such a respected worldwide newspaper organization."

One condition of the purchase was that the Upper Peninsula Sunday Times would be discontinued. Panax was to be responsible for all costs and liabilities involved in the discontinuance. The publication of the paper ceased at the time of the agreement.

In October, the Trinity Company, Inc., a subsidiary of the London Post and Echo Limited of Liverpool, England, purchased the Illinois and Indiana newspapers and printing plants for a price in excess of $7 million.

On June 1, 1981, the Central Michigan Newspapers, Inc. purchased the Mt. Pleasant and Alma properties for a cash price of $1,346,579. All but $70,000 was paid on June 1. The balance was paid on June 30, subject to certain adjustments. The purchaser assumed contracts and certain liabilities of Panax related to the operations.

In connection with the sale, the purchaser required that John McGoff enter into a consulting agreement for a five year period for a fee of $50,000 per year.

On August 21, 1981, Panax sold the Detroit area newspapers to Global Communications Corporation, a corporation entirely owned and controlled by McGoff. The liquidation plan, adopted at the August 18, 1980 meeting, required that all properties be settled and proceeds distributed pro-rata for the benefit of the stockholders

203

in cancellation and redemption of the outstanding common stock.

In the event of failure to dispose of all properties with the period ending on August 28, 1981, a Liquidation Trust was to be appointed to complete all unfinished business, including distribution of proceeds to shareholders. Subsequent to the liquidation announcement, numerous proposals to buy the Detroit properties were made. One signed agreement was made to purchase in excess of $30 million subject to securing financing. High interest rates and economic conditions in the Detroit area made the deal unfeasible. Failure to reach a mutually satisfactory definitive agreement with this or any other prospective buyer prompted the purchase by Global Communications. The price and terms were competitive with all other offers.

In accordance with the plan, a Liquidation Trust was established under the laws of the state of Delaware, a trustee was appointed and a Certificate was filed to terminate the corporate existence of Panax.

The company's stockholders received cash distributions totalling $15.00 per share in 1981 and it was estimated that they would receive from the Liquidation Trust further distribution of at least $15.00 over the next ten years, assuming the various notes and other assets could be collected at face value, all known claims could be settled and no unforeseen claims arose.

In 1980 when the public announcement to liquidate Panax caught publishers off guard, various versions for the action were expressed in subsequent stories. One respected national business magazine attributed the decision to loss of circulation and advertising arising from controversies relating to South Africa, federal investigations and termination of two editors in the Upper Peninsula. One newspaper financial analyst claimed that newspapers with a strong ideological slant were in trouble.

In reality, these factors had no bearing on the action. They were incidental and at the best no more than annoyances. Taken alone, these incidents would not have resulted in liquidation.

The action was consistent with the way of the entrepreneur, John McGoff. It was good business to get out of this particular business at that time. In his own words, he had built Panax into an ever-expanding company by borrowing, buying, building, merging and selling. During his twenty-one years at the helm, he had shown no hesitancy to cast off unprofitable operations. When it was advantageous to sell profitable properties, such as the Ypsilanti Press and the Missouri TV and radio stations, he made the moves purposely and promptly.

In 1979 and early 1980, after selling the Texas, Virginia and Florida papers, an attractive offer was made for the Upper Peninsula group. These papers had a special meaning to him. Their acquisition in 1966 had afforded McGoff the most gratifying experience of his business career. He looked back on the successful conclusion of the vexingly extended negotiations with nostalgic warmth. An overtone of intimacy was associated with the Upper Peninsula. Aside from the profitable operations, he had pleasant links with Northern Michigan University, Operation Action UP and many friends in the area. He admired the independent spirit of the people in the area. He identified with them as his kind of people. He regarded the three dailies as flagships of his journalistic fleet. Although the Sunday Times, originated in 1978, had been a financial drain during a period of economic instability generally, he held stubbornly to his belief that it would pay off eventually.

His first reaction to the thought of relinquishing these prized possessions generated an emotional wrench. Howbeit, he demonstrated again his capacity to temper sentiment with pragmatism.

As the negotiations entered into the decisive stage, legal counsel advised that sale of the properties as a routine disposition would be a taxable transaction. The company would be required to recognize a long term gain, except for certain items of recapture. It was estimated that the tax would be $6 million. As a part of a liquidation plan, Panax would not be subject to a capital gains tax.

After evaluating the possible liquidation values of all Panax assets and the probable profitability in the future, it was concluded that liquidation would be advantageous to stockholders.

The price was right. The offer for the Upper Peninsula papers exceeded book value by $18 million. Remaining assets represented eighty-five percent of total assets at the end of the first quarter in 1980 and accounted for eighty percent of the revenues for the same quarter; eighty-three percent of revenues for fiscal 1979.

The timing was right. Local economies were suffering a recession in some of the communities where Panax published. This took on particular significance in Southeastern Michigan, location of the bulk of the remaining properties. Prospects for rapid recovery of the automobile industry were less than optimistic. Panax did not anticipate a favorable year in 1980. The first quarter disclosed a loss close to $700,000. The first six months offered little improvement.

Even in 1978 and 1979, profit from operations was discouraging. Net profits for each year had been realized by sale of printing plants or newspapers.

Payment on the long term debt during a regressive business period of undeterminable length was a strain on net revenues. At the end of 1979, long term debt exceeded $15 million. Over $8 million of the debt was at interest of three-quarters of one percent above prime rate.

Historically, Panax paid low dividends, choosing to acquire more assets. Prices for the common stock had remained low. With an estimated realization of $70 million for all assets, the decision to liquidate was a bonanza for shareholders, a sound business decision all around.

Other less tangible contributory elements influenced McGoff to make the proposal. When non-profitable divisions were sold in 1979, Panax was reduced to twenty nine non-daily and six daily newspapers, plus two printing plants in Illinois. A new thirty thousand square foot printing facility in Macomb County, Michigan, printing all the Detroit papers, was scheduled to handle large scale commercial printing in 1981.

Earnings were bound to improve as the economy revived. The more compact structure of the diminished operations would be easier to control. Corporate staff could be kept at a minimum. Concentration on profits for the more limited chain could have been productive.

That future had no appeal for McGoff. He was uneasy with the status quo. His entrepreneurial drive demanded action. He needed the daily challenge of growth, new ventures, expanding horizons. With fluctuating high interest rates, he recognized the folly of increasing debt load in the immediate future. Removing opportunities for growth incised incentive. His interest waned. From the incipience of his business career, he insisted work should be enjoyable. At the board meeting called to hear his proposal for liquidation, he announced, "I said I would get out of the business if it ceased to be fun. Well, it has not been any fun for the past couple of years."

Harrassment by federal agencies and the unsparing publicity

were paired reasons. McGoff ascribed the irksome conduct of the federal agencies to unrelenting attention by the press. In turn, he had convinced himself that his unceasing clash with the liberal faction in the publishing industry induced spleenful approaches to his activities.

Aside from the philosophical slant, right or left, he believed many of the news practices were detrimental to the national interests and inevitably would lead to federal controls. His entreaties for voluntary restraints through a publishers' code of conduct had been ignored, ridiculed or opposed. His public criticism of his fellow publishers, he contended, fostered below the belt press punches against his business and personal affairs.

One former employee agreed. Marianne Kryzanowicz, a former reporter for Panax has been quoted as saying, "I know him as a kind and compassionate man. John is a magnetic person. I think he is the victim of the very industry that he has invested his life in. Maybe it's his power and influence but I really think the media are out to convict him for his views."

A less complimentary view was attributed to Robert Skuggen, a former Panax editor. He was credited in a Detroit News story with the comment, "I think he's a very vindictive man who is trying to use his own media empire to further his own views. He sees himself in some sort of holy war against the liberal establishment press."

McGoff's views about the liberal press remained unaltered and unalterable. He was proud of his position. He wore any scars from his fight as badges of honor. He was aware of such criticism as Skuggen's. He was remindful of the resistance; indifferent to the consequences. As a target of advocacy journalism, his criticism had become more personal, less intellectual, more astringent, less fulfilling, although the zest of battle endured.

McGoff's long time friends and business associates refuted any accusations of vindictiveness in his behavior. Other executives in the company pointed out that he offered Bob Skuggen the General Manager's job of the new Upper Peninsula Sunday Times in 1978, even though Skuggen resigned as Editor of the Marquette Mining Journal in 1977 for what he termed "philosophical differences". Subsequently, numerous captious statements about McGoff were attributed to Skuggen. Still, McGoff bore no personal grudge and tendered the offer because he considered Skuggen a competent editor. To Skuggen's credit, feeling as he did, he refused the offer.

McGoff claimed he had no hit list, no time to think of getting even, no plan of vengeance although he admitted to being human enough to sense a subcortical glow when any of his detractors fell from grace.

Despite emotional links to the company that he created with nothing but a few dollars of his own, some borrowed money and fire in his heart, he suffered no pangs of regret as he dismantled it, piece by piece, just as he built it. He viewed the dissolution as the beginning of a new chapter in his business career, not as an end to a twenty-one year continuous drama. He looked ahead, not back. The venturous story went on as exciting new developments unfolded. That is the way of the entrepreneur.

He phased in this new chapter with the same irrepressible urge to acquire more tangible properties, take on new challenges, augment his prestige and achievements. While completing the liquidation process, his high level energy was directed to expansible projects for his private company, Global Communications Corporation and its various subsidiaries. He did not abandon the publishing business with the sale of Panax. The Sacramento Union and the chain of weekly newspapers in California remained intact, at the time unaffected by the intentional interment of Panax.

However, in March, 1982, he sold his 50% interest in these properties to Richard Scaife, his partner in the California operations. McGoff had purchased these papers in 1974 for around $8 million. He had reaped substantial profits each year of operations. He sold half interest to Scaife for $10.8 million in 1977. With the sale of the other half, he more than quadrupled his original purchase price in a period of seven years.

McGoff's immediate priority for acquiring new businesses, after the decision to dismantle Panax, was focused on expansion of his Watersedge subsidiary, operator of Furlow Tours, several travel agencies and other leisure-related enterprises. The travel industry fascinated McGoff—all phases of it, including its moneymaking potential. The travel industry encompasses a wide range of business operations. The National Tourism Policy Study, conducted by the United States Senate, defined the travel industry as "an interrelated amalgamation of those businesses and agencies which totally or in part provide the means of transport, the goods, services, accommodations and other facilities for travel out of the home community for any purpose not related to local day-to-day activity."

Worldwide, spending for travel amounted to $504 billion in 1979. This exceeded the Gross National Product in all nations except the United States, Russia, Japan and West Germany.

Expenditures in the United States in 1979 were $126 billion for trips of one hundred miles or more from home, totalling about eighteen percent of American family discretionary purchasing power. The American Society of Travel Agents estimate expenditures in the United States will reach $220 billion by 1990, figured in 1979 constant dollars. Although impractical to estimate the 1990 figure in inflated dollars for that future period, an average seven percent annual rate would puff domestic travel spending to $482 billion.

One additional development enhanced the potentiality of the travel business. In 1979, an influx of twenty-one million foreign visitors to the United States spent $10 billion. This served as a wholesome tonic to the travel industry and magnified the role of this business to the U.S. economy. It promised rich rewards for anyone prepared to capitilize on it.

It was logical to expand his travel interests in Michigan, a major travel/tourist state. In the mid sixties, the travel/tourist business in Michigan rocketed into the second largest income and job producing segment of the economy, outranked only by industrial production. Michigan's combined land and water-covered area make it the largest state east of the Mississippi River. A mammoth two-peninsula state with four of the five Great Lakes on its borders, it wraps a thirty-two hundred mile Great Lakes shoreline around eleven thousand inland lakes, thirty-six thousand miles of fishable rivers and streams and seventeen million acres of quiet forestland. It is one of the nation's most attractive year-round vacation and recreation states.

Peopled with fur-traders, missionary-explorers, lumberjacks and adventurers, Michigan's history lingers to capture the imagination of visitors. Stockaded forts, picturesque covered bridges, Indian burial grounds, deserted mining towns and numerous historic sites remain as monuments to the state's rich heritage. This romantic aura of yesteryear creates a unique blend of year-round appeal when combined with present day sun, sand, scenery, snow and accomodations ranging from rustic cabins to plush hotels.

Three National Forests atttract between five and six million visitors annually. In 1979 travelers spent up to $4.8 billion in the state, benefiting directly more than thirty-five thousand business firms. For every dollar spent directly by tourists, another seventy-eight cents is generated. This multiplier effect resulted in a total travel impact of up to $8.2 billion total expenditures, supporting eighty-five thousand jobs.

McGoff's first effort to strengthen holdings in the travel business was a bid for several resort hotels and combination ski/golf resorts in the Grand Traverse Bay area. They could serve as the focal destination for many of the packaged tours as well as centers for business conferences and conventions. When these proposals failed to materialize as rapidly as he desired and at terms acceptable to him, he shifted his interest to a new service in Michigan.

He purchased a ship, the Bay Queen, and initiated a new service. Buying a restaurant in Charlevoix, Michigan, to prepare meals for two daily three-hour trips on Lake Michigan, the new attraction was successful from the first trip. Serving lunch on the first trip and dinner on the evening trip, providing entertainment and music for dancing, the new attraction drew capacity patronage of 300 guests for each trip during this first season of operations in 1981. The service will operate between May 30 until October 31 each year. Profits and response have been far beyond expectations.

In 1980 he acquired sole ownership of the Beaver Island Navigation Company. This company provides ferry service from Charlevoix, Michigan to Beaver Island, carrying passengers and supplies to the island, located in the northern part of Lake Michigan about 38 miles from Charlevoix. Back in the middle of the nineteenth century, Beaver Island was the site of the settlement of the splinter Mormon group which accepted the leadership of James Strang after the assassination of Joseph Smith. He dominated the settlement until his own assassination.

Today the island has a permanent population of around 500. This increases to more than 3000 during the summer months. It has one hotel and a number of motels as well as summer homes. Attached to Charlevoix County politically, the children attend the Charlevoix schools. Accessible by boat only, the navigation company operates three boats daily during the summer months and one during the winter months from December through March. It has proven a profitable operation.

Two restaurants were purchased in the Lansing area, one near Williamston and the other on the west side of the city. Both are high class restaurants catering to a well-established following. These restaurants will be used as stopover points for the packaged tours when appropriate.

Several years before McGoff liquidated Panax, he purchased an Amtrak pullman car with the idea of converting it to a private car for lease. When the condition of the car was deemed unsuitable for this purpose, he acquired a Seaboard pullman car and converted it into a luxury recreational vehicle for rail passengers. Built with a stainless steel body, the car has sleeping accomodations for ten passengers and two crew members. Included in the elegancies are a sound system, video tape capabilities, heat, air conditioning, a dining room for six and a stainless steel galley.

Looking ahead at the time, he anticipated a market for this type of train travel as business executives return to more relaxed business cross-country travel in an energy-short future. It is available for rental in the United States, Mexico and Canada. Arrangements have been made for use on Amtrak's routes to Washington and New York from Detroit.

Beginning soon after his decision to dispense with the Panax operations, his newspaper column was discontinued. His speaking engagements were curtailed to an occasional appearance. Although his public utterances were diminished, his interest in political affairs continued. Inspirited by the new national leadership, he directed his activities to organizational and fund-raising support programs.

Unadorned by corporate bureaucracy from its inception in 1974, Global Communications operates efficiently, profitably and effectively as a decentralized system. Staying detached from operating details, which he does not relish anyway, McGoff functions in areas of his preference: planning new ventures, buying, building, expanding, evaluating results, selling when and if it seems appropriate. With a small corporate staff, management problems are minimal. Reserving the privilege of final decision, he has delegated details to his associates. His travel schedule, personal and business, remains heavy. Never a desk-bound executive, he prefers to confer directly at the site of action. Owning a Gulfstream executive plane, he can take off at a moment's notice and usually does.

211

McGoff reached a level of financial independence at a relatively early age. He could fulfill his consulting committments for the next ten years, clip coupons from personal investments, sell the Detroit papers when interest rates drop and live the leisurely life of the semi-retired. Untempted by the thought, he glided smoothly into a new flurry of activity in a new phase of his business career, pleased with the past, confident of the future, eager to cross new Rubicons.

The new diversified business operations have met expectations and more. The Detroit newspapers demand considerable attention. The perpetual watch for new acquisitions occupy time, effort and thought. He claims that he is busier than ever before and is having more fun in his work than at any time in his career.

He continues to work with unabated ebullience. It is no longer a matter of pyramiding wealth, although that is happening, too. At this stage of development, intangible factors other than financial gain become dominant motivating forces.

This is characteristic of the entrepreneur generally. McGoff, in common with the most successful entrepreneurs, possesses an irresistible impulsion to succeed, a quenchless desire to achieve. He derives an exhilarating satisfaction when any of his undertakings produce favorable results. He has an intolerance for slovenly performance, an aversion to mediocracy, a compelling urge to pursue excellence in anything he does, whether of major or minor significance, whether in business or personal affairs. As soon as he makes an addition to his business holdings, he wants another. The same holds for his personal tangible possessions: more property, more homes in different locations, more ships, more cars, more of any material for bounteous living.

This need for material proof of his worth dates back to his early life as one of six children in a poor family living in a rental home, possessing only the bare necessities of life. As a pre-adolescent, he pinched pennies, earned from his newspaper route, enough to buy a bicycle. This gave him his first feeling of pride of ownership. It has never subsided. The more he owns, the more he wants. In watching his parents scrimp to buy food, clothing and to pay the rent, he fantasized a life where he could afford to buy anything he wanted at any time without worrying about the cost. This boyhood fantasy became a reality as he moved into the upper income brackets. He still gets an intoxicating thrill with each new purchase. The pleasure increases in proportion to the importance of the acquisition. This accumulation of visible possessions, apparently, satisfies a subconscious need to compensate for the deprivations of youth.

The built-in desire to achieve, to excel, to acquire, to have, to hold applies in particular to the entrepreneurs who came from poor families; who started with nothing and made it big on their own. This observation is supported by ample empirical evidence as well as numerous scholarly studies over a period of years.

In 1964, Michigan State University made an in-depth study of entrepreneurs for the U.S. Small Business Administration. Extensive interviews were conducted with a wide variety of entrepreneurs. The study revealed that entrepreneurs themsleves viewed their childhood as preparation for independent careers free of the conformity and rules established by others. Only 3 percent of the fathers of entrepreneurs came from the big business world. More than 73 percent were products of farmers, owners of small businesses or skilled or unskilled laborers. In the subsequent book, *The Enterprising Man,* the authors support the claim that much of the entrepreneurs' drive to achieve and be successful stems from memory of poverty and insecurity in childhood. Remember that McGoff had said, "Being poor is the most powerful incentive anybody should need to get as far away from it as possible."

In 1970, the authors of Organization Makers: A Behavioral Study of Independent Entrepreneurs, analyze the differences between the independent entrepreneur and the administrative entrepreneur who moves up the bureaucratic ladder in hierarchial organizations. Again, these studies reveal the need of the independent entrepreneur to escape from the insecurity of younger experiences and the rejection of authority and occupational restraints set by others.

In The Power of the Corporate Mind, the psychological impact of frustrations and dissatisfactions in early life is related to development of attitudes that make "entrepreneurs entrepreneurial."

Numerous case histories of individual entrepreneurs indicate that these compulsions keep them going at full speed long after financial security has been secured. They are the same driving forces that dominated their actions at the beginning of their careers. Few of them started in business for the prime purpose of becoming millionaires. Naturally, they wanted to better themselves but many of them reached heights that exceeded their dreams. This was secondary, in many cases, to doing something well, to achieving something worthwhile and to experiencing incredible satisfaction in the recognition and prestige accorded them as they moved up in the world of success.

Other McGoff qualities shared by most entrepreneurs in varying degrees, include an abundance of energy, persistence in pursuing his undertakings, willingness to depart from the traditional methods, processes, procedures and approaches. He accepts risk as an essential part of doing business, is unaffrighted by failure but thinks success, accepting failure and disappointments of some ventures as challenges rather than defeats. He works best in meeting challenges. He has a limitless capacity for work, is irreconcilably resistant to dissuasion from a course of action, once he is committed. He has strong convictions, expresses them freely, courts controversy by his statements on public affairs and accepts criticism as a price for non-conformity and independence of thought.

At an early stage of his business career, he recognized integrity as the most important ingredient to be considered in the process of borrowing money. He built an early reputation in financial circles for his integrity and trustworthiness. His ability to maintain the confidence of conservative banking institutions, who still grant him multi-million dollar loans, is the best testimony of their respect for his business ethics.

That is the way of the entrepreneur. McGoff is just one of countless thousands of free wheeling individuals that possess some or all of these qualities. Each has a singular style peculiar to that individual's personality, character, type of business, strengths and weaknesses. Each is different from the other. Each has similarities to the others.

William J. McCrea, Chairman of The Entrepreneurship Institute, has conducted extensive research of entrepreneurs and made analytical observations in the many forums that he directs around the country. He says that entrepreneurs have nothing in common and everything in common. He discusses these characteristics of most entrepreneurs in an article in the 1980 summer issue of his magazine, "The Entrepreneurs".

Some of them, not previously mentioned here are:

- They are honest with themselves and demand honesty from their associates.
- They prefer respect to being liked, classify themselves as introverts, have a high degree of self-confidence and listen to their own drumbeat.
- They would rather give advice than take it, at a young age worked at things they found relevant and ignored the areas they decided were dull.
- They despise routine tasks and foist them off to subordinates although they do a conscientious job on routine but necessary details during the start up phase of business.
- They need to feel a sense of control over their lives and this is a determining factor in their frustration with large corporations.
- They prefer to give orders rather than follow them, are goal-oriented, love challenges and problems.
- After reaching a comfortable income level, they work more for self-satisfaction than money, seldom change lives drastically after becoming wealthy and hang on to their old circle of friends.

These qualities are shared by entrepreneurs all over this land. They are succeeding in businesses of their own choice, after starting with nothing more than an idea, a hope, a resolve to keep trying in spite of setbacks, a moral fiber to sacrifice personal pleasures for achievement that may not have been apparent at given times. That is the way of the entrepreneur.

John McGoff is not replicable. He is one of a kind. Yet he emblematizes multitudes of a kind that reflect the spirit of the entrepreneur. Each of the others is one of a kind. Each of them reflects that spirit. These ambitious, restless men and women are ill at ease with the status quo, the accepted standards of average performance, the philosophy of confining personal aspirations to limits set by others. They are unsatisfied with whatever position they may have reached at any period of life. That does not mean they are dissatisfied with life; there is a distinction. These unsatisfied enterprisers are happy, financially secure, perpetually eager to do better no matter how well they may be doing at any time. They seek new levels of accomplishment as they clear previous levels. These are the paradoxical pace setters of society, idealistic, practical, dreamers and doers. They advance the standards in society by advancing their own standards. They do not wait for opportunities to find them. They make their own opportunities. In so doing, they open opportunities for others.

That is the way and the spirit of the entrepreneur, the essence of free enterprise, the diastolic and systolic forces that keep it vibrant. These are the perpetuators of the system, these ordinary people with extraordinary vision, energy and initiative. They reflect the enterprising spirit of those hardy souls who braved the seas, suffered the hardships, risked their fortunes and dedicated their lives to settle and found this country. These colonizers had fire in their hearts. The entrepreneurs of today keep that fire burning radiantly. They have that same spirit of independence, love of freedom and courage to take chances. The fire in their hearts keeps America the land of opportunity.

The End